One Man's Climb

A Journey of Trauma, Tragedy and Triumph on K2

One Man's Climb

A Journey of Trauma, Tragedy and Triumph on K2

Adrian Hayes

PEN & SWORD
HISTORY

AN IMPRINT OF PEN & SWORD BOOKS LTD
YORKSHIRE – PHILADELPHIA

First published in Great Britain in 2018 and reprinted in 2019 by
Pen & Sword HISTORY
An imprint of
Pen & Sword Books Ltd
Yorkshire - Philadelphia

Hardback ISBN: 9781526745378
Paperback ISBN: 9781526751652

Typeset in Palatino 11/14 By SRJ Info Jnana System Pvt Ltd.

Printed and bound in the UK by TJ International Ltd.

Pen & Sword Books Ltd incorporates the Imprints of Pen & Sword Books Archaeology, Atlas, Aviation, Battleground, Discovery, Family History, History, Maritime, Military, Naval, Politics, Railways, Select, Transport, True Crime, Fiction, Frontline Books, Leo Cooper, Praetorian Press, Seaforth Publishing, Wharncliffe and White Owl.

For a complete list of Pen & Sword titles please contact

PEN & SWORD BOOKS LIMITED
47 Church Street, Barnsley, South Yorkshire, S70 2AS, England
E-mail: enquiries@pen-and-sword.co.uk
Website: www.pen-and-sword.co.uk

or

PEN AND SWORD BOOKS
1950 Lawrence Rd, Havertown, PA 19083, USA
E-mail: Uspen-and-sword@casematepublishers.com
Website: www.penandswordbooks.com

Photograph Credits: All images Adrian Hayes unless otherwise stated

Song Credits:
Page 99: *Landslide*, Fleetwood Mac - Nicks, S. Warner Bros Records, 1975
Page 192-3: *Everglow*, Coldplay - Berryman, G, Buckland, J, Champion, W, Martin, C, Parlophone Records Limited, 2015

TO ALEXANDER, CHARLOTTE AND NICKLAS
MY LONGINGS, MY LOVES, MY LEGACY

FOREWORD

I FIRST MET ADRIAN IN 1992 in Salalah, southern Oman, when he, like myself twenty-five years earlier, was serving on secondment with the Oman Armed Forces, whilst I was completing the expedition to find The Lost City of Ubar – the ruins of a city that existed 3,000 years ago in southern Arabia. We have met up again on my subsequent visits to the region and make contact every so often. On our most recent get-together he mentioned how his life had unwittingly followed much of mine – army officer, special forces and Oman, together with tackling the world's extremes in the mountains, poles, deserts and jungles. I am humbled that, as a teenager growing up in the New Forest in southern England, he considers me one of his greatest influences and I was delighted to write the foreword to his first book, *Footsteps of Thesiger,* which traced his journey by camel and foot across the Empty Quarter of the Arabian Desert.

Unlike me, Adrian has always been a mountaineer first and foremost and, having accomplished some impressive feats on all terrains in his life, I wasn't entirely surprised when he told me he was returning to the mountains to attempt, arguably, the greatest of them all – K2. I've always felt a cold shiver at the merest mention of the world's second highest mountain and the appalling statistics on it make for sombre reading. I fully accept, therefore, that for the vast majority of people it is unfathomable why anyone would want to risk their life climbing it.

And yet that viewpoint, whilst completely understandable, undermines the very essence of an intrinsic human spirit and desire to push the boundaries beyond what may seem like common sense, whether it is in the mountains, poles, underwater or even into space. There are few major accomplishments in any walk of life without there being some risk; the skill is to minimize it as much as possible. On K2, that is inherently difficult and the huge risks and low success rates are undoubtedly largely in nature's hands. Luck will therefore always play a part in either surviving or succeeding and Adrian fully acknowledges that he was extremely fortunate with both of his two attempts on the mountain.

One Man's Climb is a remarkably honest and transparent account of the challenges, both externally and internally, that anyone who dares to take it on experiences. I congratulate Adrian for this fascinating read, for attempting K2 and for becoming one of only a tiny handful of Britons who have reached the top – and lived to tell the tale.

RANULPH FIENNES

CONTENTS

INTRODUCTION

IT WAS NEVER MY INTENTION TO WRITE A BOOK on the story and momentous events that occurred on K2 in 2013 and 2014. The initiative was only conceived when I caught up with Sequoia Schmidt in Los Angeles in June 2016, on one of my regular trips to the US. Sequoia, whose significance will become evident in this read, had become a good friend after my 2013 attempt on the mountain and, as a successful book publisher in the US, I wanted to get her advice on my planned second book on leadership and personal development.

'The book I'd really like you to write is on K2,' she replied to my surprise.

'Really?' I exclaimed, 'Is there still a market for adventure books?'

'Yes, if it's a good story – and yours is a superb one!' came her response.

And so started the long process of writing and completing this work, with my previously planned book remaining on hold for the present. From the start, however, I was determined that this wouldn't just be 'another adventure book', even if it is a powerful story. Rather, one in which I could include some lessons from my other hats as a leadership, team and personal coach, sustainability campaigner and passionate advocate of increasing consciousness, mindfulness and awareness; a *The Monk Who Sold His Ferrari* (Robin Sharma, HarperCollins 1997) or *The Alchemist* (Paulo Coelho, HarperCollins 1988) enveloped in a true story of life and death, at the very edge of existence on earth.

In addition to the story itself and 'lessons from the top' came a third major component. That is a deeply personal story in my private life that was so ingrained with my attempts on K2 that it became impossible not to include it in this book – whilst being as respectful and sensitive as I possibly could to others involved. Indeed, writing the book from January 2017 became a cathartic exercise from the intense experiences I've had since 2012.

The combined result is what I sincerely hope will be a universal book that appeals to men and women of all ages, passions, pursuits and persuasions – from mountain lovers to armchair adventurers; self-growth gurus to nature lovers; romantics to humanitarians.

And if the resultant perspectives and views of our own lives in the world below – and of the world itself – strikes a chord with those reading this, then a main objective has been achieved. It shouldn't take one to climb K2, of course, to recognize the preciousness, beauty and frailty – or indeed the unsustainability, denial and failings – of our lives on earth. Sometimes, however, we all need a profound experience to change our way of thinking, acting and being. I hope everyone who reads this work is absorbed, touched and, above all, discovers something for themselves from it.

Adrian Hayes
August 2018

PART ONE

CHAPTER ONE

YOU'RE CRAZY

ONLY THOSE WHO WILL
RISK GOING TOO FAR CAN
POSSIBLY FIND OUT HOW
FAR ONE CAN GO.

– T. S. ELIOT

'OH NO! YOU'RE NOT, ARE YOU?' exclaimed a good friend with a look of total disbelief on his face. 'Please don't tell me you are. It's way too dangerous! It's crazy to want to do this,' he added for good measure.

It was September 2012 and I'd barely uttered a word other than to say I was returning to mountaineering and my next expedition was going to be big. Very big. Possibly my apprehensive complexion gave it away. But his reaction confirmed what I'd already practised for the previous eight months, bar to a few close friends – that this was one quest I'd be keeping quiet about until I left. This mountain was best explained within the walls of my mind and heart rather than to anyone else.

One of the paradoxes of goal setting is that, once a goal is conquered, the floodgates often open and an innate hunger can drive you to seek ever greater challenges. Having climbed since I was 17 and been mountaineering and adventuring in many terrains since then, summiting Everest in 2006 was a catalyst of sorts. It drove me to accomplish major goals in the polar regions and desert in the following five years. Now the mountains, my original passion, were calling me back. However, I wasn't returning to hike up Ben Nevis. No, the appetite was whetted. Huge challenges were my forte. That meant going back to one of the fourteen 8,000-metre peaks in the world, the so-called 'eight-thousanders'. And amongst those giants and in mountaineering as a sport, there was simply no bigger challenge than the world's second highest mountain.

K2. 'The Savage Mountain'. 'The Mountaineers Mountain'. 'The King of the Mountains'. By any description it had long represented the holy grail of mountaineering, the ultimate reward and the Olympic gold medal of the sport. A simple two syllable word which, for many, defines the greatest feat of mountaineering on the planet. K2 may only be the second highest peak on earth, and more than 200 metres shorter than big brother Everest, but there the comparisons fade away. Why such accolades?

For starters, K2 is remote. Located in the Karakoram Himalayas on the border of Pakistan and China, it is so remote that it takes a seven-to-eight-day trek on a glacier just to reach its Base Camp from the last settlement of Askole – itself only reachable by a day-long drive by a 4WD over winding and often washed away mountain tracks. The trek to K2 along the Baltoro glacier is twice the length of the Everest Base Camp trek. And, unlike the latter, there are no villages or settlements along the way, with everything having to be carried in by hundreds of porters. It is a tough trek.

Indeed, K2's very name is a result of this isolation, being so far from any settlement that it never fully acquired an ethnic name. Its syllable, derived from the Great Trigonometrical Survey of British India, remained, adding to its entire mystery. Italian climber Fosco Maraini once summed up this uniqueness as: '… just the bare-bones of a name, all rock and ice and storm and abyss. It makes no sense to sound human. It is atoms and stars. It has all the nakedness of the world before the first man – or the cindered planet after the last.'

The northerly latitude and location of K2 also lends itself to its notorious weather – a highly unpredictable and volatile climate, with storms occurring frequently. There is rarely any extended period of good weather at K2 and, with usual heavy snowfall on its upper slopes, trail breaking is a constant challenge, avalanche dangers abound and rock fall is a daily hazard. Added to these challenges is that climbers have to be totally self-sufficient on its dangerous slopes. On Everest, if things go wrong a helicopter can carry out a rescue up to a height of around 7,000 metres. On K2, even getting a helicopter to Base Camp is a highly complicated and costly business and nothing will rescue you once on the mountain.

If all of this wasn't serious enough, the sheer steepness of K2 and the technical climbing required, combined with its enormous height, makes the mountain such a formidable challenge to overcome. From Base Camp, its slopes soar a further 3,600 metres to the summit with no respite – the greatest Base Camp to summit distance of any mountain on earth. It starts steep and ends steep, averaging sixty degrees, with many vertical rock bands and eighty-to-ninety-degree ice slopes to climb. Underpinning these risks is the one of altitude. Altitude which, as one climbs, will affect the body's performance, will make a climber unwell, and will eventually kill.

It is this combination of high altitude, sustained steepness, technical requirements, notorious weather, snow conditions, avalanche dangers, rock fall hazards and remoteness that comprises the hazards of climbing K2. As one American reporter recently wrote, scaling its lofty heights ends up reading like a plan to beat the last level of a video game: avoid falling rocks and deadly avalanches, scale House Chimney and Black Pyramid, climb the notorious Bottleneck under 150-metre tall ice seracs that could give way at any moment, don't fall off the side of the mountain and you'll reach the magical summit.

Those who do reach the top form an illustrious club. Prior to the 2013 season, K2 had seen just 331 climbers, including only six Britons, reach the summit since its first ascent in 1954 – seven of which were disputed. That figure compared to over 4,000 who had conquered Everest in the same period – a number that had risen to over 5000 by 2018. No one may succeed on K2 for many years, such are the difficulties and conditions.

Notwithstanding this low success rate, its high death rate makes for even grimmer reading. Before 2013, eighty-one climbers had died on K2, making a death to summit ratio – the somewhat morbid statistic used to measure how dangerous a peak is – of 25 per cent. Or, put more starkly, for every four climbers who reach the top, one dies trying. Only Annapurna in Nepal, the tenth highest mountain in the world, has a higher death to summit ratio, but is a much lower altitude peak, technically easier with its fatalities due primarily to an avalanche-prone section of the climb. K2 combines nearly as high a risk with being a brute of a mountain to scale. The first three Britons to reach the top all died on their descents. The first five women to the summit also died, either on K2 or a few years later on other mountains, leading to a superstition that K2 was cursed for women. And if any climber is fortunate enough to reach the summit, he or she has the greatest possibility of dying on the descent of any mountain on earth. The mountain widely deserves its reputation and name as the 'Savage Mountain'.

With such low odds of reaching the top and such high odds of being killed while doing so, readers may be forgiven for questioning the sanity of anyone who attempts this notorious mountain. And why there may be increasingly more climbers willing to risk their lives for it. Many books have been written on the reasons why people climb mountains and most climbers will state, with apparent conviction, that they thrive on the challenge; that climbing makes them feel alive; that being in the extremes of nature galvanizes them; that it is the people they meet along the way that inspires them and so on. Many will say they do it to raise awareness or funds for a cause. And many others will say they 'do it to show others that they can too'. Sorry, but some of this is not being entirely honest. All play an important part in why climbers, myself included, put up with extreme coldness, tiredness, hunger, discomfort and even pain just to slog up to higher elevations all over the world. And, similarly, why countless others embark on all sorts of alternative adventure sports. These reasons, however, can mostly be satisfied on a weekend hike up Table Mountain. None of them justify or explain why someone wants to climb a mountain as dangerous as K2.

The real and most important reason and answer, which few climbers will admit or be fully aware of, is *significance*. One of the basic drivers of human behaviour and needs – to be significant. It is what has driven mankind's actions since time forgotten and, no matter what shape or form, we all have some intrinsic need to feel or be valued. The only difference is the scale of that value. The majority of people will find it in normal circumstances such as getting married or being a parent. Many will display it in material means, such as a smart car, a beautiful house or a good job. For others, it means reaching the top in their profession or sport. And, for a few, it takes on a meaning which has propelled the human thirst for expanding our horizons, conquering and stretching boundaries in all walks of life.

However, as in so many areas of our lives, the internet and, in particular, social media have given significance an even greater meaning. The comparison of our lives with the rest of the world is now in open and full view every single day. Consciously or subconsciously, our place in society is constantly measured against others and becomes even more of a motivation. On Facebook and other social media forums, at a stroke we can receive recognition from hundreds of likes, well wishes, compliments or congratulations for such simple matters as our birthday, our new house or the exotic destination we are going to on vacation – even the airport we are transiting through. If we haven't much to show ourselves, we can receive the same through our children. The recognition makes us feel good and gives us instant gratification – which is all caused by our bodies releasing a powerful neurotransmitter, dopamine, into our system. And dopamine is something we find difficult to ignore, the so-called Kim Kardashian of neurotransmitters.

Coupled with the impact of the internet is the evidence of a gradual, possibly profound, shift in awareness and consciousness taking place in the world. An increased striving to find a greater meaning, purpose, direction and our place in a highly unstable, uncertain, stressful and, some would say, technology gone crazy world. The implications, consequences and outlets of this shift range far and wide and some manifestations may presently be confusing, flawed, or even chaotic, but we are in a time of great change, some good, some concerning. And one consequence of this evolving awareness is of vastly multiplying numbers of people now concluding that there is more to life than working twelve-to-fifteen-hour days to boost a corporation's annual results.

Nowhere is this desire for greater meaning more evident than in the worlds of fundraising, sport and adventure. For the charity world, fundraising in the 1970s used to be via a sponsored walk and a novelty. In the 1980s it had progressed to a sponsored run or a marathon and was special. In the 1990s and 2000s it had become a skydive, an adventure or a mountain and was amazing. Nowadays, I personally receive an online charity fundraising request almost every week from some acquaintance, or stranger, doing some great challenge for some great cause and, notwithstanding the noble aims, has become routine. Indeed, so routine has it become that we are in distinct danger of 'charity overdose'. Most of them are worthy quests, generally enacted with the greatest of intentions, but many boil down to wanting to find this ever-increasing need for personal significance, purpose and a meaning.

In the sporting world, too, not too long ago anyone who ran a marathon was considered a fitness addict; those who entered a triathlon a fitness freak; and the few who participated in an Ironman triathlon considered total nutcases. Now, whether it is marathons, triathlons, Ironman or countless other sports, it has become commonplace – millions of people all over the world entering sporting pursuits which were once only participated in by an elite few. And, as merely competing in these has become routine, subconsciously fuelled by the huge number of likes, encouragement and congratulations we receive on social media, that drive for significance is pushed even further – getting that sub x-hour time, winning that age group, or moving to an even bigger challenge, such as an ultra-marathon.

In the adventure world, this desire for significance has exploded. Whether it is dog sledding in Canada, kayaking down the Colorado or climbing Kilimanjaro, there are now millions of people participating in the great outdoors – all proudly showing it on Facebook, Instagram or elsewhere. With thousands of organizations who will satisfy the demand, what was once considered well-nigh impossible is now very achievable. And, as with sport, as each boundary becomes 'normal', greater and greater numbers of people will seek to push those boundaries further, longer, faster, harder and higher, ever more propelled by their ability to *share* their accomplishments worldwide.

Summiting the world's 8,000-metre peaks are an extreme consequence of this human desire to push boundaries – they are a place where accomplished climbers are prepared to measure the risks and say 'what the hell' anyway. Previously the preserve of the world's foremost mountaineers, and often only possible if you were famous or connected enough to be invited on a national funded expedition, they are now being attempted by mountaineers with great technical skills, ability, mental toughness, extreme fitness, and sufficient time and money, in a personal drive for significance. That is the underlying reason ahead of the other joys of climbing. And, for those of us in the extreme adventure world, increasingly connected to each other via social media channels, it is becoming easier to hook up to form a team, organize a logistics supplier, provide documentation, arrange support and make an attempt happen.

The only problem with all of this is that, if significance is the major driver and need in your life, you will never be satisfied. And, secondly, that dopamine has been found to be highly addictive. This combination has, firstly, led to the numerous, if harmless, cases of attention seeking on social media we all find from time to time. In the charity world, meanwhile, the resulting recognition in the astonishing number of congratulations, well wishes and awards we receive on the great works we are doing in the world can sometimes take on the greater mantle – some fundraisers or charities, particularly those involving celebrities, have seemingly become more about the person than the cause itself.

Go farther down this slippery slope, and it has led to the increasingly dark side in the lengths some people are prepared to go to achieve this recognition. In professional sport, the use of performance enhancing drugs in athletics and other sports has been around for some time, but it is the explosion of drugs in *amateur* sports that is now so profound.

In the polar world, the desire (or desperation) for extensive publicity, albeit some promoted by sponsors, PR companies and television, has resulted in increasing 'economies with the truth' – for example, failing to distinguish between a seven day, 'last degree' walk to a pole with a two month 'all the way' expedition from the coast, a difference akin to trekking to Everest Base Camp and summiting Everest. Or, on polar or other expeditions, such as river journeys, desert crossings and sailing feats, failing to mention various forms of support, shortened journeys, means of travel and so on.

In the mountains, it's evident from a disturbing increase in teams' tents, food or equipment being used by other climbers at high altitude, something that would never have taken place decades ago. And, unacceptably, lying about reaching a summit – of the disputed summit claims for K2, a few were, according to those on the mountain at the same time, blatant lies. Other mountains have had similar cases, with one Indian couple even going to the extent of photoshopping themselves on the summit of Everest in 2016!

If we can't get this significance ourselves, then the lengths we are prepared to go to may transfer to some unwise, many would say dangerous, attempts through our children – the example of 13-year-old American, Jordan Romero, climbing Everest is one. Or 14-year-old Dutch sailor, Laura Dekker, attempting to sail around the world another, both fully encouraged, primarily for the purpose of recognition, by their parents even if they weren't fully aware of the psychology behind their desires.

Some readers may, by now, be questioning this notion of significance and how much of it is a driver in our lives. Some may wish to remind me of people who lead incredible lives, do great works for charity or perform impressive feats, largely unknown to anyone. And indeed there are many thousands of such people across the world. Their lives and works however, are still motivated by *significance*, even if it's purely internal. For instance, the dedicated charity worker who performs his or her duties for a lifetime, eschewing all publicity, will still obtain recognition – only it will be from those unfortunate but eternally grateful souls of all afflictions they help day after day. In today's connected, social media addicted and celebrity obsessed world, however, such silent gladiators are in severe decline. At some stage, someone, somewhere will feel the urge to write, report or film them; others to nominate them for an award or honour. And, consciously or subconsciously, most of the recipients will be secretly pleased they did.

So where do I and K2 fit into all of this? As much as I would love to write that I am different from everyone else and attempt my challenges purely for the sake of self-fulfilment, self-growth, connection with nature, learning and much more, that is not being honest. Yes, I've always dreamed big – as a 12-year-old I had pictures of polar explorers and mountaineers on my wall, was obsessed with travelling the world, wrote down my goals, including living on a desert island, summiting Everest, walking to the North Pole and much more. Most of these 'plans', as I called them, all came true. Beneath the dreams and goals, however, existed a deeper core value of freedom, wanting to be different, to escape from a struggling childhood, to achieve the extraordinary and a determination to experience everything I possibly could in my life. All of these entailed a desire for significance. Even when, years later, I passed selection for 21 Special Air Service – part of the British Special Forces – and wasn't allowed to tell anyone, it was still significance in my inner world.

K2 was the latest in a long line of experiences and challenges I had set myself in all areas of the outdoor world for this same reason. I am passionate about the world and speak, write, blog and campaign on many contemporary issues on our planet. I do this, in my own small way, for the world. I am also passionate about people and hence through my professional work in leadership development, team coaching and executive coaching, I do this for people. And I am passionate about expeditions, adventures and the natural world. I do this, however, with one or two exceptions, for myself.

Others attempting the mountain may have their own specific motivations, reasons and explanations but everyone is primarily driven by the significance it brings – internally, externally or both. However, I have never heard of anyone who has climbed K2 without telling anyone. Some cynics of mountaineering have slated that nobody would climb any serious mountain if no one knew about it. Probably true, but that doesn't stop with mountains. Would an Olympic athlete train brutally for four years to strive to win a gold medal if no one knew about it? A multinational CEO sacrifice his family life, leisure and health by working eighteen-hour days for self-gratitude only? A tightrope walker set a world record for a dangerous endeavour without anyone recording it? No, of course not. We all need significance in our lives. For me, it just so happened that this latest goal was going to be one of the most challenging and certainly the most dangerous that I had ever attempted.

CHAPTER TWO

A HISTORY OF DISASTER

K2 IS NOT SOME MALEVOLENT
BEING, LURKING THERE ABOVE
THE BALTORO, WAITING TO
GET US. IT'S JUST THERE. IT'S
INDIFFERENT. IT'S AN INANIMATE
MOUNTAIN MADE OF ROCK, ICE
AND SNOW. THE 'SAVAGENESS' IS
WHAT WE PROJECT ONTO IT, AS
IF WE BLAME THE PEAK FOR OUR
OWN MISADVENTURES ON IT.

- ED VIESTURS

K2'S HISTORY IS DARK, dire, depressing and sometimes diabolical. It is a history full of underestimation of the mountain's dangers, poor decision-making and all too often death. And it is a history frequently filled with egos, crass leadership and, sometimes, human behaviour at its worst. At the end of this chapter, the reader can well be forgiven for holding the most contentious view of not just the mountain, but those of us stupid enough to risk climbing it.

The mountain was discovered and measured in 1856 by Briton, Lieutenant-Colonel Thomas George Montgomerie of the Survey of India, and it was given the symbol K2 – K for Karakoram and 2 because it was the second peak measured in the Karakoram range. Montgomerie plotted the peak from Haramukh and immediately recognized its great stature. It was also given the name Mount Godwin-Austen for the peak's first surveyor, Colonel Henry Haversham Godwin-Austen, a nineteenth-century English geographer, whose expedition five years later carried out the first physical survey of the Baltoro region and undertook an exploratory mapping of the district. To him we owe one of the first descriptions of the Baltoro glacier. The mountain is known in Chinese as Qogir Feng and Chogori (meaning Great Mountain) in Baltistan, but neither name gained widespread recognition and K2 remained.

The first attempts to climb K2 via the North-East Ridge were undertaken in 1902 by Oscar Eckenstein, Aleister Crowley, Jules Jacot-Guillarmod, Heinrich Pfannl, Victor Wessely and Guy Knowles. After several serious and costly endeavours, the team retreated after reaching 6,525 metres, their lack of success being attributed to deficiency of modern climbing equipment, weatherproof fabrics, the difficulty of the challenge and sickness. There were also issues regarding questionable physical training, personality conflicts and poor weather conditions.

The notorious Crowley, an accomplished climber who had achieved many important solo climbs in the Alps, was known as a fervent occultist. He had offended just about everyone involved in black magic in the early twentieth century, yet found his way onto the K2 expedition. Further bad omens occurred when the expedition leader, Eckenstein (inventor of the 10-point crampon) was arrested in Kashmir on suspicion of being a spy. Rumours circulated that William Conway, the then president of the Alpine Club, had arranged for Eckenstein's incarceration because of a previous conflict between them during an expedition in 1892.

When Eckenstein was finally released three weeks later, suffering from a respiratory infection, and joined his team at Base Camp, he walked into a debate about which route to take. Crowley, who was afflicted by malaria and spending a lot of time in his tent with a high fever, wanted to attempt the South-East Ridge, but the team decided on the North-East Crest. On their subsequent failure, Crowley took out his revolver and threatened Guy Knowles who retaliated by kneeing Crowley in the groin. After further debate and some resolution, the team regrouped and planned for a second attempt. This time, they tried via the saddle between K2 and Skyang Kangri (the Staircase Peak, 7,545 metres).

Here Crowley redeemed himself with his superb mountaineering skills and by rescuing Pfannl, who was suffering from pulmonary oedema, by insisting on taking the sick man off the mountain. The decision saved Pfannl's life, but prevented the team from reaching the peak.

After the expedition, Crowley's life took a downhill turn when he descended into heroin addiction, which caused his behaviour to become more bizarre. At one point he became convinced that his wife was a bat and forced her to sleep tied upside down in a closet at night. His involvement in unnatural practices, such as eating human excrement and flesh, and enjoying sexual communion with freaks of all shapes and sizes, drew from the public the opinion that he was 'the wickedest man in the world'. By the time of his death, Crowley's reputation was not that of a talented climber or that he made the first attempt on K2, but that of an infamous black magician. Many years later, he was immortalized by artist Sir Peter Blake on The Beatles' album cover of *Sgt. Pepper's Lonely Hearts Club Band*, where his image stands between Mae West and Indian guru, Sri Yukteswar Giri.

The next expedition to K2, in 1909, was a large Italian endeavour under the leadership of Prince Luigi Amadeo Giuseppe (Duke of Abruzzi) the grandson of King Victor Emmanuel II of Italy. Its members produced a very good account of the expedition with photographs and accurate maps of the Baltoro area. They reached an elevation of around 6,250 metres on the South-East Spur, now known as the Abruzzi Spur (or Abruzzi Ridge). This would eventually become part of the standard route, but was abandoned at the time due to its steepness and difficulty. After trying and failing to find a feasible alternative route on the West Ridge or the North-East Ridge, the Duke declared that K2 would never be climbed.

In 1938, Charles Houston led a party of young Americans on a full reconnaissance of all possible routes on the southern face of K2. After spending a good part of the summer in difficult and unrewarding exploration, they worked out a feasible route to the great snow shoulder lying below the summit cone. With time and food running out, they reached a height of about 7,925 metres before abandoning any summit attempts.

This route was then used a year later by legendary German-born mountaineer, Fritz Wiessner, who, along with his deputy,

American Jack Durrance, led a fateful expedition to K2 in 1939. Wiessner, Pasang Dawa Sherpa and millionaire climbing and yachting enthusiast Dudley Wolfe, reached a camp more than 7,000 metres above sea level. With Wolfe too exhausted to go on, Wiessner and Pasang continued climbing and reached a height of over 8,400 metres, just 200 metres short of the summit, before Pasang insisted they turned back. They tried again, but failed the following day. Five days after leaving the high camp, Wiessner returned with an injured Pasang to find a badly sick Wolfe alone with just a few supplies. No provisions had reached him from lower camps, so all three went down to the next camp, which they found had been stripped bare by their teammates, who were convinced all three men were already dead.

Wolfe was again left on his own for a week while the two others, already suffering frostbite, went further down the mountain to organize a rescue. Three Sherpas apparently reached Wolfe but, after bad weather descended, all four were never seen again, the mountain's first victims. The deaths caused a fierce argument between Wiessner, who blamed Durrance for the tragedy, with the latter countering that, as an inexperienced climber, Wolfe should never have been allowed on the expedition. Wolfe's body was discovered many years later, in 2002, by Spanish climber, Araceli Segarra, who found bones, fragments of trousers and a mitten with Wolfe's name on. Appearing to have died alone in or near his tent, the discovery also appeared to dispute the assumptions that the Sherpas had reached him.

Wiessner never had another chance to reach the summit. Had he made it, he would have been the first man to reach the summit of an 8,000-metre peak, eleven years before the first successful conquest of Annapurna. He would have also summited the world's second highest mountain without the use of supplemental oxygen, a feat forty years ahead of its time.

Charles Houston returned to K2 to lead the 1953 American expedition. After several weeks on the mountain, the team had barely established camp at about 7,772 metres when a blizzard broke. It continued to rage for two weeks, by which time a young geologist, Art Gilkey, developed phlebitis in one leg and was unable to walk. When the storm finally abated, the other five members of the party were faced with the almost impossible task of dragging and lowering Gilkey down the mountain in his sleeping bag. Within a few hundred yards of the next camp, one man slipped, climbing ropes became entangled and the five men began to slide off the mountain. By a magnificent piece of belaying, Peter Schoening – the youngest member of the party – succeeded in holding all five men, although Houston lapsed into unconsciousness. After securing Gilkey to ice axes on the steep slope, the five men found a bivouac site on relatively safe ground and, less than an hour later, went back to bring in Gilkey. He was not there and was thought to have been swept away by an avalanche. The stricken party then endured an appalling time trying to descend the mountain with a severely weakened Houston – who had prepared to jump off the mountain to his death in order to save his teammates. 'I knelt in the snow and said the Lord's Prayer,' he later wrote. 'Next thing I can remember is being grasped by strong arms and helped into Camp 4.' Houston gave up climbing after the tragedy, cancelling his plans for a further expedition to K2 in 1955. Despite the failure and tragedy, the courage shown by the team gave the expedition an iconic status in mountaineering history.

The following year an Italian expedition finally succeeded on K2, with climbers Achille Compagnoni and Lino Lacedelli summiting the mountain via the Abruzzi Spur on 31 July 1954. The expedition was rife with tensions from the off as a young, highly accomplished alpinist, Walter Bonatti, had proved himself to be easily the most capable of surviving high altitudes, and yet the more experienced Lacedelli and Compagnoni were chosen as the climbers to reach the summit. The resultant success was highly controversial after it later emerged that Compagnoni and Lacedelli had left 24-year-old Bonatti and Pakistani Hunza porter, Amir Mehdi, who had carried up oxygen for the two lead climbers, to sleep on a ledge at 8,100 metres. Whilst both survived the night, Mehdi later lost all his toes due to frostbite.

The names of the summiteers were not released until the return of the expedition. When it was announced, Compagnoni and Lacedelli, who also claimed they reached the summit without oxygen, were celebrated as national heroes, with Bonatti's reputation sacrificed for the greater good of restoring national morale in the aftermath of the Second World War. Bonatti took revenge in his own way: solo climbs, first ascents, and new technical routes, including a first ascent of 7,925-metre Gasherbrum 4 in 1958. In his accomplishments, he proved that he was one of the best climbers of his generation, if not in all of climbing history, until he gave up mountaineering in 1965.

Thirty years after reaching the summit of K2, Bonatti wrote about the 1954 expedition in his autobiography, *The Mountains of My Life*, displaying proof of his innocence, and including a photograph of Compagnoni and Lacedelli wearing oxygen masks on the summit. Efforts in the 1950s to suppress these facts to protect Lacedelli and Compagnoni's reputations as Italian national heroes were also brought to light. And in a book released in 2006, an elderly Lino Lacedelli finally confessed to the truth and attempted to call Bonatti to apologize. The Italian Alpine Club, however, still declines to formally confirm that Compagnoni and Lacedelli used oxygen.

The story of bitterness and animosity continued into the 1970s. Galen Rowell's book, *In the Throne Room of the Mountain Gods*, records a particularly vitriolic American expedition to the west side of K2 in 1975, led by the brothers Jim and Lou Whittaker. The team split into rival factions and one climber, Fred Dunham, responded to 6.4-foot Lou Whittaker's physical presence by recording in his diary: 'There is only one way to handle a guy like Lou who shoves his weight and size around … with an ice axe in the back of his head or a bullet between the eyes. There is no other way for a smaller person to get justice.'

On 9 August 1977, twenty-three years after the Italian expedition, Ichiro Yoshizawa led the second successful ascent, with Ashraf Aman as the first native Pakistani climber. The Japanese expedition took the Abruzzi Spur and used more than 1,500 porters.

The third ascent of K2 was in 1978, via a new route, the long and corniced North-East Ridge. The top of the route traversed left across the East Face to avoid a vertical headwall and joined the uppermost part of the Abruzzi route. This ascent was made by an American team, led by James Whittaker with a summit party of Louis Reichardt, Jim Wickwire, John Roskelley and Rick Ridgeway. Wickwire endured an overnight bivouac about 150 metres below the summit, one of the highest bivouacs in history. This ascent was profound for the American team, who saw themselves as completing a task that had been begun by the 1938 team forty years earlier.

Another notable Japanese ascent was that of the difficult North Ridge on the Chinese side of the peak in 1982. A team from the Mountaineering Association of Japan led by Isao Shinkai and Masatsugo Konishi put three members, Naoe Sakashita, Hiroshi Yoshino and Yukihiro Yanagisawa, on the summit on 14 August. However, Yanagisawa fell and died on the descent. Four other members of the team achieved the summit the next day.

The first climber to reach the summit of K2 twice was Czech climber Josef Rakoncaj, He was a member of the 1983 Italian expedition led by Francesco Santon, which made the second successful ascent of the North Ridge on 31 July 1983. Three years later, on 5 July 1986, he reached the summit via the Abruzzi Spur, after summiting Broad Peak solo, as a member of Agostino da Polenza's international expedition.

Earlier that summer, the first woman to summit K2, Pole Wanda Rutkiewicz, reached the top on 23 June 1986, but would die six years later whilst attempting Kanchenjunga, the third highest mountain in the world, having reached the top of eight eight-thousanders. Liliane and Maurice Barrard who had summited K2 the same day as Rutkiewicz, fell during the descent on the Bottleneck couloir, having been climbing alpine style. Liliane's body was found on 19 July at the foot of the South Face, the first woman to die on K2.

That summer, in what is now known as the 'Black Summer of 1986', a further eleven climbers died in seven separate incidents, from an avalanche, falls, crevasses, rock fall and exhaustion. By the end of July, eight of these deaths had occurred, including Italian, Renato Casarotto who fell into a crevasse in the icefall just above Base Camp. Then, in early August, a newly formed group of international climbers, who had failed on various routes in different teams in the previous weeks, attempted a summit via the normal route. For unexplained reasons, they chose to spend an extra day at Camp 4 on the Shoulder at nearly 8,000 metres. When they returned from the summit the following day they found themselves fighting for their lives in a six-day storm. Of the seven who were trapped, only two, Austrians, Kurt Diemberger and Willi Bauer, survived the ordeal and ended up being criticized for leaving climbers to die in their tents at Camp 4. One of those was British climber, Julie Tullis, the second woman to die on K2.

With deaths occurring in many years prior to and after 1986, in 1995 the mountain experienced another prolific number of fatalities. The most publicised was that of Briton Alison Hargreaves who, in May that year, had become the first woman to solo Mount Everest without oxygen. On the summit push on 13 August 1995, New Zealander Peter Hilary, son of Sir Edmund Hilary, decided to turn back, noting that the weather which had been fine for the previous four days appeared to be changing. Hargreaves reached the summit of K2 – only the fifth woman to have done so – at the extremely late time of 6.45 p.m., accompanied by Spaniard, Javier Olivar, followed by American, Rob Slater, Spaniards, Javier Escartín and Lorenzo Ortíz, and New Zealander, Bruce Grant. All six would soon die on the descent in a violent storm, which, with winds in excess of 100 miles per hour and with no shelter or fixed ropes, resulted in them literally being blown off the mountain. Canadian, Jeff Lakes, who had turned back below the summit earlier, managed to reach one of the lower camps, but died from the effects of exposure.

The death of Hargreaves caused much controversy, as a mother to young children, climbing high and distant mountains while leaving them behind. It sparked debates across the US and the UK over the incommensurability of motherhood and mountaineering, provoking a scrutiny in ways which fatherhood does not. Ironically, her son Tom Ballard (with whom she was five and half months pregnant when she made the first British female ascent of the North Face of the Eiger in 1988) became an accomplished climber and has set his sights on K2.

With Barnard, Tullis and Hargreaves all dying on K2, Rutkiewicz dying on Kanchenjunga and Chantal Mauduit of France, the fourth woman to climb K2, dying on Dhaulagiri, the eighth highest mountain in the world, in May 1998, the superstition of K2 cursing any women who attempted it arose.

2004, the fiftieth anniversary of K2's first ascent, saw many teams on the mountain commemorating the anniversary, including two Italian teams attempting the mountain from Pakistan and China. The anniversary season started with tragedy almost immediately when, on 10 June, three South Koreans were found dead in their sleeping bags in a crevasse, after an avalanche struck Camp 2. Shortly after, on 29 June, five porters drowned, caught in a swift-moving stream while carrying luggage to Base Camp for the Italian expedition. The season did produce a record number of ascents, however, with forty-eight undisputed summits in three separate waves. Edurne Pasaban, from Spain, finally broke the women's curse of the mountain when she summited K2, lived to tell the tale, and still lives to this day.

The worst single accident in the history of K2 occurred four years later, on Saturday, 2 August 2008, when eleven climbers were killed. With what later transpired as miscommunications, flawed assumptions, and poor coordination between the six teams launching a summit attempt, an absence of ropes and subsequent delays caused queues on the notorious Bottleneck. The first death occurred when Dren Mandic, a member of the Serbian team, unclipped himself from the fixed lines to overtake another climber, but as he did so, he slipped and fell to his death. With a recovery operation launched to lower his body, a Pakistani high-altitude porter, Jehan Baig, then also fell to his death.

The subsequent delays all resulted in the summit being reached much later than normal safety guidelines, with some of the eighteen climbers who summited that day reaching the top as late as 8 p.m. In the ensuing darkness, a large section of the 150-metre vertical ice seracs above the Bottleneck broke off, killing Norwegian, Rolf Bae, who had turned around 100 metres from the summit, and severing the fixed lines. With little or no equipment to descend safely, the remaining climbers were left stranded above the Bottleneck and, over the course of next two days, with two more ice serac collapses, nine more would die, including Irishman, Gerard McDonnell, the first Irishman to summit K2. Rolf Bae's wife, Cecilie Skog – who had reached the North Pole with Bae in 2006, the year before I did – survived, and Pemba Gyalje Sherpa, who launched several rescue attempts, was named the 2008 National Geographic Adventurer of the Year for 'extreme heroism under trying extreme circumstances'. The tragedy was documented in Graham Bowley's *No Way Down: Life and Death on K2* (HarperCollins 2010), and Nick Ryan's feature film, *The Summit*, which was released in 2013 to critical acclaim.

In the following three years, despite several attempts, nobody reached the summit from Pakistan. On the Chinese side, a team of four world-class climbers succeeded on 23 August 2011, including

Austrian female climber, Gerlinde Kaltenbrunner – who became the first woman to climb all fourteen of the world's 8,000-metre peaks without the use of supplemental oxygen.

Along with this grizzly history, comes the disputes. K2's records show an uncomfortable number of claimed summits prior to any other team arriving or when other teams had departed. Among or in addition to these, there were at least seven disputed summits before 2013, where climbers had failed to produce sufficient (or sometimes any) evidence that they had reached the top, some claiming to have done so under the most extraordinary of circumstances. Several individuals and organizations attempt to keep track of all Himalayan 8,000-metre peak ascents and casualties, including ExplorersWeb, Elizabeth Hawley's Himalayan Database, Eberhard Jurgalski and Bob Schelfhout-Aubertijn. However, whilst raising a 'disputed' status is one thing, getting a climber formally stripped from official national records is more difficult.

One summiteer who was officially stripped of his summit of K2 was Austrian Christian Stangl, who claimed to have reached the top on 12 August 2010 in a four-day epic solo attempt. Doubts on the credibility of his claims surfaced immediately, with his supposed 'summit picture' appearing far lower than 8,611 metres, no GPS coordinates, and no witnesses to his feat. Under increasing pressure from ExplorersWeb and others, he eventually broke down and confessed in a television interview. To his credit, he returned to summit the mountain in 2012, and also became the first person to complete the '3 x Seven Summits' – the three highest mountains on every continent. Had he not confessed, however, he would have been yet another name to add to the collection of fakes blighting the integrity and ethics of alpinism.

This is K2's controversial history and one which is unlikely to end any time soon. Journalist Mark Horrell succinctly summed up this poor track record in 2014, writing 'K2's history, more than any other Himalayan peak, is unspeakably dark, tragic and depressing. It's a history littered with corpses of those who underestimated the mountain and perished after making unwise decisions, and one that has frequently been darkened by the worst aspects of human nature.'

It is hard to argue his summary.

CHAPTER THREE

THE SEEDS ARE SOWN

IN THE MIDST OF EVERY CRISIS
LIES GREAT OPPORTUNITY.

- ALBERT EINSTEIN

THE IDEA OF CLIMBING K2 had barely crossed my mind since I started climbing in my teens, or since adventuring became part of my professional work in 2006. Other challenges had taken over and my then most recent expedition – the forty-four-day crossing of the Arabian Desert in the footsteps of legendary British explorer Sir Wilfred Thesiger, in late 2011 – had consumed me fully for two years of planning, preparation and execution.

Despite this, I'd read many books on K2 and, in early January 2012, the first embers of thoughts for the world's second highest mountain started to appear in my mind. It was no sudden urge and commitment though, and too many problems clouded the vision. The high risks were one matter – serious enough to put most sensible people off even attempting it. For myself, though, it was the low success rates, coupled with these high risks, which were even more of an issue. They were pitiful. High risk, high reward is one thing; high risk, low reward something else. If the disaster of 2008 wasn't bad enough, the fact that no one had summited from the main Pakistan side in the past three years did little to inspire any confidence that it was worth the time, effort and cost.

There were other issues also. Being out of the high-altitude mountaineering scene for five years, with my usual climbing friends all with other plans, meant trying to hook up with others via the internet, climbing associations, a local logistics supplier or expedition organizer. There were very few options and many doubts. 'Double hatting' with Broad Peak, the 8,051-metre neighbouring twelfth highest mountain in the world, was one practice, the feasibility of which I questioned. Attempting K2 by the supposedly less avalanche-prone and safer South-Southeast Ridge, the 'Cesen' route, as opposed to the normal South-East Ridge, the Abruzzi Spur – though nothing was 'normal' on K2 – was another. However, the absence of any successes seemed to suggest that one or both practices weren't working. Rumours were heard that a new international expedition, led by Nepali brothers, Dawa and Mingma Sherpa – the first Sherpas to summit all fourteen eight-thousanders – was heading to K2 in 2012 with a strong team in support. Nothing was certain, however, and there was little to alleviate my concerns that this mountain was one step too far.

Notwithstanding these concerns, there were other and greater priorities to tackle. One was the certain matter of writing a book about my desert expedition – always part of the sponsorship deal with the Abu Dhabi government. I'd hoped to have the book, *Footsteps of Thesiger*, completed by June 2012, but writing a book, for me at least, requires a concentrated period of uninterrupted time, space and focus, and my life was anything but that. By May 2012 I'd barely written three chapters.

Above all, however, it was my personal life which caused the greatest anchor to K2 progressing any further than thoughts. As a father of two children whom I adored – although abroad from them much of the time after separating and divorcing from their mother a few years earlier – the thoughts of my son, Alex, and my daughter, Charlotte, always created guilt and doubts in my mind. It was just too selfish, too dangerous and too reckless to put them at risk of losing their father, I would tell myself. In addition, my partner, someone whom I loved dearly, whilst supporting my expeditions fully, was totally against the idea of K2, begging me to promise her I would never attempt it. Any thoughts of K2 were firmly put on hold.

As so often happens in life, however, events that summer then took on an uncanny twist. In June 2012, the first fires were lit of what would end up being a five-year, heartbreaking, debilitating and damaging battle, through the UK's family law courts, for contact with my children. That was followed by my partner saying she needed her 'own space' and, soon after, calling time on our relationship. It was a double whammy which left me reeling. In Pakistan, meanwhile, on 31 July 2012, a thirty-strong group of climbers led by Dawa Sherpa, summited K2. The die was cast. Knowing that K2 was possible with some good support in place, free of the promise my partner had begged me to make, and devoid of any contact with my beloved children, I made the decision to attempt the mountain the following year.

Readers will justifiably see a flaw in my reasoning above – that of my kids. I hadn't lost them, they were still there and probably needed me more than ever. But, prevented from seeing them, and in the emotional trauma which resulted, I needed something to channel my thoughts. Writing *Footsteps of Thesiger* provided it in the short term, K2 provided it for the future.

It is often the case with humanity that, when the chips are down, it can often bring out the very best in us. I say 'can' as it isn't always the case – stress, loneliness, depression, disease and suicide are all testimony to what can happen after a crisis. On the other hand, there are countless examples where the most debilitating of events have inspired men and women to achieve the most remarkable of outcomes. One notable example is Louis Zamperini, a Second World War hero who drifted in the ocean for forty-six days after his plane crashed and was then captured and tortured as a Japanese POW, but survived despite all the odds. The remarkable adaption to a crippling disease by Professor Stephen Hawking, another. Or the multitudes of lesser known cancer sufferers, given six months or so to live and whose feats or inner strength become an example to us all. It's all a matter of perspectives, mindset and mental toughness.

I cried more than once for my absent children that summer, but, in the depths of that despair and heartache came creation. It manifested itself in the book that I buried myself writing from sunrise to sunset each day, and which became far more personal than I had ever envisaged. And it manifested itself in my thoughts and plans for this mighty peak far away. We write the script of our own lives.

With Dubai being my former base – though increasingly away from there in recent years – the UAE and Oman mountains became my training ground for the forthcoming quest, as they had been for many of my recent endeavours. The mountains, which rise to 2,000 metres in the Musandam peninsula and to 3,000 metres in the Hajar mountains farther south in Oman, provides a superb terrain for training during the winter months in the northern hemisphere. For climbing, numerous barely touched limestone crags abound all over the region, offering traditional and sports climbing routes up to moderately high grades. For hiking, the barren, sparse landscape, with very few tracks, offers hard trekking on loose rock, wadis, dried up waterfalls and steep escarpments. It is a tough hiking country, and countless super-fit sportsmen and women from the UAE have found that a long day's hike on such unstable ground leaves their legs unable to function for a week. The difficulty in route finding, also, is such that satellite navigation is secondary to having a feel for the land. Many a group relying on GPS have become lost in the mountains, where even a few metres off can mean missing a distinct ledge or goat track. Being benighted overnight is relatively common.

Musandam, the long finger of the Arabian peninsula which pushes north to Iran, nearly splitting the Arabian Gulf from the Indian Ocean, was my prime area, being nearest to Dubai. Aside from its training potential, it also offers a fascinating cultural insight into the people and history of the Arabian Gulf. Unlike the rest of the Gulf, which has a long history of repeated invasion and colonization, the Musandam Peninsula has always been too rugged to be readily invaded. As a result, its people, the Shihuh tribe, have been largely isolated from the rest of southern Arabia and are culturally and linguistically different from their Arab neighbours in the UAE and Oman. And unlike the Bedouin, from whom most Arabs in the UAE trace their roots, the Shihuh are not nomadic wanderers of the desert, but farmers. Centuries ago, when there was far greater precipitation than today, they created an impressive structure of high-altitude terraced fields and sophisticated water collection and storage systems in their mountain stronghold, with gullies feeding large stone cisterns known as *birkahs*. Nowadays, with a dryer and hotter climate unable to support agriculture, most of the villages are in ruins, but many have been rebuilt to be used as weekend huts for the now urbanized Shihuh.

With this stark, rugged beauty and the abundance of fascinating remnants from past civilizations, the area is a haven for the relatively small number of enthusiasts, who venture from their 4WD's cruising the modern cities of Dubai and Abu Dhabi, to explore the mountains. The only downsides are the lack of greenery and the shortness of the season – both due to the Gulf's intense climate. The heat which hits the region for most of the year means that hiking is only possible between mid-November to end-March, with serious trips a month shorter at each end. Outside of this season, it is too hot to venture outdoors for lengthy periods in the day, although rock climbing on shaded crags offers an extended season.

That mid-November to end-March main season always worked perfectly for the Nepal Himalayas climbing period of April–May. K2's location, approximately 1,500 kilometres north-west in Pakistan, and the subsequent later climbing period of mid-June to early August, however, meant that I would have to find other means or countries to ramp my training up in the critical two months prior to departure.

My normal training regime comprises of keeping a very high level of all-round fitness – running, cycling, swimming, triathlons, weight training, rock climbing and hiking. Then, four months in advance, I focus with a full intensity on specific training geared to whatever endeavour I am embarking on, in this case hiking and climbing. In my view and experience, it's hard to keep that level of intensity and focus for much longer than four months, and I am sometimes slightly cynical when I hear of athletes 'training for four years' for a race or event. Yes, their overall goal may have been four years' hence but with many interim goals and rest periods within that time.

To take full advantage of the UAE's trekking season, I would also have to commence specific training much earlier than normal, albeit with a gradual build-up of intensity as opposed to a full-on assault. Following racing Ironman Western Australia in early December 2012, my first training hike took place on 28 December with two erstwhile outdoor friends on the famous

'Stairway to Heaven' – an exposed hike and climb which follows ancient 'staircases' built into a cliff by the Shihuh tribes centuries ago. The hike that should have lasted eleven hours ended up over seventeen hours, due to taking some wrong lines down the mountain and ending up at the head of numerous cliffs – an epic that exemplified route finding difficulties in the region. It caused me a stiffness in my legs for a week, aptly proving that fitness is totally sports specific. The hiking and rock climbing continued over the following months, complemented by running, cycling, stair climbing, gym work and rock climbing at one of the local climbing walls.

Aside from training, I needed to find a teammate or teammates. I was introduced to Canadian Al Hancock, from Edmonton, who unsuccessfully attempted K2 in 2012 and was intending on returning in 2013. He had already summited four eight-thousanders – Everest (twice), Manaslu, Cho Oyu and Shishapangma – and had attempted Broad Peak as well as many smaller altitude peaks, so was well experienced. After several emails, we arranged a Skype call.

'Hey Al, good to finally meet,' I started.

'Hi there, Adrian. Good to meet you too!' he replied in a distinct Canadian drawl.

'What happened to you on K2?' I asked after we'd been chatting for a few minutes.

'Oh, man! I had one issue after another, and in the end was on a different rotation schedule. I was bummed,' he answered.

He told me the story of what had happened in 2012 and the experience and knowledge he had gained. We expanded our chat to cover how we got into climbing, our other experiences and additional elements of our lives – not to check each other out, but to gain some rapport. A former oil industry senior supervisor in the response team, he'd been a competitive bodybuilder in his early years, becoming a regional champion and competing in several national championships.

'Al, I've met all sorts in the great outdoors, but bodybuilding to mountaineering is a first,' I joked.

'Yeah, right buddy!' he laughed. 'But you know there are some things which are very common in both – extreme discipline, focus and clear goals.'

And he was right. Although never a bodybuilder, I'd been a gym goer for most of my life and so perhaps understood more than most the value of weight training. On finishing bodybuilding, he'd moved into mountaineering as a new outlet for his physical energies and, having climbed for twenty years, was now concentrating entirely on the eight-thousanders – even giving up his oil industry job in the pursuit. I liked his assertive, confident and entertaining manner and we gelled immediately.

'Adrian, K2 is mighty steep, serious climbing. You have to be ultra-vigilant, totally focused and need a lot of luck,' he advised as we neared the end of the call.

'Yeah, I've read enough to gather that,' I replied.

'You seem to have a great track record and I'd be pleased to team up with you and give it a crack.'

'I'd be pleased too, Al.'

And so the de facto British-Canadian team for K2 2013 was formed. I felt a distinct sense of relief. The buddy system is vital in high-altitude mountaineering and many a disaster has occurred when climbers have been stranded on their own. Here was someone who spoke the same language as me, was well experienced, had been on K2 before and with whom I clicked. It had the makings of a good partnership. We agreed to use the inaptly named Seven Summits Trekking (SST), the expedition organizer formed by Dawa and Mingma Sherpa, as our logistics provider and Nazir Sabir Expeditions (NSE), the company founded by the former K2 West Ridge summiteer of the same name, as our partners in Pakistan. With their successes of the previous year, it also seemed a good tie up.

Searching for any further direct information I could find, I made contact with a number of climbers who'd succeeded or failed on K2. One of these was French climber Fabrice Imparato, who'd successfully summited K2 in 2012 on Dawa Sherpa's team on the Abruzzi Spur, but had previously failed attempting the Cesen route in 2009. I was curious to hear his comparisons and he willingly agreed to meet in London one evening, where he was now working.

'What's your view on the Cesen?' I asked after we'd had a drink and the usual small talk.

'It's crazy!' he laughed. 'Safer from avalanches, yes, but the climb from Camp 3 to Camp 4 takes eleven hours!'

'Seriously?' I expressed with surprise, knowing that the climb from Camp 3 to 4 on the Abruzzi was the shortest leg of that route.

'Totally. We were utterly spent when we reached Camp 4 in 2009 and had no strength to launch a summit attempt. The guys who'd arrived hours before on the Abruzzi were laughing at us,' he joked.

The picture was distinctly clearer and the reasons for the lack of successes on the Cesen route between 2009 to 2011 partially answered. Fabrice also enlightened me on the 2012 summit success the previous summer, which nearly ended in tragedy. He explained that a Chinese climber was short roped to three Sherpas descending the mountain 150 metres from the top, when the Sherpa at the front fell, dragging the other three with him.

'None of them managed to self-arrest and they tumbled down at full speed before disappearing into the clouds!'

'Crikey, you serious?'

'Yes! Later we found that they had managed to stop in a small crevasse after falling 200 metres, and they traversed to the route before continuing their descent.'

'Whew, one fortunate escape.'

'They were very lucky and a total disaster narrowly avoided!'

Fabrice was invaluable in giving me some pertinent advice and I thanked him wholeheartedly. We kept in touch.

My former agents and PR company, Professional Sports Group (PSG), had been sourcing sponsorship since the previous autumn but the offers hadn't exactly flooded in. I'd secured continued commitment from my regular and enthusiastic support sponsors – satellite communications company, Thuraya, and UAE distributor, Xtra-Link; hotel group, JA Resorts; California Chiropractic and Sports Medicine Centre of Dubai; website producers, Ten Twenty; Middle East sports company, MEFITPRO; Dubai Podiatry Centre; and outdoor garment manufacturer, Marmot, together with their UAE distributors ZSI Trading. A major sponsor, who would provide the main funding, however, was proving harder to find. PSG thought that there was something in the risks of K2 that was possibly making it unattractive to corporations, which I somehow suspected. Few companies would be willing to put money into a project where the key player might get killed!

Nevertheless, we continued approaches and in early 2013 received a lucky break when a major manufacturer, whom I'd delivered a seminar to, expressed interest in supporting the upcoming expedition. I take my sponsorship commitments extremely seriously and a sponsorship proposal always consists of a full package of PR and media benefits, branding opportunities, internal leadership and team development work and external ambassadorial duties, such as product launches, client events, promotional shoots, opening supermarkets, kissing babies or whatever.

One key attraction of our K2 proposal was the offer to take four employees on an Everest Base Camp (EBC) trek in May, when I would deliver a discussion topic on some aspect of personal growth, leadership or team development each night. Aside from the benefits to the company, it would also assist my training by allowing a trek at altitude in a month when the UAE heat would be kicking in. And, most importantly, would allow me to tag on a climb of 6,189-metre Island Peak after the Base Camp trek had been completed. Nepal is a country very dear to my heart from my eight years as a Gurkha officer in the British army, which included several welfare treks and recruitment observations in the country; my speaking Nepali; and from many climbing trips in the Himalayan kingdom. Returning after a gap of a few years would therefore be both very rewarding and beneficial.

The deal was agreed, and contracts were signed in February 2013. The company hasn't or won't be named, unfortunately, as the day before we embarked on our trek – having undertaken much preparatory work such as employee selection, equipment preparation, photo shoots and suchlike – we received a telephone call from the company's marketing department. The call strangely asked us not to undertake any PR work on the trek as 'some internal procedures needed to be cleared'. That was the first sign of what would end up being a three-year battle to obtain money from what was a binding contract. Oblivious to this at the time, however, the trek went ahead as planned with four gallant employees, who were keen, eager to learn and great companions.

On the trek up to EBC I took the party to meet Lama Geshi in the small Sherpa village of Pangboche. He is the senior lama in the Khumbu region of Nepal, and third in line behind the Dalai Lama. It is traditional for many Everest parties to visit the Lama to receive a blessing, and all our Everest team of 2006 had been received by him in April 2006. It would be an honour to see him again – and, for K2, I would take every blessing I could.

Pemba Sherpa, who was accompanying us on the trek, led us into the monk's home and we sat down in hushed reverence as we greeted the Lama. Now 82 years old, he had visibly aged since my last meeting, having suffered a stroke a few years earlier, but was still fully alert. Pemba translated Lama Geshi's Tibetan into English as the ceremony got under way. One by one we accepted a personal blessing, and a sacred thread and a *kharta* (the traditional Tibetan Buddhist ceremonial silk scarf that represents purity and compassion) were tied around our necks. We then received a personal greeting card which we would take to Everest Base Camp.

When it came to my turn, Pemba explained to Lama Geshi where I would be heading in the summer, which prompted an exchange of questions and answers in Tibetan. Lama Geshi proceeded to write a card for me, which would be my duty to take to the summit of K2 if successful, before giving his blessing. Aside from the sound of some crows crying in the village, you could have heard a pin drop.

'The Lama give you blessings and safety for climb K2,' Pemba quietly uttered.

'Thank you Lama,' I replied.

'The Lama say you live long and happy life,' Pemba added.

'It's not always been happy, but I'll take the long bit!' I replied, laughs from everyone, including the Lama, breaking the suspense.

The ceremony concluded by him throwing rice into the air, touching foreheads and holding hands. It was a magical and mystical hour of complete presence, ending up with smiles, laughter and fond wishes all round.

When we reached EBC after eleven days, I met up with an old friend, Henry Todd, the leader of our 2006 expedition and one of the most experienced and successful expedition leaders on the mountain. He was back again with a new team of eight climbers.

After greetings, general chat and some very welcome warm tea, he asked me whether I was planning any more eight-thousanders. I smiled, anticipating his reaction. He'd always said K2 was utterly crazy and far too risky to attempt.

'Err, well Henry, in fact I am,' I stammered.

'I'm climbing Island Peak in a few days' time, all part of my preparation for ... K2!' I added, with a probable look of trepidation on my face.

'Really?' he exclaimed, his brow furrowed and mind in thought.

'Yep, I'm heading there next month.'

'Hmmm,' he added, disguising any personal feelings on the subject. Perhaps he'd mellowed his objections.

'Listen, I need to give you some advice. I've lost too many friends on that mountain,' he started with a serious tone.

Henry then proceeded to give me his knowledge the mountain, together with some valuable tips, including taking a clear compass bearing of Camp 4 when launching our summit bid. He explained that many a fatality had occurred in white-outs, when descending climbers had been unable to find their way back to the safety of the camp.

'Do you know Marty?' he asked. 'Marty Schmidt. Good friend of mine.'

'I've never met him but obviously well know of him,' I replied.

'He's attempting K2 this summer, you should get in touch.'

'Oh, that's interesting, will do.'

'Marty will be of much value; he's attempted it twice already.'

We spent a few hours with Henry and, for thirty minutes, another old colleague, Kenton Cool – probably Britain's most acclaimed high-altitude climber. It was great to see them both again and learn how Everest had changed in the past seven years. I was also pleased to hear that someone of Marty Schmidt's calibre was going to be on K2 – he was a very well-known and accomplished guide from New Zealand, with a host of experience.

The final and probably most important component of the trip, for me, was to climb the 6,189-metre Island Peak, otherwise known as Imja Tse, located one day's walk off the EBC trek. Having been out of high-altitude mountaineering and ice climbing for a few years, this would be a good refresher, particularly the steep ice wall which required ascending on the final summit push. After trekking to Island Peak Base Camp a few days after leaving EBC, we launched our summit climb the next morning. The ice wall was interesting – much steeper than I had assumed for what is a regularly climbed mountain. I climbed the wall using my ascenders on the fixed lines and then, given that I was fine on time, descended the wall on the lines and ascended it free climbing. Nothing too risky as the lines were a foot away in case of a fall, but it made me concentrate fully on my ice axe and crampon skills. Thankfully, ice climbing is somewhat like riding a bike – you never forget, only one's specific fitness loses shape. We summited Island Peak and eventually returned to Kathmandu and then Dubai.

By now it was mid-May and little more than a month until our departure. I was still concerned at our late arrival date of 22 June into Islamabad. It didn't stack up that, for Everest expeditions, teams gather in Kathmandu on or around the 1 April each year, take an internal flight – very dependent on weather – to the mountain village of Lukla, trek to Base Camp over ten to twelve days, conduct the necessary rotations and acclimatization in preparation for a summit bid in the last two weeks of May. By contrast, in Pakistan, we would be gathering in Islamabad, taking an internal flight – again very dependent on weather – to the mountain town of Skardu, drive and trek to K2 Base Camp over ten to twelve days, conduct the necessary rotations and acclimatization prior to a summit bid in the last two weeks of July. K2 is only 200 metres lower than Everest, so it just didn't fit that the acclimatization and rotation period would differ by a full three weeks.

I was also getting increasingly concerned that, aside from Al Hancock and myself, and recently Marty Schmidt, we'd had no updates or confirmation of other climbers or teams on the mountain. Getting a good number of teams and thus support, particularly in the form of Sherpa support, would be a vital ingredient in maximizing our chances of success. I emailed Tashi Sherpa of SST to express my thoughts on both issues, to ask him for an urgent update on other teams and to strongly suggest we get our party on the road at least a week earlier. His reply, a few days later, was a shock. He wrote saying there were no other climbers confirmed to join Al and myself, very few other teams on the mountain, and asked me to consider deferring our plans until 2014, when he promised there would be much larger numbers on the mountain.

Things suddenly became frantic. I emailed Marty Schmidt and we had a few exchanges of information. He wrote that he was going to be climbing the mountain with his son Denali and an Australian friend, Chris Warner, and that they would be attempting Broad Peak before K2. When I asked him how many Sherpas he was planning to take his reply was, 'None. We're doing both alpine style.'

I then called Tashi Sherpa to clarify and expand on his email. He said he'd heard that a Swiss team, Spanish team and Greek team were going to be there, and possibly one other. We discussed the issues of Sherpa support and how many we would need to make this viable. He replied to say that four Sherpas would be the minimum required to have the necessary support for a small expedition attempting a fixed line summit. Al Hancock and I subsequently had a Skype call to discuss the latest developments. I'd already agreed to pay for two Sherpas.

'Adrian, I'd love to contribute more, but after so many expeditions the past few years my finances are limited – one Sherpa is all I can afford,' he said when I'd explained the situation.

'Okay … look I'm determined to not let it slip this year,' I replied. 'I've got sponsorship – at least they have said they are still on board. I'll finance three Sherpas for our team.'

'Thanks buddy, I'm truly grateful,' he responded.

We agreed to forge ahead but, on the matter of commencement dates, Tashi was unable to change, saying it would take a month to secure visas. It wasn't giving me the greatest of comfort. I spent the final month on usual expedition final preparations – preparing and refining kit; training by stair climbing; some night hikes along with rock climbing at the local climbing wall; running, cycling and weight training. I also spent time sorting out my business interests and administration for when I would be away.

Although not announcing anything public until ten days before I left, I'd been telling most of my friends about my plans since the beginning of the year. The majority knew exactly what it entailed. 'He was a good man …' joked one Emirates Airline captain friend, who'd always urged me not to try K2, when I told him. He and other Emirates pilot friends regularly flew close to K2 on flights from Dubai to China and Japan, and had seen a unique view of the mountain from their flight decks. Keen to share the sights, more than a few sent me pictures, which were spectacular, if some distance away. On one flight, however, one good friend, Richard Cousins, who'd known about K2 for some time, was routed far closer to the mountain than normal on the flight corridor. His subsequent picture was the first time I'd seen such a close view of K2 from the air – a steep-sided monument soaring above the clouds and the surrounding mountains; razor sharp edges defining its shape and a 150-kilometre snow plume being blasted off the summit in the jet stream winds. It was as absorbing as it was horrendous.

I finally put a post on my Facebook page and website, just ten days before departing, as below:

THE NEXT EXPEDITION – K2
MONDAY, 10 JUNE 2013

18 months thinking about it, over a year in planning and preparation and 6 months of specific and frenetic training, this is the latest challenge I am shortly about to embark on – and there is few bigger. In the world of high-altitude mountaineering K2 is probably the greatest challenge of them all; it's risky, the success rate is low and there is no guarantee of reaching its lofty heights. And due to this, in many ways I'd be happy to keep this quiet and just go off and hopefully do it. However, I treat my sponsors support very gratefully and seriously and, as such, the PR goes with the territory. I will be blogging and posting regularly on this site from today until we head off in just 10 days' time and then from Pakistan itself. Thank you for following.

It inevitably created a great deal of reaction, mostly with people offering their best wishes but many urging me to be safe and careful.

The risks and the reactions were playing on my mind, however. Aside from our time in Nepal, over the past few months I had experienced fitful sleep at nights. I've long had intermittent problems with insomnia, not problems falling asleep – which I do very well indeed because I'm usually so shattered by bedtime – but waking up in the middle of the night. It happens primarily in periods of my life where my mind won't switch off, and is racing with thoughts or I am not at peace. And at this moment in my life, in the months leading up to K2, I definitely wasn't at peace. My thoughts usually turned to my absent children and my concerns would hit me in the depths of the night for weeks. 'This mountain is so risky, how could I be so selfish? What would they feel if anything happened to me? What grief would I give them if I was killed? Is this really worth it?' And so on. Disturbing thoughts on the merits, wisdom and safety in attempting this brutal and dangerous quest. And, although at the peak of physical fitness, also questioning whether I was as fit as I should be. I countered it by telling myself I had always excelled at the greatest of challenges, that I had a good teammate, four experienced Sherpas, a sponsor assumed on board, that I had planned this for eighteen months and prepared physically and mentally for nearly a year. But it was sabre-rattling that never totally eased my doubts that something wasn't quite right.

On my final day in Dubai I managed to fit a bike ride in with my cycling club, the Dubai Roadsters. At the thirty-kilometre break, Wolfgang 'Wolfi' Hohmann, the founder of our club and a close friend, gave a very personal and heartfelt best wishes to me in front of the assembled eighty or so cyclists, who responded with a round of applause which seemed to last a lifetime. Later that morning, at our annual club brunch, he repeated it in an even more personal way, which resulted in the same response, and touched me greatly. Leaving the brunch early to sort out some final matters at home, I gave everyone a big hug as I left – a hug more profound and sincere than 99 per cent of the hugs I've probably given before. Consciously or subconsciously, it was a natural instinct of showing, in case I didn't come back, how important a part in my life these friends were.

CHAPTER FOUR

THE TALIBAN STRIKE

WITH GUNS YOU CAN KILL
TERRORISTS, WITH EDUCATION
YOU CAN KILL TERRORISM.

- MALALA YOUSAFZAI

AT 7 P.M. ON FRIDAY 21 JUNE 2013, I left my home in Dubai for the 9.30 p.m. Emirates flight to Islamabad, laden with approximately seventy kilos of equipment, clothing and food. The flight would take about three hours. I had booked business class, mainly due to the weight I was carrying, and I was looking forward to three hours of relaxation after the frenetic build-up of the past month. The flight was never made... Completely unexpectedly, my Pakistan visa wasn't in order, and the Emirates check-in desk couldn't issue a boarding pass without it. I explained that it was in Islamabad, that all was confirmed as far as I knew, but rules are rules and I wasn't allowed to proceed. Frantic calls to Sultan Khan, the operations manager for NSE, revealed that there had been a mix-up on visas from SST, but they would try and sort matters out the next day. I couldn't believe it; after all this time in planning and preparation my expedition was off to a very dodgy and uncertain start. I returned home in a very low state.

The next morning, I immediately got on the phone to Pakistan. Sultan said they couldn't guarantee I would be let into the country, but they would send a letter which would at least enable me to board the flight that evening. They would then try and obtain a visa at the airport. There was little I could do other than to read all the warm messages that had been sent to me and plan on further refining of kit and some final admin tasks. I wasn't going to mention the delay to anyone – there was no need to and, besides, I wanted some quiet 'me' time. My telephone then rang and, on checking out of curiosity, I sat back in a chair in shock – it was my former partner, whom I hadn't seen or spoken to since September the previous year.

'You promised me you wouldn't go,' she said with concern in her voice, before even saying 'hello'.

'Well, a lot changed last summer,' I replied.

'I'm sorry. Please, please, please be careful,' she urged. 'Promise me Adrian.'

'Getting to the top is optional, getting down is mandatory,' I said, repeating legendary American climber, Ed Viesturs' profound quote. 'I won't do anything stupid.'

She ended up coming around to my house, helping to sort out some kit and taking me to the airport, this time much earlier than normal to ensure documentation was in place. Airport departures can be emotional moments for many people at times and I recalled the occasions years before that I'd kiss my children goodbye, with a deep sense of guilt, eyes welling up as I passed through the departure lounge. Once on the aircraft, however, that singular focus would take over. It had to; continuing those feelings of guilt would undermine the 'zone' I would need to get into. This departure was obviously different but, after a long hug, I left with mixed feelings and more questions than answers. The aircraft departed Dubai at 9.30 p.m. and I settled back into the Emirates business class seat, thankful to be finally under way. Little did I know what was about to happen over 2,000 kilometres away in Pakistan.

On arrival in Islamabad, it took a lot of sterling work from Sultan, plus some mentions from myself that I was a British army officer – even though I'd retired from the army eighteen years earlier – to persuade the immigration authorities to allow me into the country. After two hours and various referrals to higher ranking officials, Sultan finally secured a tourist visa for me, which was my only option given that paperwork hadn't been accepted for an expedition visa. We both breathed an immense sigh of relief.

NSE and SST had arranged our stay in Islamabad in the Intercontinental Hotel. After the stresses of the past few days I was pleased to be staying in a luxury hotel from the giant worldwide hotel group before we headed off on the expedition. When I arrived, however, I realized that 'Intercontinental' was something of poetic license. The place was a shithole. No connection at all with the international group and merely some cheap downtown Islamabad hotel which had seen justification to use the same name.

'Are you serious, Sultan?' I expressed in dismay as we entered the stifling reception, a sleeping watchman waking up to hand us a key.

'We usually accommodate the expeditions here,' he replied sheepishly.

'You don't say,' I replied with my eyes surveying the reception. 'I can see why,' I added, my hands pretending to count money.

'Ah, you have to speak with Seven Summits,' he added, laughing.

'I most definitely will,' I said in a half serious tone.

I ventured upstairs to my room with my three large holdalls and one day bag. Entering the room, I was nearly flattened by the smell of mould. Lying down on the 50-year-old mattress, my butt sunk so deep I probably resembled a foetus on its back. And the pillows had more lumps in than the inedible mashed potatoes I remember from school dinners forty years ago. I decided to forego the bed and keep the ants company on the floor with a roll mat and sleeping bag. Only not in the bag – the heat was so fierce and the air conditioning so inefficient that I slept in the buff. 'I guess I've slept in far worse places,' I muttered to myself, before crashing into a disturbed sleep.

In the morning, I wandered down to breakfast. There were a couple of Europeans in the room, some Pakistanis and some obvious Sherpas. I uttered a normal 'Good Morning' in a cheerful demeanour to see who would respond. Nobody did. Indeed, the entire room was hushed and in deep conversation. A man finally came up to me.

'Adrian sahib?'

'Yes? Tashi?' I replied, recognizing his voice.

'Namaste Adrian, welcome. I'm afraid there's been a terrible tragedy,' he immediately stated with an ashen face.

'What?' I exclaimed. 'What's happened?' I replied in Nepali.

'Nanga Parbat. Terrorists shot eleven climbers in Base Camp last night. They die. It is terrible,' he stuttered.

'What!' I uttered, my eyes looking to the ceiling and brain unable to process the news. 'Let's sit down, tell me what happened.'

Tashi explained what they knew, which would be clarified and confirmed over the course of the day. At 10 p.m. on the evening before, a group of approximately sixteen militants from the Pakistan Taliban had apparently stormed the Base Camp of Nanga Parbat, the 8,126-metre ninth highest mountain in the world, located 200 kilometres from K2 in Pakistan. Dressed in police uniforms, the terrorists killed ten climbers from Ukraine, China, Slovakia, Lithuania and Nepal, plus a local cook from Pakistan. Another twenty-five or so climbers were on rotations up the mountain at the time. Mingma Sherpa, of Tashi's company, was about to enter Base Camp after returning from Camp 1 when he heard the shots. After the attackers fled he had immediately called Tashi on his satellite telephone.

'Some of the climbers were good friends,' Tashi told me. 'Sonam Sherpa was killed and Mr Yang and Mr Rao were the most well-known climbers in China,' he carried on.

'I'm so sorry,' I replied.

'This very bad news for us; and Pakistan.'

'Yes, it is.'

I furrowed my brow, deep in thought. There was discernible shock in Tashi's face. A familiar voice then boomed out across the dining room and I wandered over to him.

'Hi, Al,' I uttered.

'Hey Adrian! Man, have you heard the news?' he exclaimed.

'I sure have, I'm stunned.'

'We all are.'

Another group of Europeans then entered the hotel – the Belgian Gasherbrum (G2) team with their leader, Dutchman Arnold Coster, with whom I had corresponded before; a total of seven climbers and sixteen trekkers. They had been sent home from the airport that morning, prevented from boarding a flight to Skardu, the staging post for all Karakoram eight-thousanders apart from Nanga Parbat, as news of the massacre reached Islamabad. Arnold, Al and myself sat down with Tashi to share thoughts, concerns and implications. They all knew many of the victims and spoke of the climbs and mountains they had shared. All of the slain climbers were experienced high-altitude mountaineers, befitting of the experience necessary to tackle Nanga Parbat – along with K2, probably the most technical and difficult of the fourteen eight-thousanders. The two Chinese, Mr Yan and Mr Rao, in particular, were the most accomplished mountaineers in China, having summited eleven and ten eight-thousanders respectively, including K2 the previous year.

It later transpired that the attackers had reportedly found their way to the 4,200-metre Base Camp by abducting two Pakistani guides, travelling thereafter by foot or on horseback. They firstly ordered climbers to hand over money, satellite phones and passports before tying their hands with ropes and shooting them in the back of the head. The Pakistani cook was killed because he was a Shia. Another Chinese climber, Zhang Jingchuan, who was in Base Camp at the time, miraculously survived the attack by making a dash in the darkness when his fellow climbers started to be shot. He avoided the Taliban by lying in a ditch before making his way to higher ground.

High-altitude mountaineering is one of the very few sports, occupations or pastimes, outside of the military in a combat zone, where death is a constant risk, continually faced and often talked about. In various studies and measurements of risk, it has been deemed *the* most risky sport of all – a full twenty-six times riskier than base jumping. An outsider observing a group of mountaineers gathered around a fire or table would be shocked at how frequently death is mentioned. Eventually the conversation will turn to some colleague being swept to his death by an avalanche on a Nepal giant, followed by someone else being killed in a fall on a Chinese peak, followed by so and so dying of altitude sickness on a mountain in Pakistan. It can all appear very casual, matter of fact and lacking any apparent empathy or emotion. But the insinuation that climbers are flippant about life and death is untrue. Most climbers will conversely say they climb to feel alive.

These deaths, however, were entirely different. Whilst it's an accepted risk of the sport to die from avalanches, falls, hypothermia or altitude, to be killed by a cold-blooded mass execution by sixteen murderers wasn't. And the shocked reaction and extreme sadness of my fellow climbers in our Islamabad hotel showed that even supposedly hard-core, death-defying risk takers have emotions and are human.

Amidst the shock and condolences, we inevitably spoke about the implications for our K2 and Gasherbrum expeditions. For, despite the tragedy, we were all determined to proceed. Part of the reasoning for this lay in the geography of Nanga Parbat, which lies in an unstable area of Pakistan. The region's main city, Chilas, had experienced much unrest and killings over the years. Nanga Parbat's relatively low Base Camp, easily accessible from Chilas, was another negative factor in assessing the risks.

K2, Broad Peak, G1 and G2, by contrast, were located 200 kilometres further east of Nanga Parbat, in the high Karakoram province of Baltistan – a province in south-east Pakistan that was always considered safe. In addition, trekking to K2's Base Camp alone required an eight-day trek on a single glacier just to reach it. These facts gave us some degree of confidence that continuing the expeditions would be safe. Our major concern would be the possibility of flights being cancelled due to weather – a frequent occurrence – and having to drive to Skardu by bus.

Some people reading this might feel that we were somewhat blasé about the risks we faced heading into the Karakoram after such an atrocity, particularly given the follow-up statement from the Taliban that all foreigners in Pakistan would be targets. Indeed, many might think we were crazy. However, it's another trait of climbers that, when faced with and dealing with risk and the possibilities of death constantly, they tend to evaluate risk with a far more evolved, logical and less emotional attitude than 99 per cent of the population. I've always taken the view that the week after a terrorist attack on an aircraft, in a shopping mall or in a country, is probably the safest time ever to fly, go shopping or visit that country. Because normally complacent police, army and security staff are subsequently vigilant. And therein lies an uncomfortable truth.

It was therefore an interesting observation that 95 per cent of all trekking tours, either already in Pakistan or due to arrive, would cancel their trips, leading to a crushing blow to the already damaged Pakistan tourism industry. Not one climber, however, either in the hotel or already trekking to their respective Base Camps, cancelled their expeditions. Most of us concluded that we faced far greater threats on the mountains we would be attempting than by the small threat of a similar terrorist incident happening again.

That decision, however, could be out of our hands. The Pakistan government, which had immediately announced that all Nanga Parbat climbers would be evacuated and all expeditions on the peak cancelled for the season, could easily issue a similar order for the other four eight-thousanders. We discussed how they could impose this when many teams were already well on their journeys to their respective Base Camps. But anything was possible.

Little was going to happen for a few days, whatever the outcome, so all we could do was wait. And wait we did – for an entire week. It was murder. The heat in a hotel with limited air conditioning was intolerable, the food grisly and the internet sporadic and slow. Not the ideal place to be with no idea of an outcome. Outside wasn't much better; with due respect to my Pakistani friends, much of Islamabad is a sight which is far from aesthetical. The air in summer is heavily polluted from traffic fumes and dust. Litter and rubbish line the streets. And, above all, poverty abounds everywhere with countless children, elderly or the maimed begging on street corners or traffic junctions, in torn and filthy clothes. Like many Middle Eastern and Asian countries, Pakistan is tragically paying for having a birth rate and population way beyond its means, one that has seen its numbers soar by an incredible sixty-three million people in the past fifteen years alone, to a total now approaching 190 million. It is a devastating state of affairs, and one to which the Pakistan government's responses over the past decades have been negligent. The entire government and civil service is built on an impossible bureaucracy, inherited from the British, but one that has barely changed since independence. Corruption is inherent and it takes weeks or months for most matters to be dealt with, sometimes years. So, we ventured nowhere other than the hotel or the shops and restaurants surrounding it.

The international news agencies had reported the Nanga Parbat murders widely, and the Islamabad office of the BBC and other mainstream news agencies were contacting us or turning up at the hotel looking for information – our hotel being the base for the remaining expeditioners in the Karakoram. As the only British mountaineer apparently in the country that summer, the British press asked me for some comments on the tragedy and our forthcoming plans. As always, some questions could only be answered by an 'it's too soon to deduce the full circumstances' or 'that information will likely become clearer in a day or two'. When asked whether we would continue our climb of K2, however, the answer was an unequivocal 'yes'.

After three days, the climbers who had been at higher camps on Nanga Parbat at the time of the massacre returned to our hotel. All of them were from former Eastern European or Asian countries. Many had their equipment trashed or burned in the atrocity. We spoke with Mingma Sherpa, the Sherpa who had been just above Base Camp when the Taliban arrived. Like most Nepalis, he was resilient to the disaster but told us in greater detail what he had experienced. It was a sobering tale.

Things were getting increasingly frustrating, with rumours, speculation and assumptions abounding. One day it all seemed likely that everything would be called off, the next that the government would be providing a military aircraft to transport remaining climbers to the Karakoram. Part of the problem was that we couldn't just get in a truck and drive a few hours to the hills. We needed to travel over 600 kilometres to Skardu, which meant either flying or driving forty hours non-stop through an entire day and night on the notorious Karakoram Highway. The highway goes straight past Nanga Parbat and the volatile city of Chilas en route and naturally there wasn't too much enthusiasm for that option. Al had made the journey the previous year when a bus, full of Shia Muslims, was stopped by police just a few kilometres ahead of his truck. The 'police' turned out to be imposters and murdered twenty-two people in the bus. He and his fellow climbers were rushed off to a safe house for twenty-four hours before continuing their journey.

Flying, therefore, appeared by far the more sensible option, but flights to Skardu were always overbooked with first availabilities often stretching to a week or more ahead. In addition, the small ATR or Fokker aircraft used didn't have the capacity to carry the equipment of the climbers and trekkers left in the hotel, which meant that a truck needed to be used whatever the options on flights. Being just two of us, Al and myself were in a much better position than the Belgian G2 team of five climbers and seven trekkers – eleven of their trekkers had already decided it was too risky and returned home. But it also became clear that one decision would be made for all.

Swiss–South African climber Mike Horn arrived at the hotel on 27 June, and we went out to dinner that night at one of his favourite restaurants. Al had met him before, but it was the first time our paths had crossed. Horn was an icon in the adventure world and there was probably no other person on earth who had achieved more all-round major goals than he had. A two-year journey around the world on the equator was one of his finest achievements; reaching the North Pole in winter with polar legend Borge Ousland another. He was also a highly-experienced mountaineer with several eight-thousanders under his belt. Instantly likeable, but mad as a hatter to some, he was an effervescent character who was extremely tactile. The only problem was that, far from 'touchy-feely', his interpretation of being tactile was 'touchy-painfully' as he grabbed you on the hand, shoulder, arm or leg with a pressure I have yet to experience from anything other than a vice. It was a pleasure to meet him and we shared adventure stories for over three hours whilst devouring continually served grilled beef and chicken – the best meal we'd eaten in Pakistan that week. Mike's two Swiss teammates were already on their way to K2 Base Camp, and he'd already decided he was going to drive to Skardu early the next morning.

'Ya fellas, you're stuck eer with no choice,' he drawled in his thick South African accent. 'I'm going before dey can pull the plug and heading strite to de mountains.'

Al and I would probably have joined him but, aside from all the other problems, I still had no expedition visa to venture out of Islamabad. I was prepared to take my chances on my tourist visa and sort out the overextension on my return – rightly or wrongly, another example of a less concerned attitude than most to what I considered a small risk. Sultan Khan was insistent that the police and army checkpoints we would cross would certainly stop me proceeding.

We therefore had to visit the ministerial offices for the supposedly simple task of sorting out my visa. Except that nothing is simple when it comes to Pakistani bureaucracy. Walking into offices that didn't look like they had seen a mop or duster since the country's independence sixty years earlier, with papers and files piled two feet high on every desk, it baffled me how anyone ever got any visa issued. With my having to repeat the procedure three times to different ministries, each time waiting hours to be seen, I was left utterly astounded at how the entire Ministry of Tourism could ever hope to entice visitors to the country with such archaic procedures in place. It took Sultan most of the week to obtain visas for both myself and our Sherpas, which also hadn't come through in time, further delaying any possible thoughts of getting away early.

Having been marooned for a week in the overbearing heat of an Islamabad hotel whose only claim to being 'Intercontinental' was the suffering incurred by a Brit, Canadian, Dutchman, eleven Belgians and eight Nepalis, we received word that our expeditions had finally been cleared by the ministries of tourism and defence. Furthermore, they announced that we would be flying to Skardu on additional flights provided by Pakistan Airways. At last we would shortly be on our way.

CHAPTER FIVE

SKARDU AND THE BALTORO

JOY IN LOOKING AND
COMPREHENDING IS NATURE'S
MOST BEAUTIFUL GIFT.

– ALBERT EINSTEIN

ON 28 JUNE 2013, Al and myself left our hotel for Islamabad domestic terminal on the first phase of our long journey to K2 Base Camp – an internal flight to the city of Skardu. Our four Sherpas had left the night before with most of the baggage to travel the same journey by road. It seemed unfair, but that is what we were paying them for.

Although the Nanga Parbat murderers had been captured, the Taliban threats to westerners were still very much alive and there was a degree of caution about overtly displaying our pale faces on the thirty-minute car journey to the airport. Unfortunately, tinted windscreens for added safety and security weren't an available option in the thirty-year-old trucks we were travelling in. As in all such 'danger zones', the real situation and actual threat on the ground, as opposed to what one might believe from watching the media, was small. Nevertheless, I've always approached any situation with a 'what if' and 'actions on' mindset installed from my military career. And, however remote the threat on the streets of Islamabad was, it's a useful exercise to go through. The problem is that inside a truck without any weapons, one is extremely vulnerable if stopped and hence why keeping driving at all costs is a prime objective. If stopped, talking one's way out of a possible confrontation may be the only real option.

We passed many police and army checkpoints en route, a completely normal circumstance in Islamabad. 'Salaam w'alaykum' (peace be with you) – the universal greeting of the Muslim world – was offered by me at each checkpoint, met with a 'w'alaykum A-Salaam' (and peace be to you) but few smiles or other interaction. With thousands of cars every hour, and in the brutal heat and dust, there was little incentive for the uniformed men to be anything else.

After thirty minutes our trucks arrived at the domestic terminal of Islamabad airport. Western tourists were now as rare a sight in Islamabad as blue skies, clouds and the sun, such is the pollution in the city. And with the Belgians booked on a later flight, Al and myself stuck out like two polar bears in a coal mine. Many people looked at us, wondering what could possibly bring two guys dressed in shorts and hiking boots to want to visit Islamabad in summer. I wondered the same myself. Most, however, simply got on with their business of getting through the mayhem of the terminal to their flights. If the international terminal was chaotic, the domestic terminal felt like a stampede in a market. It was bedlam.

We eventually reached security. Like other experiences to date, this word is also used loosely. Despite the increased threats, I managed to get through the first machines with an expedition knife and lighters not being picked up, and decided to leave them in my hand baggage rather than the one hold bag I was checking in. They passed through without issue. It was light years from the UK's ultra-extreme, some would say overzealous, procedures that require every innocuous tube of toothpaste, gel or spray to be placed in a plastic ziplock bag.

After waiting for many more hours seated, slumped or lying on our bags, the announcement finally came for boarding. On sitting down in my aircraft seat, I immediately fell asleep, barely conscious of our taking off. My slumber was only disturbed when Al shook me to show me the scenery unfolding below. Nanga Parbat was to our north within touching distance of the flight path – a vast island of ice, snow and rock soaring to 8,126 metres in a surrounding area of rural Pakistan of far lower altitude. Looking at the peace and serenity of the scenery before our eyes, it was hard to imagine such bloodshed had been inflicted at its Base Camp just one week before.

Having flown over increasingly rugged countryside with decreasingly numbers of roads and settlements, we landed at Skardu. Unfortunately, but perhaps not entirely surprisingly given the misfortunes so far, the one bag I had checked into the aircraft hold hadn't arrived. In today's interconnected world, with daily flights between cities and computerized tags for luggage, a missing bag will invariably find its way to its owner the next day. This, however, was Pakistan, a remote town in the Karakoram and bar-coded bags were probably a generation away! More concerns and delays resulted while my missing luggage found its way to Skardu.

Spectacularly located at the confluence of the Indus and Shigar rivers, Skardu is the capital of the Baltistan province of the district of Gilgit-Baltistan, situated close to the Chinese province of Xinjiang and disputed territory of Indian Kashmir. Surrounding the town, which lies at an altitude of 2,500 metres, are mountains rising to 5,000 metres whilst beyond on the Chinese border, are the four remaining 8,000-metre giants of Pakistan. The people of Baltistan speak Balti, a language similar to ancient Tibetan. Indeed, such are the similarities with Tibet in the form of culture, lifestyle and architecture, Baltistan is also known as 'Tibet-e-Khurd' (Little Tibet).

We were taken to the Concordia Hotel on the outskirts of town, and greeted by its owner, Mr Sher Ali. Long a regular staging post for Karakoram expeditions, the hotel was a haven of peace and tranquillity, with green gardens and a terrace overlooking the slow-moving Indus River drifting below. The contrast with the overpopulation, poverty and pollution of Islamabad couldn't have been greater.

A large reception was held that evening in the hotel, attended by local hotels, tourist operators, outfitters, the media and special guest, Manzoor Hussain, President of the Alpine Club of Pakistan, who had flown into Skardu the day before. In speech after speech, dignitaries apologized profusely for the massacre at Nanga Parbat and condemned the Taliban with a ferocity that was refreshing compared to the often lukewarm condemnation uttered in many countries with problems of Islamic terrorism. Each speaker thanked us graciously for our faith in the Pakistan tourism industry, welcomed us with a gratitude and warmness which was heartfelt and assured us that we were as safe as anywhere in the world in Baltistan.

The next day I tested this in practice as I walked into the town. Although Skardu sees many Western climbers and trekkers, many people still greeted us in broken English with a 'good morning', 'hello' or 'salaam w'alaykum'. Regardless of what words were said, I felt a distinct sense of safety and security. As we would later be told, the Balti were far removed from the more extreme elements of Pakistani society. And we – climbers and hikers – were their livelihood. An entire region's income was dependent on us visiting, staying in hotels, eating food and, above all, using hundreds of porters to carry equipment up the Baltoro glacier. Little wonder, then, that the Balti were so scathing of the Taliban who had endangered their entire livelihood. And as we were also reassured by everyone we met, any outsiders arriving in Skardu would be immediately noticeable in the close-knit Balti community. I concluded that we were indeed as safe in Skardu as we could be anywhere in the world.

I spent a few hours walking around the dusty town, surrounded by its stunning snow-capped mountains. The weather was a pleasant twenty-five degrees Celsius. Fresh mangoes were abundant on many outside stalls, the mangoes from Pakistan being the sweetest in the world. I bought five and asked the young boy selling them, who couldn't have been more than 9 years of age, to peel one for me to eat on the roadside. Different types of cashews, almonds and dried apricots were available in bulk, piled into twenty or more huge baskets in many shops, and the shopkeepers thanked me wholeheartedly when I bought several kilos of each. Wandering into a hairdresser to get a pre-expedition close crop, my request to 'give me David Beckham' caused much amusement and laughter from the locals. Some English traditions and icons travel to the farthest corners of the earth.

With no training of any kind possible for a week whilst we were delayed in Skardu, I took a run and hike late in the afternoon up to the ancient mountain fort called Kharpocho (King of Forts), located on a hill dominating the town. The fort was constructed by Ali Sher Khan Anchan, who ruled over Baltistan until the end of the sixteenth century. Hiking up to the fort from the Indus River required some steep hiking and scrambling in places – the side facing the town, meanwhile, was a sheer escarpment. Little wonder that the fort probably received only sporadic visitors. I thus had the entire mountain and the ruins of the fort to explore for myself. Perched on the edge of the escarpment with clear views over the town and surrounding country, I could see why old Ali Sher built it. Given the effort it took me to climb up, I wondered if any possible invaders even bothered.

We were keen to get on our way and commence our long journey to K2 Base Camp. But here, yet again, we faced possible delays as our liaison officer hadn't yet arrived and needed to be with us for the journey. Liaison officers (LO) are part of the regulations imposed by the Pakistan government, and every Karakoram expedition is appointed a junior officer from the Pakistan Armed Forces to accompany the expedition throughout its length. Rehmat Ali, Nazir Sabir's Skardu manager, told us that, in previous years, an LO would often arrive late and join teams on the trek in, or even at Base Camp. Following the events at Nanga Parbat, however, clear instructions had been remitted that liaison officers were to travel with teams together through the heavily militarized early stages of the journey. That meant waiting. I took the opportunity of the delay to have a meeting with Al.

'Al, are you free to have a chat?' I asked.

'Sure, what about?' he replied.

'Well, I don't do anything with any group of people without having some team agreements in place.'

'You mean putting all our cards on the table? Great idea, I'm on board. How long we need – twenty minutes?'

'I reckon a good few hours …'

I then proceeded to go through a comprehensive list of agreements I had drawn up over the past few years, which I use to varying degrees in my work in corporations, right through to people staying at my house. Everything, from agreeing what our objectives for the journey were, to toilet habits, our individual boundaries, to agreement on what we would do in the case of disagreement, was aired. Anything which could possibly affect how we worked as a team was put on the table, discussed and an agreement reached. I wrote everything down in a makeshift 'charter'.

Some readers might think this somewhat over the top, but I have found through teaching, training and my own bitter experience, the vital need for these rules. That is, unless you get agreements in place at the beginning of any couple or group of people embarking on a task, project or even a life together – and review them regularly – misunderstandings, misassumptions, friction, conflict and chaos can result. We needed to speak openly, honestly and transparently on about thirty or so points which could all impact on how effectively we worked, lived and gelled together for the next two months. Which would also be a key determining factor of how successful we would be.

One agreement, above all, was sacrosanct – the permission and agreement that either of us could say anything we wanted to the other, good or bad, without the other taking it personally. That agreement, provided it was done with unconditional positive regard for the sake of the team, was critical in creating the total trust that we would need on K2. Far too often, whether it's between teammates, friends or couples, things get left unsaid for fear of the other's reaction. That issue can then fester and build over days, weeks or months before reaching such a crescendo that it finally comes out in an explosive rage, causing irreparable damage to the relationship. Leaving things unsaid, unease at reactions, distractions and festering prevents the open and transparent communication which every high-performing team needs to succeed. And whilst such distractions are detrimental in any environment and team, on K2 it could make the difference between safety and missing a hurtling rock flying down a mountain face. Our 'chat' lasted five hours.

'Great session, Adrian, thank you!' Al said as we finally finished.

'Pleasure mate. It's well worth the time invested, believe me,' I replied.

'Oh, I sure do.'

'Let's grab some lunch.'

Weeks later, when a strong argument did indeed ensue between us high up on K2, we had a charter in place, which we could refer to.

Our liaison officer, Flight Lieutenant Rizwan Haider from the Pakistan Air Force, arrived on the 29 June. That meant we were free to complete the final paperwork process – a briefing at the

Ministry of Tourism in town. The K2 team (Al Hancock and myself, plus our four Sherpas and our LO) and the Belgian G2 team were duly taken to the said ministry to receive a briefing and sign expedition papers.

With clearance obtained and our departure from Skardu confirmed for the following day, an almighty packing operation got under way at the Concordia Hotel by hotel staff, Nazir Sabir staff, porters and our Sherpas. At times the amount of kit, equipment, food and supplies being sorted, moved and stacked resembled the baggage terminal of Heathrow Airport on the busiest travel day of the year. 500 tons of luggage were somehow loaded in, on and above ten Mark 1 Toyota Land Cruisers arriving at the hotel in the afternoon in preparation for the eight-to-ten-hour drive to Askole.

The following morning, we all crammed into the trucks; Al, Rizwan and myself staking our claim on a vehicle with open sides to allow some fresh air to alleviate the pain. We agreed on a roster of the three of us rotating round the relatively spacious front seat with the two cramped seats in the back. 'Relative' is emphasized – we were competing for every seat with bags, food boxes and everything bar a live goat for a dinner. I'm sure I saw one of those loaded too.

Al had warned me that this stage of the journey was the most uncomfortable road trip I was ever likely to face. I wasn't to be disappointed. It was a bone-crunching expedition by itself, with our old 4WDs shuddering over every rock, divot or trench encountered. And if that wasn't bad enough, I was feeling utterly wretched from something eaten the night before. Nothing was digesting in my stomach and I suffered in acute pain for the nine hours of the journey.

Several sections of the road were damaged by landfall. Our drivers somehow navigated the trucks along narrow two-metre-wide sections of the road, the outermost tyres dangling on the edge of the bank, which dropped seventy-five metres down to the Braldu River. At one point the road was considered too dangerous for us to stay in the trucks and everyone walked, eyes constantly on the unstable steep slopes above us. How it was deemed too hazardous for us to be in the cars, but not our gallant drivers, is a pertinent question.

Finally, after nine miserable hours, we arrived in Askole – without doubt the most arduous road journey I have ever undertaken. I probably looked like death and certainly felt like it, but death would have been a relief. Askole is notable as being the final remote settlement before the wilderness of the Karakoram. Situated at an altitude of 3,300 metres, it was a village that looked like something out of the Middle Ages. Houses built of wood and sand mashed together in tight communities. Women were only seen toiling the fields around the town. Although already veiled and most wearing face masks, any attempts at taking a picture or video was met with a turning of their backs or even aggressive gestures that this was *haram* (forbidden). I've lived in the Middle East for many years and knew this wasn't a scene isolated to Askole alone, but even so, whilst women's rights and lives are slowly evolving, there is a long way to go.

Although we may not have been completely welcomed by the women of the village, it was in Askole that we vividly saw, in the most visual way, how vital we were to the local economy. Hundreds of men and boys gathered on the edges of our fenced compound hoping to get chosen for portering duties. Dressed in little more than rags and with some looking as young as 12-year-olds, it was hard not to feel both a degree of satisfaction at our helping the community, coupled with distinct guilt at the comparison of their tattered clothing to our high-tech gear.

What the selection criteria was I have no idea, but somehow Muhammad Nafees Khan (Nafees), and his team from Nazir Sabir, chose, assembled and delegated the roles of nearly 150 porters to carry the mass loads to K2 and G2 Base Camps. All the bags were weighed and allocated to a porter in the second phase of the operation. We would be trekking with a small day pack; they would be carrying three holdalls, barrels or equipment weighing forty kilos or more.

'It doesn't look as though "elf and safety at work" has quite reached Askole,' I joked to Arnold Coster in an exaggerated British union accent.

'Yesh, Adriaan, I think yer rright,' he acknowledged in his mellowed Dutch.

'If this was the UK, the unions would have downed tools and called a national strike!'

'If zish was Holland you'd shee a room full of shivil shervants with bucketsh of regulashuns and rrules. You'd sit with yer mouth full of teeth!'

'Ish zhat sit or shit, Arnold?' I asked, mimicking the Dutch accent to its fullest.

'Probably boath!' he roared.

The next day, 1 July 2013, we all left Askole early to commence the long trek to K2 Base Camp, starting with an anticipated six-hour hike to a camping spot called Korofong at 3,500 metres. A trek to an 8,000-metre mountain, Base Camp is always one of the most enjoyable parts of any expedition and this was no different. Within an hour of leaving the village the entire panorama of the Karakoram unfolded before our eyes.

The Pakistan the West reads about or sees in newspapers, or on TV, is invariably one of terrorism, the Taliban, suicide bombers, corruption, poverty and unstable governments. Here finally was the Pakistan few of us see – a spectacular and largely deserted landscape of ice-capped mountains, green valleys, streams, waterfalls and rivers. It was stunning.

'Al, I don't mean to be unsociable, but don't wait for me,' I said after an hour when stopping for a call of nature. 'I actually love to walk on my own on treks in.' I added.

'I'm the same!' he exclaimed. 'I want to get my thoughts in order, listen to music and enjoy nature.'

'Yep, you've got it. Great, we're aligned. I'll catch you in a few hours.'

As Al carried on, I had a pee, a drink and some food, strapped on my pack and set off ten minutes behind. Aside from the dodgy 'Hotel Intercontinental' bedrooms, this was the first time I had been alone since arriving in Islamabad. And I needed that time and space. Devoid of the bombardment of information from emails and social media channels which our modern lives and technology overwhelms us with, I soon entered my own world of deep thought, appreciation of nature, contemplation and focus. Alone in my thoughts, sights, sounds and smell, my mind marvelled in the presence of sharp sculptured peaks coming into view.

I reflected on the future with the forthcoming climb of K2. The deep concerns about our delays, the shortened time frames and the challenges ahead were eased somewhat by our finally being on the move and the beauty of my surroundings. We were now on our way and I entered that mindset of focus, positivity and getting 'into the zone'. The steep climbing was ten days or more away; this was time to get my mountain legs back, my equipment, systems, acclimatization and my mindset honed.

And I finally had time to contemplate on the journey over the last eighteen months that had led me here. It had been a torrid twelve months plagued with trauma, despair and heartache. I thought of the many times this expedition never looked like it would happen and the challenges we'd faced. I thought of all my friends heading off on their summer vacations around the world with their partners and families. And, above all, I thought of my children. Deep thoughts of longing, love and missing them intensely. I wondered how they were; what they would be thinking; whether they even knew where I was. I had no idea of the answers to those questions; all I could do was think of them and send my heartfelt love over the thousands of miles that separated us.

At such times of deep thought and contemplation, time has no meaning. I may have thought about something for two minutes, twenty minutes or two hours, it made no difference. Plugging in some music at stages took me even further into another world. It was my own form of meditation – a practice that, to the dismay of many in the coaching and self-development world, I don't, can't and won't do. I allowed myself to smile, remembering the various shocked reactions of those in the profession who would exclaim such platitudes as, 'How can you possibly NOT meditate?' Well, here in the high Karakoram, in the most stunning landscape on earth, with some New Age, Enya or reiki music in my ears, I was on as deep or even deeper frequency than sitting cross-legged on a floor in a London flat.

Sometimes, I'd be snapped out of my deep thoughts by a porter passing me with his forty-kilo weight on his back. Or by the sight of a crow swooping down the raging river. Or a minor avalanche on distant peaks. But then I'd return to my zone. The hours whittled away in bliss.

'Hey, Adrian!' Al shouted as I turned a corner. 'How you doing, buddy? The camp's about ten minutes away. Let's walk in.'

'Man, I needed that day. Finally got my thoughts in order, I'm focused and in a good place,' he added.

'You said it,' I replied. 'An amazing day. What I desperately needed.'

We walked into Korofong and camped for the night – a sheltered clump of trees with some terraced platforms for the multitude of tents. It was a long way from Nepal's lodges and teahouses, but at least the government had constructed some toilets. I put my tent as far away from possible snoring companions as I could.

The journey over the next week followed a similar pattern. Up at first light, tea and some eggs, a packed lunch provided by the cooking team and on our way by 6 a.m. The route meandered up the Baltoro valley, eventually hitting the moraines of the Baltoro glacier. Each day the track became progressively more rugged and the trek between camps longer as we slowly gained altitude. It was hard trekking with a lot of steep sections, loose rocks and route finding on a glacier which sometimes stretched to a kilometre in width – far removed from the well-marked and easy trails of Nepal.

As the route became ever more rugged, any concerns of a Taliban attack on K2 Base Camp disappeared into near obscurity. No terrorist would want, or be able, to trek so long up such a hard route without a team carrying tents and supplies. And, if they did, they would be immediately noticed by the army of porters trekking up and down the glacier. And, finally, just in case they did try, there were a couple of army checkpoints to cross. Of the numerous challenges we would be facing, being shot by a masked coward was the least of our worries.

On 4 July, we heard that an Austrian team had summited Broad Peak, the twelfth highest mountain in the world, whose Base Camp was only a couple of hours' trek from K2. Although welcome news that conditions were already good enough to summit, it peeved me off that here was a team summiting a mountain only 600 metres lower than K2, and yet we hadn't even reached Base Camp. Nanga Parbat strike or not, it reinforced my concerns that the entire expedition was woefully later than it should have been. We later read that only one climber had reached the main summit, although six had reached the fore-summit.

On 5 July, Al and myself approached Concordia Camp, where the Baltoro glacier takes a distinct junction: the northerly glacier leading to Broad Peak, K2 and the Chinese border and the southerly glacier heading to the Gasherbrums. Concordia is notable in that it is the first time that K2 is visible at any point on the trek in, due to the mountains and escarpments which line the glacier. I thought I'd savour the moment for posterity.

'Al, I don't want to see K2 for the first time appearing slowly behind the mountains. I want to see it in all its glory, in full!' I said.

'Great idea,' he laughed. 'Walk alongside me and I will tell you when to look.'

As K2 slowly appeared, I kept a steadfast look at my feet and the ground in front, refusing to be tempted to look to my left. After five minutes, we reached a point where Al said I could turn. I dropped my bag and decided to hand him my video camera to record the moment. As I turned to face K2 for the first time, my reaction, completely unscripted, was captured on film.

'Oh my God!' I laughed, followed by a period of silence as I tried to comprehend the sight.

'Wow … wow! That looks steep! In fact, that looks incredibly steep! How are we going to climb it?' I joked, turning to Al behind the camera.

'One step at a time,' he answered.

'Anyway, mountains look much steeper the further you are away from them. When you get closer they are far less steep,' I commented in a mock attempt to explain my reaction. 'But that is impressive.'

And so it was. The first sight of the mountain literally took my breath away. There, finally, in full view on a perfect sunny and warm day was K2. *The* K2! The greatest challenge in high-altitude mountaineering in front of my very eyes. It was a sight that provided some sensory overload. The steepness was sobering: sheer raw edges launching from the glacier floor to the summit. The Abruzzi Spur was visible on the right skyline; the Cesen to its left; the 'shoulder' of K2, the site for the final Camp 4, looked to be the only place on the entire mountain which wasn't a near vertical wall. It was a mesmerizing scene, and I stayed gazing at it for a full five minutes.

Yet, despite the sensory overload, there was also something strangely reassuring about actually seeing it. The uncertainty had somewhat dissipated. Up until this moment in time, K2 had only ever been a name, pictures, a statistic, a fierce reputation, a mystery, a complete unknown and a complete uncertainty. Now, finally it was there for real, right in front of my eyes. And for all its steepness, some degree of uncertainty had dissolved.

And therein lies the lesson – another basic human need, that of our need for certainty. We, as a species, don't do well with the unknown. The known, good or bad, is far easier for us to process. Examples abound in all walks of life, but the most notable is one of a health scare. A woman who discovers a lump in her breast, or a man who discovers a lump in his groin, is hit by a sense of concern. The doctor he or she sees says it may or may not be cancerous and refers them for a scan and biopsy. The earliest appointment is six weeks away. When the results come, if it's benign there is an obvious massive sense of relief. Yet, conversely, if people find it is malignant there is often an acceptance, an eerie calmness and a determination to fight the 'Big C'. The uncertainty has gone, he or she has cancer and 'we're going to fight it!' But it is that six weeks of unknown, prior to the good or bad news, that is so distressing for us. It eats away at us, preys on our minds, is never far from our thoughts and affects our entire essence in a life diminishing ebb.

Mountaineering is full of the unknown and uncertainty, of course. There is no guarantee of a 'finisher's medal', no pre-booked 'summit picture', no money-back refund if you don't make the summit. It is total uncertainty, even for something as profound as one's continued existence. And yet a degree of uncertainty had now been relinquished. The unknown which had consumed me for months, causing all sorts of anguish, largely disappeared. At that moment, I saw the mountain which I would be living on, forming a deep connection with, and forging an intense relationship with over the coming weeks. It was real, it was magnificent, it was hugely challenging, but, finally, it was known.

We stayed at Concordia for an hour, chatting to the Belgians and some Pakistani HAPs (high-altitude porters), taking photographs and videos and drinking tea. It was all quite a party atmosphere in the warm sunshine. Finally, it was time to bid farewell to Arnold and the Belgians who were heading to the G2. They had become good friends in the two weeks we'd been in Pakistan and we were sorry to see them go.

'Best of luck guys. Wave to us from the top!' shouted one as we headed in our separate directions.

'First team to summit and back here buys the beers!' someone else shouted.

And then we were down to seven – myself, Hancock and Lieutenant Rizwan, together with Lakpa, Mingma, Nurbu and Nima. Our army of porters were ahead or behind. As it was getting late we stopped at 4 p.m. to camp, setting up a table and chair on a perfect day in full view of the mountain. The next day, Saturday, 6 July 2013, we trekked a further hour to Broad Peak Base Camp, stopping for thirty minutes to chat to teams there. And after a further hour and a half, we reached K2 Base Camp. The first phase of the journey was complete.

CHAPTER SIX

BASE CAMP

HOME ISN'T WHERE YOU'RE
FROM, IT'S WHERE YOU FIND
LIGHT WHEN ALL GROWS
DARK.

– PIERCE BROWN

FOR THOSE WHO HAVEN'T EVER visited a Base Camp of an 8,000-metre or high-altitude mountain, they can be inspiring or disappointing, beautiful or a blight, a place to strive for or a place to get away from. Located at anywhere between 4,100 metres and 5,300 metres, the highest Base Camp in the world (Mount Everest) is conveniently situated at the maximum height of any permanent human settlement on earth. That honour goes not to a Himalayan settlement, but to a Peruvian mining village in the Andes called La Rinconada. The interesting fact about this 5,100-metre-elevation village is that the miners have tried to settle higher, but all attempts have eventually failed due to a gradual physiological deterioration of their bodies. Given that mountaineers will spend up to two months climbing an 8,000-metre peak, the same rules apply and hence why most Base Camps will be located around this height – the maximum elevation to aid acclimatization, balanced with the need for a flat, safe and stable location with good water supplies. For those eight-thousanders with lower Base Camps, or those with long treks from camp to the mountain, an Advanced Base Camp (ABC) is usually established up to a height of 5,800 metres or so, with some degree of facilities.

Situated at just below 5,000 metres, K2 Base Camp is located on a narrow spur of moraine on the mountain side of the Baltoro glacier. It is the last piece of real estate composed of rocks and relatively flat ground, before the moraine gives way to broken ice, boulders and the streams of the glacier. A few more continued hours trek up the glacier leads to ABC, located just short of the Chinese border, but that area, otherwise known as 'crampon point', is primarily to store some ice climbing equipment in a few tents, as opposed to a camp for sleeping. To enable an early start when climbing the mountain, some teams sleep at ABC the night before, but most use the relative comfort of Base Camp as their launch station.

With glacial streams on both sides of the moraine, the site has ample supplies of water and when the sun shines, usually in the mornings, it can be warm and pleasant. Conversely, it can also be a place of heavy snow, precipitation and white-outs, making it a quite inhospitable. At night, temperatures plummet to minus twenty degrees Celsius or lower.

Trekking over a glacial ridge on our last day of the trek in, on 6 July 2013, we saw the multitude of tents, grouped in their obvious teams, leading up to the top of the moraine. Due to the narrow width of the moraine, the tents were well stretched out – a distance I would later calculate at over 400 metres. The community of those attempting eight-thousanders is growing and although we didn't know exactly how many teams and climbers would be there, Al was sure to know some. We did realize that we would probably be the last team to arrive.

The first group we met were the Japanese team, an eight-strong group, though only six would be climbing. They gave us the usual warm and genuine welcome I have come to experience of the Japanese, offering us tea, soft drinks and food. Had we stayed any longer, I'm half convinced they would have bought out sushi, sake and a karaoke machine, but we bid our farewells after ten minutes to move on up the moraine. Although only one in the team spoke reasonable English, we learned they were the first team to establish base at K2 and had set up fixed lines to Camp 1.

The next team we met were the Spanish team of Alex Txikon, Felix Criado and Benjamin Salazar (Mexico). Alex had passed us on the trek to Base Camp so we already got to meet him – a vastly experienced high-altitude climber with ten eight-thousanders to his name. Felix was met for the first time, but Al knew Benjamin from a previous climb and immediately started to share news of climbs and mutual friends. They were a friendly trio.

The next tent belonged to Zdravko Dejanovic from Macedonia, who we'd all call 'Macedonia' thereafter, not for any other reason other than it was the easiest way he could be referred to. He appeared in some distress after a fall out with his Argentinian teammate, who'd apparently left Base Camp taking critical supplies and equipment with him. We asked Zdravko how he intended to climb the mountain alone and with missing equipment, which he struggled to answer other than to say he would find a way.

'I've seen this before,' Al muttered as we left his camp area. 'Guy on his own, no teammate or Sherpas. He'll let all the other teams fix lines, ride in the carriage behind, ask to borrow kit, use our tents and so on,' he added.

'Yeah, his teammate seems to only have been firmed up a few weeks back. It all seems a bit haphazard,' I added. 'Whatever, we should help if we can.'

We then approached an open space which offered a good spot for our camp. Within a few minutes, the quickest of our thirty or so porters would be arriving with tents, holdalls and barrels of food and supplies. The first job was to dig and flatten platforms for our tents, comprising a kitchen tent, mess tent, store tent and sleeping tents for all in our party – two climbers, four Sherpas, a cook, an assistant cook and a general assistant. It took a full day of digging to get the platforms laid and main tents erected, and a further day to get the mess tent, additional cook tent, store tent and toilet tents constructed.

For the latter, two were situated on the side of the moraine closest to the mountain, about forty metres from and below our tents. All the teams up the moraine placed their toilet tents the same side of the moraine, with water collected on the other side to prevent any possible contamination. Comprising of a large hole dug into the ground and rocks piled up to create a platform, it served its purpose adequately, although in Nepal body waste is 'performed' into barrels and carried out. Not so in Pakistan, but the small numbers at Base Camp meant the earth could absorb the wastes.

There is always a sense of homebuilding and housekeeping when setting up one's own tent. Given my sleep issues, I wanted mine as far away as possible from both the cook tent and other tents to spare me from the inevitable noise of early morning clatter, late night revelling or anytime snoring. My tent was therefore placed the farthest up the moraine I could go before being deemed out of territory. Ironically, I usually sleep better on expeditions than I ever do at home - due undoubtedly to realigning with nature's clocks and rhythms, rather than the artificial 'social jetlag' increasingly prevalent in today's society.

Your tent is your home, a place of solitude, contemplation, thinking, reading, calling loved ones, diary writing, and planning and preparation for up to six weeks. A place to return to for recuperation and replenishment after exhausting forays and rotations up the mountain. It is the one known certainty amid a lot of uncertainty in high-altitude mountaineering. As such, it bestows on me – and most mountaineers I know – a need to have that home as neat, tidy and organized as possible, with everything in its place. Messiness and untidiness grate on me back at home; in a Base Camp tent it might mean losing or mislaying a vital piece of equipment. There is no place for anything other than OCD cleanliness and tidiness.

We had got to know our Sherpas very well since arriving in Pakistan. Lakpa Sherpa was the leader, a young, bright 22-year-old with a fashionable hairstyle. He'd summited K2 in 2012, spoke excellent English and was keen, proactive, polite and always helpful. I gelled with him immediately. Mingma Thinduk Sherpa had summited K2 twice before, in 2007 and 2012, and if successful, would be the first person to top the mountain three times. He was obviously highly experienced and competent, but now into his late thirties, didn't seem as motivated as the others, with several remarks alluding to his family and ceasing high-altitude climbing, giving me some cause for concern. Chheji Nurbu Sherpa (Nurbu) was the third Sherpa of the team, a likeable and fun guy, very strong and competent, who'd also summited in 2012. The fourth Sherpa, who was on his first visit to Pakistan, was Nima Dorje Sherpa, a quieter climber who tended to let the others do the talking.

We also warmly befriended our Pakistani cooks on the journey in. Sultan Aziz, known as Aziz, who we later learned was a mechanic as well as a cook, was probably more adept at fixing equipment rather than cooking, but he produced good dishes when needed. I half expected to find nuts, bolts or a spanner in our soup, but he seemed to separate his increasingly flexible duties admirably. He was accompanied by Ghulam Mustafa, known as Mustafa, as the assistant cook and Ali, the general helper. Ali was one of those people who was pure salt of the earth. Kind, caring and always smiling, nothing was ever too much trouble and he never complained about anything. All three were shining examples of the people of Baltistan and of Pakistan.

The final member of our party was our liaison officer, Lieutenant Rizwan. Cheerful and supporting, he became a good colleague during the journey. He was also honest about the liaison officer policy, saying it was a 'jolly' that the nominated officers could and would use to visit their families whilst the teams climbed the mountain. That meant he would trek to Base Camp, ensure we were safe and settled, and then go away for a month or so, returning when it was time to leave. We didn't mind this, for whilst Base Camps are great places for rest when you've been climbing and hauling loads up a mountain, they are bleak if you must stay there for six weeks at a stretch with no similar goal.

I proceeded to wander farther up the moraine. The next team up was the Greek team of Alexander Aravidis and Nikolaos Mangitsis. As they were closest in location, we would frequently visit each other's mess tents to chat, share stories and food. Alex and Nico were Greece's premier high-altitude climbers. Without being disrespectful to their country, they were probably Greece's only high-altitude climbers! Alex was very strong, stern and serious most of the time, but with a dry sense of humour that came out regularly. Nico, conversely, was all smiles and warmness. They were good neighbours.

At the top of the moraine were the Swiss team of Mike Horn, Kobi Reichen and Fred Roux, and I visited them shortly after arriving. As mentioned, we'd met Mike in Islamabad, but it was the first time I'd met the others. German-speaking Reichen and French-speaking Roux were alpine climbing instructors, and their pedigree and abilities would later become apparent. They were like racing cars on crampons, leaving everyone in their wake, including Horn. Whilst Fred was in his thirties, Kobi appeared to be well into his fifties, proving that age really doesn't matter on the mountains. Visiting their tent, one knew you were going to end up laughing; not taking things too seriously was their way at Base Camp, assisted by the first-class wine, cheese and salami they had somehow managed to bring all the way up to 5,000 metres.

And finally, located between the Greeks and the Swiss would be the New Zealand team of Marty Schmidt, his son Denali and Australian Chris Warner. They were all on Broad Peak when we arrived but called in at Base Camp a few days later to say hello, stopping in our mess tent for a good couple of hours to chat. As I wrote earlier, Marty and I had exchanged emails prior to the trip, but it was the first opportunity I'd had to meet him, or any of them, in person.

Marty, 53, was born in California but had moved to Australia in 1988, then New Zealand a year later - receiving New Zealand citizenship due to his then wife, Joanne Munstein's work in the country. A former US Air Force pararescue jumper and a mountain guide for thirty-eight years, he ran Marty Schmidt International Guiding (MSIG) out of New Zealand. A highly-experienced mountaineer, he'd summited Everest twice and reached the top of five other eight-thousanders without oxygen, in addition to a host of other achievements across the world. K2 had always eluded him, however, and it was his third attempt on the mountain. 'I've climbed a lot of the world's biggest mountains, but K2 is the one I love and respect the most,' he was quoted as saying before leaving for Pakistan. 'I'm just called to it all the time. I want to show the world what it's like.' He came across as very assertive, independent-minded and somewhat opinionated, but also very welcoming, generous and communicable.

Denali, 25, named after North America's highest mountain, was a ski patroller at Bear Valley Ski Resort in California who had recently graduated from California College of the Arts in San Francisco. Widely talented and a phenomenal skier, he was also an extremely strong climber who had climbed and guided regularly with his father since his teenage years. He came across as a very mature 25-year-old, a genuinely nice guy, softer spoken than his father, very friendly and interested in others' stories as opposed to talking about himself. Despite his extensive mountaineering experience, it was his first time on any 8,000-metre peak and he was about to attempt two back-to-back: Broad Peak followed by K2. Any doubts on his adaptability to high altitude were later dismissed when he and his father powered past us on one rotation. They were both exceedingly fit.

Their teammate, Chris Warner (not to be confused with the American K2 climber of the same name) was a Canberra-based Australian who had his own rope-access cleaning and maintenance company. Having previously climbed with Marty, he had an extensive track record of all-round adventuring since his teens and did it for the love of the outdoors more than anything else - there was no website listing his exploits. Chris had been on K2 in the tragic year of 2008 but was fortunately not part of the fatal summit attempt of 31 July, which killed eleven climbers. He was humble and, like Denali, friendly and interested in others more than himself. I clicked with them all.

Thus, seven teams comprising twenty foreign climbers from ten nations, together with seven climbing Sherpas, converged for the 2013 K2 attempt. Seven teams, all with their own characteristics, values, strengths, cultures and energies, but sharing one major goal – to summit this mighty peak. Some readers might conclude that with all this assumed alpha-male-dominated camp, there might be problems with egos, cliques or superiority complexes, but there was none of this. Everyone at camp was experienced and competent to varying degrees and this reflected in the relationships we all formed. As a sociable guy, I spent much of the time visiting, chatting, drinking or eating with all of my extended teammates and, in a small Base Camp of only twenty climbers, one gets to know other climbers very well indeed, and the bonds became strong. Information sharing, support and cooperation were abundant. Aside from the isolation, one reason for this is that everyone on K2 was playing with risk and death, which is a great leveller. And although one or two could possibly drift into A-male labelling, my own view and experience with close-knit teams on expeditions or in the Special Forces' four-man patrols, is that there is no room for all that testosterone flying around if you want a high-performing team. Far from being an alpha male, I call myself a Zulu female.

With poor weather preventing any movement onto the mountain, the aforementioned risks would be all too obvious when I visited the Gilkey Memorial a few days after settling into Base Camp. The memorial, named after Art Gilkey, who lost his life in the 1953 attempt on the mountain, is the gathering place for all who have died on K2, Broad Peak, G1 and G2, and is located on a rocky outcrop 500 metres from the bottom of the Base Camp moraine.

I wanted to visit it on my own to fully feel what I knew would be a sobering experience. Walking down the glacier for twenty minutes, passing the Japanese tents at the end, I trekked across the wider moraine to reach the start of the rocks. Scrambling up the loose scree, I eventually came to the first plaques. And then they all loomed into sight. The rock pillar was covered in them – simple metal plates carved with names and dates, together with other more elaborate plinths bought in by fallen climbers' families and friends on later pilgrimages. Many photographs, equipment and other memorabilia dotted the landscape.

Some were names from the past I was all too aware of – Briton Alison Hargreaves and Irishman Gerald McDonnell, to name two. Some were familiar from the K2 summiteer list, which contains the names of those who died on descending. Most, however, were killed without reaching their goal and were names I had never seen.

I sometimes stop by graveyards when I'm running through the New Forest back in the UK, finding them both deeply sad and yet a place to gain wisdom. They are a stark reminder of both the fragility and, above all, shortness of our lives on earth. A place from which to gain some semblance of gratitude for the healthy, fit and active life I am still living. And one to remind me that it will all be over in the twinkle of an eye and to savour every day to the fullest. But graveyards primarily contain the remains of those who, subconsciously, tried to avoid or prolong death for their entire lives. The vast majority of headstones will be of elderly people, most of whom will have died of a disease or of old age.

The Gilkey Memorial, conversely, was entirely full of 'headstones' of young, supremely fit people, all of whom had willingly exposed themselves to the possibility of death. Staring at the names, their ages and the photographs, it all seemed such a sad waste of a life. So futile, so stupid and so selfish. It was one thing seeing the plaque and picture of a Polish climber killed twenty years earlier, but at least he was at peace. He wouldn't ever know the grief and pain he would have inflicted upon his poor parents, his sister, brother or, if he had them, his children or partner. A pain that could last a lifetime. A pain he would never know, but would be felt every day by those he left behind.

I stared in silent contemplation at the memories of these climbers frozen in time; the silence only being interrupted by the wind blowing across the barren glacier far below me. The sky was grey with thick clouds forming over the mountains. It was a bleak day to match my bleak feelings. We all bore a great deal of responsibility to spare our loved ones the same fate.

CHAPTER SEVEN

UNEASY SIGNS

IT IS WHAT YOU DON'T EXPECT
... THAT MOST NEEDS LOOKING
FOR.

– NEAL STEPHENSON

FOR THOSE NOT AWARE OF HOW one climbs an 8,000-metre mountain, here is a brief summary. It normally takes six to eight weeks in total because of the single greatest challenge in climbing big mountains – altitude. Although 5,300 metres is the maximum height of permanent human habitation in the world, even getting a helicopter straight to this height, to shorten a trek in, would make 90 per cent of climbers ill within twenty-four hours. If you could get a helicopter to the top of a high eight-thousander (which you can't), you'd be unconscious within minutes, due to the lack of oxygen.

At 6,000 metres, people can survive for a few weeks, sometimes even months, and there is one documented case of a man surviving for nearly two years at 5,950 metres. At this height, acclimatized climbers may expect to feel well, have a reasonable appetite and be capable of climbing with loads and at speeds comparable to lower elevations. At 7,000 metres, the situation changes with tiredness and lethargy increasing, appetite being lost and physical exercise becoming impossible. Above 8,000 metres is inhospitable to sustained human life and hence why such heights are often referred to as the 'death zone'. Therefore, the critical process of acclimatization is essential to anyone attempting an eight-thousander, a process which can be slow – often laboriously slow. If one shortens this process, you risk suffering from varying stages of acute mountain sickness (AMS), pulmonary oedema, cerebral oedema, strokes or other illnesses. Altitude kills all too frequently.

Whilst all the twenty climbers at K2 Base Camp had one shared goal, the way in which we attempted it would vary somewhat. The one factor in which we were all on the same page was that all the teams would be climbing the Abruzzi Spur; the Spanish and Kiwi teams had abandoned thoughts about attempting the Cesen route.

The first matter of variability was on the type of climbing we would be adopting. The usual way of climbing any eight-thousander is by the so-called 'expedition style' or 'fixed line' climbing, where camps are stocked at various locations on the route in a series of load carries or 'rotations'. This method also involves the setting up of fixed lines on technical or dangerous sections of a climb, comprising thin rope fixed by bolts or ice screws on the route. When a climber ascends a route, he or she clips in an ascender to the line which acts as a 'safety catch' in case of a fall. A second means of attachment, of a karabiner attached to the climber on a sling, provides an additional security – particularly at crossover points of lines at bolt locations. Although in theory it provides a heightened degree of safety, accidents still do happen. On an ascent, the line is used purely as a safety link, as opposed to hauling oneself up. On steep sections of a descent, meanwhile, a climber will abseil down the line, putting his entire weight and trust on a thin rope attached by some hopefully secure connections. Add chronic fatigue and oxygen depletion, then the potential for human error increases dramatically – most deaths on 8,000-metre mountains occur on the descent. On K2, given the steepness of the route, 90 per cent of the Abruzzi Spur would need to be 'fixed' – with lines having to be replaced each year due to previous year's ropes being buried or worn away. That would require over 3,000 metres of rope.

The other method of climbing is alpine style, where, in the ideal scenario, a climber carries all his or her food, shelter and equipment as he or she climbs, eschewing fixed ropes and porters, and normally climbing in one push. It is regarded as the purest form of climbing, involving limited logistics, less time overall and reduced time at altitude. Without lines or porters, it is also less expensive. However, rejecting the use of fixed lines increases the dangers substantially.

In 2013, all but two of the teams would be climbing using fixed lines. The Swiss and New Zealand-Australian teams would be climbing alpine style. Whilst this caused no consternation between any teams, there is and was an area of blurred parameters – climbing alpine style on a virgin route is one thing; climbing it on a route where a fixed line is just a metre away in case of an emergency is altogether different. And, regardless, both teams would still undertake rotations to stock higher camps. The reason for going alpine style was thus down to saving costs on Sherpas and lines and the old chestnut of significance, even if 99.9 per cent of the general public aren't aware of, or care about, the difference.

The second variable plans of the teams was the inclusion or otherwise of attempting Broad Peak prior to K2. My concerns on the limited timeframes in the Karakoram to attempt both were documented earlier in the book. In 2013, all but two of the teams would be solely climbing K2, however the New Zealand-Australian and Greek teams would attempt Broad Peak first.

Thirdly was the teams' individual choices to use oxygen or not. Again, the prime driver for this is status, even if it means little to those outside of high-altitude mountaineering. The Swiss, Kiwi and Greek teams weren't using oxygen, whilst the rest of us were. My view on oxygen is very simple and is a view shared by Kenton Cool amongst others. That is whilst I have immense respect for those who climb without it, my health is more important than status. Scientists cannot precisely determine the long-term effects on our brains of prolonged time at altitude. All I know is that, after I summited Everest in 2006 without oxygen for all but the final two hours of the ascent, and for none of the descent, something happened to my brain cells. Some readers might conclude that those of us who do such dangerous and stupid activities probably don't have too many brain cells to lose in the first place! Whatever, my long-term memory and an ability to remember people's names – something I used to excel at – were affected notably.

Fourthly, was the matter of using Sherpas in support. This is a practice which can also cause some divided opinions amongst climbers, particularly the more elite. The simple counter is that Sherpas have been used on 8,000-metre peaks for all the last century, due to their phenomenal ability at altitude. And they have been paid accordingly. All that has changed in the last twenty years is the increased use of them. The Spanish, Greeks and ourselves were using Sherpas, others not. However, as is often the case, all teams would eventually reap the benefit.

The last matter is one which has also become increasingly blurred – that of the supposed commercial expeditions versus private ones. 'Commercial expeditions' were launched in 1993 on Everest by New Zealanders Rob Hall and Gary Ball. The aim was simple – providing expedition logistics and support for competent and experienced climbers who did not have the connections, name or influence to join hitherto often government-funded expeditions to major peaks. The practice has grown considerably and, nowadays, one will find expeditions on most of the 8,000-metre peaks being organized by providers. The blur comes in that, aside from probably Everest, Cho Oyu and Manaslu, the three most common 8,000-metre peaks attempted, one must still find and assemble potential teammates to get enough climbers to form that team. And, secondly, all the teams on K2 were 'commercial' in that we were all using Pakistani logistic providers, porters, transport systems and so on. The only difference was how much we would use.

Regardless of all these variables, however, there were and are no shortcuts with big mountains. Climbers, whatever method used, had to climb using their own legs from Base Camp to the top and back again, although we would all be on our own timeframes on the mountain.

One factor, however, would dictate our movements more than any other – the weather. As previously written, the weather in the Karakoram is notably unpredictable, with satellite weather forecasts already proving highly unreliable on the trek in. When there was good weather, most of the teams would be at some stage on the mountain on load carries or setting up camps. When the weather was bad, which it usually was, 100 per cent of us would be in Base Camp.

Aside from ABC, located at approximately 5,300 metres, K2 has four camps which require setting up on the mountain, whatever form of climbing one is undertaking. Camp 1 is located at 6,100 metres; Camp 2 at 6,700 metres; Camp 3 at 7,300 metres; and Camp 4 at 7,800 metres. Some of these altitude gains are hefty and beyond the general principles of a maximum altitude gain of 500 metres in any one day. As I would shortly find out, the steep terrain on K2 lends itself to no other choice of camp locations.

I'd read much about Camp 1 being exposed with little flat ground, but being secure with little history of avalanches. Camp 2 is also located on exposed steep terrain, and renowned for being an extremely windy and cold place. Camp 3, whilst situated on less steep ground, is known as the most avalanche-prone camp on the mountain. Camp 4, meanwhile, located on the 'shoulder' of K2, is the only camp located on flattish ground and relatively avalanche free.

Expedition climbing has changed its practices over the past few years on the most beneficial number of rotations and time spent in these camps in the preparation phase. Ten years ago, three rotations were the norm on many mountains, including sleeping a night at Camp 3 – a camp situated anywhere between 7,000 and 7,600 metres depending on the mountain. Nowadays, the more common procedure is to merely touch Camp 3 on a second rotation, i.e. climb up to it and return to the lower Camp 2 to sleep. The argument goes that sleeping above 7,000 metres, even just for one night, has detrimental effects on the body that outweigh the benefits of acclimatization. As a consequence, two rotations have become the standard practice on eight-thousanders. My cynical self has sometimes questioned whether the increase in this practice has more to do with shortening the length of the expedition, and thus the costs, than what is beneficial to acclimatization.

On 9 July 2013, the combined seven Sherpas at Base Camp conducted their puja, the Buddhist ceremony of blessing which all Sherpas hold prior to climbing on the mountain. All the teams, except the Kiwis and Greeks who were on Broad Peak, attended. With the poor weather preventing any full climbing, I then took a foray up to ABC with Lakpa Sherpa to set up a storage tent, dump some gear and get some minor acclimatization in.

ABC is a two to three hour trek farther up the Baltoro glacier, for which one treks in either hiking boots or climbing boots, depending on one's preference. I chose the former and so took my heavy boots in my pack. Aside from fixing lines to Camp 1, the Japanese team had placed marker posts along the glacier to point to the safest route. However, they were placed a long distance apart and it would be easy to veer off route, particularly after snowfall obliterated tracks.

Leaving the last rocks and broken ground of the Base Camp moraine, the first hour or so of the trek to ABC was relatively easy going and considerably easier than the moraine. The glacier then became progressively more varied and broken, with the route weaving its way past numerous crevasses. After two hours trekking, we entered the final jigsaw of the glacier, which required some scrambling up ice slopes and crossing of ice bridges over deep crevasses. Finally, we reached a further moraine with a dirt track leading to ABC.

'Here is Abruzzi Spur!' Lakpa shouted, pointing to the wall of rock and ice leading to his left.

'I can certainly see!' I replied, trying to take in the sight above me.

Looking up the spur, the mountain didn't just ascend but soared for as far as the eye could see. The steepness and distance was quite breathtaking – 3,300 metres into the atmosphere with no end in sight. It was a scene out of *Avatar*, *Lord of the Rings* and *Star Trek* combined, but without any mythical castle hovering in the clouds. If the view from Concordia, one week before, had been profound, this created an even more 'in the face' experience.

We set up a tent and I put on my Millet climbing boots – hefty double boots that, to outsiders, look like something an astronaut would wear. Venturing over the loose rocks to the start of the ice slope, which angled approximately forty–fifty degrees, I put on my crampons, strapped the ice axe onto my harness, and climbed up a few hundred metres. The forty-five-kilometre-per-hour winds didn't make it particularly pleasant, but I had greater worries – I had developed a chest infection and it wasn't getting better, indeed it was getting progressively worse. After thirty minutes on the ice, we returned to Base Camp.

On 14 July 2013, the weather finally turned and Al and myself proceeded on our first proper rotation to Camps 1 and 2. As with all rotations, it had two purposes: to acclimatize and to deposit clothing, kit and equipment that would be needed in the higher camps for a later summit push. Due to the delayed start, it was very possible that there might not be time for a second rotation, so we packed enough food for four days, planning overnighting at both Camps 1 and 2.

We left very early in the morning for ABC, stopping there to deposit hiking boots and a few other items. And then it was onto the Abruzzi Spur. The climbing route followed the edge of the rock-composed spur; lines were fixed on this rock whilst we would generally be placing our feet on the easier terrain of ice and snow next to the spur. Several mixed sections would require us to climb purely on rock – always a bit tricky wearing crampons.

There was nothing easy about climbing to Camp 1 that day. It was long, steep and with no respite, aside from one rock pinnacle where we could take our packs off and stop for lunch. My chest was on fire and my throat felt like sandpaper, affecting my breathing greatly, which in turn affected my movement and speed. With the weather worsening as the day progressed, it was a tough day from start to finish and took me around nine hours – far longer than normally expected.

Clambering up the final steep seventy-degree snow slope on a gully west of the main ice slopes, I hauled myself onto the ledge which housed Camp 1 feeling well spent. Al had arrived a good hour earlier. Before me was a sight that aptly reinforced what K2 camps are all about. Five tents strung together with countless ropes, tethers and ice screws on a small fault line that provided a break in the steepness of the Abruzzi.

'Wow! I see what you mean Al,' I croaked as I collapsed into the tent, boots and crampons hanging out the vestibule.

'This is it, the only piece of flat ground from ABC until Camp 2,' he replied.

'Unreal; where's the toilet?'

'The steep gully just there,' he said, pointing to the left.

The tent was squeezed tightly between two others, with rocks and ice protruding through the tent floor and the sides falling away into deep pits – another reality of the vain attempts to construct a flat base on hard ice and rock. As always, a hot brew brought some life back into my chilled bones and, with my boots and crampons still on, I ventured outside to have a 'number two'. 'Crap Alley', as we named it, was a scree slope which fell steeply away to the Baltoro glacier 1,000 metres below. It was full of dried and frozen excrement and a corresponding smell. Traversing gingerly across the gully with ice axe in hand, I wasn't sure whether it was the fear of sliding 1,000 metres down the gully or one metre into a pile of human waste that was the more worrying. Either way, that's the reality of human life – and waste – on mountains. Business done and hands sanitized, I went back to our tent to rest.

Al and myself spent two nights at Camp 1 to acclimatize. The altitude gain from 5,000 metres to 6,100 metres had, as fully expected, caused my head to pound badly so there was no way I was fit to proceed up to 6,700 metres on the second day. Indeed, I wondered whether it would subside by the third morning. As always, Advil, a brand of ibuprofen, was my best friend but it required more than I was happy consuming and, even then, not completely subduing the pain.

It was an uncomfortable place to spend two nights, but at least the weather was good in the middle day which enabled us to get out of the tent to walk around. The only problem was there wasn't anywhere we could actually walk to! Behind us, just a foot from the tent edge, was the steep gully we'd climbed up. To our right was the even steeper, exposed and avalanche-prone ice slopes east of the Abruzzi Spur. In front of us, within a few metres the Abruzzi resumed its relentless upward path; to our left was 'Crap Alley'. No room at all, therefore, for any stroll around the camp and all we could do was rest, sleep, eat and read.

On day three of our rotation, Al, myself and Mingma Sherpa, who'd arrived the night before with a second tent, started the climb up to Camp 2, located a further 600 metres higher at an elevation of 6,700 metres. Unlike the climb to Camp 1, the route to Camp 2 required climbing on rock much of the time, with several vertical rock bands to ascend. None of them would cause any technical problems at sea level, climbing in rock boots with bare tops and a cooler at the base, but this was at well over 6,000 metres with difficult weather, heavy packs and wearing double boots and crampons.

The climb to Camp 2 required total commitment and, several times, rocks came raining down from above, requiring one to be 100 per cent alert all times. It took around six hours before we reached a small piece of flat ground below the famous House Chimney, where we stopped for a break. This area was sometimes called Lower Camp 2 as, with some digging and levelling, it had space for one or two tents.

House Chimney is a thirty-metre climb in a chimney of approximately ninety-degree angle, and is considered one of the most technical sections of the climb. It did require some hauling and pushing, which at the altitude we now were, caused some exhaustion, but was overcome without any major problems. The biggest concern was a massive boulder precariously perched at the top of the chimney, with a rope around it supposedly keeping it in place. The chimney wasn't a place to hang around.

The weather had been poor all day but, once we emerged from the shelter of the chimney, the full force of Karakoram winds hit us. Camp 2's notoriety as an extremely windy location didn't disappoint: fifty-kilometre-per-hour winds hit us the moment we hauled ourselves past the boulder, battering us relentlessly as we climbed the final forty-metre ice slope to the camp. On reaching the strewn-out debris of Camp 2, we hastily built up a tent platform and erected a tent, with the wind hitting us with its full force in what was a near white-out. With fingers losing their sensation and the cold beginning to bite, we needed to get out of the storm fast. Al dived in the tent followed by myself, both of us only having time to take off our crampons.

'Get in, Mingma!' I screamed in Nepali. 'Let's get out of this!'

'Throw your bag! Shut the tent!' Al shouted.

'Fuck! The zip's broken!'

'Guys, we gotta get in!'

It was mayhem. The wind, snow and ice were filling the ripped tent as Mingma tied up the crampons and ice axes with a rope. He finally fell in, looking as white as a sheet, which, for a Nepali, is saying something. I somehow partially closed the outer tent behind him with the broken zip. Al was hyperventilating, running his hands to get some life back into them. I was frozen solid. Bags, boots and food were strung everywhere. The floor was freezing. We needed our sleeping mats, sleeping bags and an urgent brew, but there was no space to move on the narrow platform the tent was sat on. I gradually manoeuvred myself to the far side of the tiny space and managed to lay out a sleeping mat. Al got his mat out, ripped out his sleeping bag and climbed in to try and warm up. Mingma gallantly fought through the mess to find a stove.

'Man, what a place!'

'What a wind!'

'Slow your breath … breathe deep!'

'Get the thermos out!'

This was our welcome to Camp 2. If Camp 1 was a sobering experience, Camp 2 was even more stark. Outside of Antarctica, I had rarely experienced such wind, which had made a mockery of the forecasts. There was no flat space at all, with tents built on platforms of snow, rocks, previous year's tent remains and other debris. The entire area was strewn with ripped tents and other old equipment, and the snow littered with yellow urine stains and human excrement. It was a hellhole. And, once we'd settled down, it didn't fail to resonate that if the world's press latched onto a 'Rubbish on K2' story, as Everest has been accused for many years, they would have a field day. The only mitigating factor was that infinitely fewer people ever reached this hell on earth.

We finally sorted ourselves out and, as darkness fell, got a brew and some food on. There was no time or inclination to do anything but crawl into our bags and try to sleep, which was difficult given the tiny space we were in. To my left side, the built-up platform, and consequently the tent floor, fell away sharply into the abyss, and I struggled to maintain some balance to avoid falling over the edge with only a thin tent floor supporting me. I had a piss into my pee bottle and poured it out through a zip next to me. To my surprise, I heard the contents seemingly hit the top of what sounded like another tent. Peering out through the zip in the howling wind, I confirmed that my dehydrated urine was now adorning the top of a tent three metres below us.

'What a place, I just poured my pee all over a tent below,' I exclaimed.

'Whose tent?' Al asked.

'It's okay. It's only the Spanish …'

The wind didn't cease the entire night or the next day and we remained rooted in our tent the entire time. The only ventures outside were, firstly, to gather some fresh snow in a stuff sack for boiling water, a difficult search given the absence of snow caused by the high winds. And, secondly, to go for the inevitable crap, an even more precarious experience. Whilst 'Crap Alley' at Camp 1 was at least situated on rocks and didn't require dressing up, any sojourn outside our tent at Camp 2 required boots, crampons and ice axes to be worn or carried, such was the ice and steepness of the terrain. Many tragedies on big mountains have occurred when going to the ablutions, particularly at night, and we weren't going to take any chances. The 'toilet' at Camp 2 was located on a small sloping rock field to the edge of the camp, not a dangerous location once you were there, but climbing down and over to it entailed some careful placing of feet. In the bitter wind, the toilet operation was a quick experience.

The snow and debris platform we'd built up wasn't anywhere near large enough to fit our tent on. As a result, apart from the side I was sleeping on falling into an abyss, the end facing south, where our feet lay, also fell away steeply. We ended up putting our packs in the deepening holes and laying sleeping mats on top to try and create some level base. On Mingma's side, the broken outer tent zip resulted in wind and snow blowing in whenever the inner tent was opened, which caused him to move closer to the middle. And finally, the head side of the tent arched upwards with the slope of the mountain, resulting in little place to put anything. The result of all this was three climbers practically sleeping on top of each other along with a ton of equipment. Any slight movement caused a chain reaction in the tent.

One of those movements was peeing. I have never managed to pee into a pee bottle laying down and have to adopt a squat position to perform the operation, which inevitably caused some disturbance in the tent. Mingma, like most Asians, was more discreet about the process. Al, meanwhile, had mastered the art of doing it laying down, but even that still required a lot of huffing and puffing for him to get into position. Peeing in pee bottles in a tent is all part of expedition life, but having your teammate urinate a foot from your face, along with the inevitable passing of wind to accompany it, wasn't quite what the 'great outdoors' promotes.

I also discovered an annoying trait about my teammate. He peed a lot. And I mean a lot. The problem was his pee bottle was tiny – no reflection on his personal statistics I hasten to add (that's what he told me at least). Whatever, it was the smallest Nalgene bottle one could buy and barely held a single piss. As he was in the middle of the tent, he needed someone to empty it outside. Step forward the urine refuge collector sleeping to his left.

'Hey, Adrian, sorry to wake you up buddy; can you empty my pee bottle out the side?' he asked in the middle of the night.

'Al, when's your birthday?' I grunted, after one urine expulsion into space.

'4 November. Why?' he replied.

'Can I buy you a present – a kind, true and heartfelt present that you will remember me by in case anything ever happens to me?'

'Yer so kind!' he said with an unsure anticipation. 'And what may that be?'

'A damn proper pee bottle!' I groaned. 'Your test tube is good for a cat!'

On day five, having been hit by ferocious winds the previous three days, the wind finally dropped. We were tired, battered and bruised, but at least we had a chance to get back down to Base Camp; many occasions on K2 have resulted in teams being stranded at high camps for a week or more due to the weather.

Leaving a large stuff sack of food, a cooker and gas canisters which we would only require on our next climb to Camp 2, it was a relief to pack up the remainder of our kit and get moving. Using a Figure 8 device or, in my case, my preferred and quicker Italian hitch, we climbed or abseiled down to Camp 1 over several hours, rocks regularly piling down from above us. At Camp 1 we dropped off sleeping bags, mats, goggles, a spare sock set and some other equipment ready for the next arrival at that camp and descended to ABC and on to Base Camp. Our gruelling rotation was over.

It was now 17 July and, as with most of the climbers at Base Camp, that was it for the acclimatization phase – one accelerated rotation was all we would be able to manage. Marty, Denali and Chris, and Alex and Nico arrived from Broad Peak, with all bar Nico having summited whilst Al and myself were at Camp 2.

'Hey guys, congratulations!' I said as they arrived at our tent.

'Awesome effort in just a few weeks,' Al added, reflecting the short time they'd taken.

'Thanks guys. We were lucky with the small weather window,' Denali replied.

'Well done on your first eight-thousander, Denali!' Al responded.

'Yes, you know Broad Peak isn't as easy as people make out,' his father added.

It was now down to waiting for a five-day weather window for a summit attempt – the number of days climbing it would take to reach the top. The weather closed in again and the wait began. We spent the next week in and out of others' camps.

On one social visit to the Kiwis' camp, Marty and Chris were sleeping in their tents with only Denali in the mess tent.

'Hey Adrian, come on in, want some tea?' Denali offered, as I arrived.

'Thanks, will be great. How you feeling?'

'I'm good, thanks. Feeling strong.'

'You did amazingly well for your first eight-thousander!'

'Well, my Dad taught us a lot as kids. We've grown up on it. I've been reading about your exploits – amazing stuff. What's the polar world like?' he asked.

We chatted for a good hour and, as I'd found to date, Denali was more interested in other people's work and exploits than his own, continually asking on my own life – a humble characteristic that I greatly admired. He was very different from his irrepressible father.

Whilst the Broad Peak climbers were fully acclimatized and fit, I was becoming concerned at how our own timelines were playing out. One sole rotation, caused by the Taliban strike on top of an already late arrival in Pakistan, was nowhere near enough time at altitude to fully acclimatize, and we'd had precious little actual climbing. My chest and throat were still infected, I had bad haemorrhoids and concerns on both my physical strength and health. I had further doubts on our food supplies, particularly the quality of food we'd sourced from local suppliers – it containing inadequate calories to cater for the demands of high altitude. With the Greeks' Sherpa abdicating from further climbing due to an injury, I also felt concerns on whether there would be enough of us to carry and fix lines or share trail blazing.

It was the weather, however, which was the greatest worry. It had been poor for most of the limited time we'd spent at Base Camp or on the mountain, and both weather and snow conditions weren't good. And with these predicaments, casualties on other mountains started to mount up. A German climber, Heidi Dana, had already been killed on 7 July at Broad Peak, when she stopped for a picture on a makeshift bridge over a glacial stream at Base Camp. The bridge collapsed, she fell into the icy waters and was eventually found dead 100 metres down the stream under a rock. Cause of death was either by drowning, hypothermia or a heart attack from shock. That was a pure accident, but the subsequent fatalities were caused by a combination of weather and human error.

On 9 July, a Polish climber, Artur Hajzer, died on G1 after a fatal fall. Then, on 18 July, we were all alerted to an unfolding crisis on Broad Peak with three Iranian climbers being stranded at a high camp after summiting the mountain on the sixteenth. Attempting a new route, they were at an unclear location, exhausted, without oxygen and with little food. Communications were being made from the climbers to an Iran station, who were relaying messages back to Mike Horn, who subsequently coordinated with Broad Peak Base Camp. It was increasingly confusing and chaotic, and their plight was discussed at length by the Swiss, Kiwis and myself at the Swiss camp the next day – the Greeks were indignant as they believed the Iranians had stolen equipment and food from their tents at Camp 3 on the mountain, nearly jeopardizing their own safety.

'There is no ridge at 7-4!' Schmidt senior insisted when Horn and Roux relayed where the climbers were.

'There is NO RIDGE AT 7,400; the ridge starts at 7-8!' he bellowed.

'We agree, but that's what they said on the radio?' Roux replied

'Who said that on the radio?'

'Iran!'

'How did they get that information?'

'From the guys sitting on the ridge at 7-4!'

Laughter interjected the chaos. It was a pantomime, but no one knew the seriousness of the situation at that stage. Marty, Denali and Mike Horn eventually decided to head up to the unknown ridge location with oxygen bottles to try and help the climbers – an immense act of selflessness from all three. Unfortunately, they failed to locate anything, the situation worsened and, after the last call was received on 20 July, the Iranians were assumed lost the next day.

At the same time, we started to receive yet more bad news that three Spanish climbers had also gone missing on G1, after summiting the mountain on 21 July. They were also pronounced dead two days later. Eight fatalities already weren't a good omen.

We continued resting, recuperating, preparing equipment and liaising with all the teams over the week, above all comparing weather forecasts. The critical matter was the wind – we could not venture to the highest camps with anything over twenty-five-kilometre-per-hour winds, but most days showed forecasts well above forty kilometres per hour. Finally, on 22 July, amidst a continued white-out and snow at Base Camp which had lasted since our return from Camp 2, we began to see a short weather window looking possible for the period 25–29 July. It didn't look perfect and it wasn't long, but it presented what might be the only possibility to launch a summit attempt. A meeting was held with all the teams on 23 July at our mess tent, and a collective decision was made for summit day on 28 July 2013. That would mean leaving Base Camp on either 24 or 25 July, depending on whether teams would be staying at Camp 1 or climbing direct to Camp 2. Amid a lot of uncertainty, poor weather, the mounting fatalities and less than ideal preparations, it was all systems go.

CHAPTER EIGHT

ALL IS LOST

I AM ABOVE THE WEAKNESS
OF SEEKING TO ESTABLISH
A SEQUENCE OF CAUSE
AND EFFECT, BETWEEN THE
DISASTER AND THE ATROCITY.

– EDGAR ALLAN POE

THE LAST FEW DAYS BEFORE a summit push of a major 8,000-metre peak is a mixture of extreme busyness and eerie calm. Everything up to this point, from the first plans eighteen months ago to the year-long preparation and the month in Pakistan, had been the supporting act, a gradual build-up to this time. This was now it, the main feature, the headline act, the attempt for the summit. And that headline act would all lead to the climax – the final climb from Camp 4 to the summit and back to Camp 4. The stakes were high, the pressures enormous and the realities daunting.

The Sherpas busied themselves sorting food supplies to take up the mountain and checking oxygen systems. I meticulously prepared, repaired, checked, re-checked and re-re-checked my equipment. Some was already deposited at ABC, Camp 1 and Camp 2, but there was a lot to check and refine. Above all, I needed to cut down on weight wherever I could to attempt to mitigate my illnesses and subsequently compromised fitness levels. That presented a fine line between weight-saving and safety however, and erring on the side of caution usually won. We also needed to carefully check our oxygen systems and food supplies, with the one rotation not giving us the opportunity to deposit the former, or stock enough of the latter, up the mountain.

Along with all this preparation and much liaison with other teams, came some inevitable personal thoughts, but these tended to be subservient to the greater urge to focus on the goal ahead. Similar to soldiers in a conflict zone, it was so much easier for us here. We were comparatively in the known and, even if the outcome was wholly uncertain, everything could be physically seen, heard or felt. It was far harder for those back home, who were in a place of total uncertainty; their only way of knowing what was happening from the Facebook or website posts from myself or other teammates.

My team at Professional Sports Group in the UAE would be managing posts on my behalf when we left Base Camp – all updates being transmitted by a satellite phone call on my Thuraya XTS. With weight such a factor, it wasn't feasible to take the heavier IP Plus data transmitter up the mountain and pictures would have to wait until our return.

The last night at Base Camp naturally caused me to sink into some deep thoughts. The weather cleared briefly and, before I retreated to my tent for the final time, I looked up at K2, its snow and ice glistening in the moonlight. It ebbed a powerful sway, so seemingly close to touch and yet so far to reach. It exuded a magnetic pull and attraction, yet a repulsion to distance itself. It was a friend yet a foe. Which would it be in the following five days, I asked both myself and the mountain that I looked at, striving to find the answers in the unknown. The calm before the storm, the stillness before the action, the peace before the mayhem, only time and the cosmos would tell.

In seminars I deliver, people sometimes ask questions to do with God or faith, to which I have a stock reply. That is to, firstly, thank the person for the very understandable and perfectly sensible question, and then to say: 'My beliefs, or non-beliefs, are personal to me and I prefer to keep them that way. And it's my personal view that if more of the world kept their own beliefs, or non-beliefs, personally to themselves rather than to impose, force, encourage or, perhaps over time as mankind evolves, even to display, then our very divided world would be a much more peaceful and stable place.'

I am going to keep that mantra here. For whether I say I am an atheist, agnostic, lapsed Christian, evangelical, Buddhist, Jewish,

Sikh, Hindu or Muslim, I will alienate someone. My beliefs or non-beliefs at that moment were personal to me and it doesn't matter to anyone else what they were. What I will say is that they were as deep that night as might be expected.

We rose very early the next morning, at 4 a.m. It was freezing cold and snowing lightly, as per the forecast. Scoffing down a hastily cooked breakfast, we gathered our bags and prepared for departure. My pack was extremely heavy, our Sherpas' even more so. Aziz, Mustafa and Ali gave us a big hug as a farewell. We passed the puja shrine and all of us tossed rice into the air, bowed our heads and paused for a brief ten seconds of private thoughts. And then it was off.

The trek to ABC was less secure than before, with much of the route being buried by snow, and it took longer than normal to reach. The Japanese, Spanish, Greeks and Macedonia would be joining us on the route in the morning as well, intending to camp at Camp 1 that night. The Swiss and Kiwis would be trekking to ABC much later in the day, spending the night there and climbing directly to Camp 2 the following day. Everyone had their own preferences, but Al and myself were firm in the belief of spreading out the ascents to lessen fatigue.

The climb up to Camp 1 was also longer than anticipated, due to our heavy packs and some deep snow. My legs and lungs weren't performing brilliantly, but far better than our first rotation to Camp 1, and enough to maintain a slow but steady pace. 'It isn't a sprint, it's a marathon,' I kept reminding myself. 'It all comes down to the final summit night. Keep it steady and slow.' It was a relief to finally reach Camp 1 in the mid-afternoon after a long day.

We arose on the following day not to the expected and forecast clear skies and sunshine, but to more cloud and snow. The snowfall would continue all day. Leaving at a relatively later time than normal, we commenced the steep climb up to Camp 2. Al and myself continued at our steady pace, climbing with the Japanese and Greeks at various times. Midway through the ascent, Kobi Reichen and Fred Roux passed us. They were indeed extremely strong. Mike Horn followed nearly an hour later and we shared a few pitches before we let him pass. Then Marty, Denali and Chris Warner caught up. Fully acclimatized and fit from Broad Peak, they also looked supremely strong. There was no way I would have had any possibility of keeping up with them.

All of the seven teams reached Lower Camp 2 within a short time of each other, minus our Sherpas who had left much earlier and were pushing to Camp 3 to drop loads. As the Swiss started to ascend the House Chimney, with the Spanish next in line, the rest of us took a break. The Kiwis and Greeks were camping at Lower Camp 2 and we all had a chat. The atmosphere was positive and fun, and there was a lot of banter.

'Forget about digging your platforms. Get that brew on for us poor folks,' Al said.

'You sure you're gonna fit two tents on here fellas? Come on up to Camp 2 – big party tonight!' I added.

'In that wind! We'll leave the party to you. We're keeping warm down here,' Denali responded.

'Yeah, good point. Make sure you dig enough space for us to join you.'

'Anybody got a pneumatic drill in their packs? Or a JCB by any chance?'

After the Swiss, Spanish, Japanese and Macedonia had entered the House Chimney, Al and myself bade our farewells to Marty, Denali, Chis, Alex and Nico, and slowly ascended the vertical chute. Exiting the chimney and clambering up the final steep ice slope to Camp 2, I immediately noticed that it wasn't ice, but deep snow. Much deeper than expected. And, contrary to all of our forecasts, it was still snowing with poor visibility. When we finally reached Camp 2, we encountered everyone milling around outside their tents. There was obviously some important discussion ensuing.

'What's going on fellas?' Al asked, as we arrived at the gathering.

'Adrian, Al, I think we have problem,' Lakpa replied.

'It's all over!' Kobi Reichen interrupted, as he passed us. 'Conditions too bad. See you next time!'

'Lakpa?'

'My Sherpas climb to Camp 3, but very deep snow. Some place waist deep. They fall back and slide in one small avalanche.'

'Really?' I expressed in concern.

'They drop equipment in cache halfway. Back here now. They say too dangerous to go up.'

'Well … okay, let's have a chat with everyone.'

Al and myself quickly spoke to the Spanish, Swiss, Macedonia and the Japanese.

'Mike, are you going to try again next week?' I asked as he hauled his pack on and started to descend.

'No, we've all got commitments next week: Kobi and Fred on climbs and I'm joining my ship,' he replied. 'That's it for us. Good luck!'

'What you reckon guys?' Al asked, turning to the others.

'We go with other team say,' Endo, of the Japanese team, uttered in broken English.

'We're going down,' Benjamin replied, referring to the Spanish team. 'I think K2 may be over this season!'

That alarmed me. Going down was one thing, aborting the expedition entirely different. The Swiss had already pulled the plug, and now the Spanish were looking dubious. It was obvious that nothing sensible could be achieved by pushing on up now, but my mind was already thinking to next week.

'Okay Lakpa, you go down now,' I said. 'But I, for one, want to stay here an extra night to get some acclimatization in. What about you Al?'

'I'm good for that too,' Al interjected.

'Let's regroup tomorrow in Base Camp and see where we go.'

And so the combined Sherpas, Swiss, Spanish, Japanese and Macedonia all descended to Base Camp, leaving Al and myself alone at Camp 2. Our aims were entirely sensible. Whilst there was no question of continuing now, the weather could easily turn better in a week and we wanted to be fully acclimatized for a second summit push, which I, for one, was determined to attempt.

'Adrian, I don't think we'll be coming back to Camp 2,' Al said as we brewed some tea.

'The Swiss have called it a day, and I know Benjamin well. He's not coming back, nor the other Spanish.'

'Al, I haven't spent the last eighteen months preparing for this and paying out for three Sherpas for it to be called off before we've even given it a go,' I replied indignantly. 'I'll do whatever I can to get us back up.'

'I'm with you. I just think we need to expect some bad news.'

We were fully aligned, but we ran over the implications and possibilities throughout the evening. It was calm weather, and we were the only climbers on the mountain. I slept relatively well, but my mind was already on Base Camp the next day.

The next morning, Friday, 26 July, we finally rose to the clear weather and sunshine that our weather systems had forecast, providing the best views we'd had since setting foot on the mountain. Buoyed up by the warmth, we packed up our gear and descended the House Chimney. When we reached Lower Camp 2, below the chimney, voices could be heard from one of the tents, which was a surprise given our assumptions that we were alone.

'Morning guys. Who's here?' I shouted as we approached the tent, not knowing if it was the Kiwis or Greeks.

'Hey, Adrian, Al! Come on in!' Marty answered as he peered through the tent.

Al and myself sat down by the entrance in the warm sun and the guys passed us some tea.

'We thought everyone had gone down!' I said.

'So did we!' Marty responded.

'We stayed on to get some acclimatization in. What are you guys doing?' I asked.

'We're going up!' Marty said emphatically.

'Really?'

'Yep, you bet we are. We're gonna go up to Camp 3 today and check it out; if it's good, we'll push on tomorrow; if it's bad, we'll come back down, simple as that. All this bullshit going around about quitting! Hell, this is an 8,000-metre peak – not a vacation! When it snows, you get snow!' he bellowed.

'Yeah. There was a lot of talk about it all being over,' Al interjected.

Up to this point only Marty had spoken, but then Chris piped up, with what seemed like a degree of hesitation.

'I'm actually coming down,' he said.

'Oh … !' I exclaimed in surprise, shooting a glance at Marty and Denali to look for any sign of tension.

'I've chatted at length with Marty and Denali and they're fine with it; it's my decision,' he went on.

'I just don't think we're strong enough, just the three of us, to break trail for the summit. So, for me, there doesn't seem much point in going up just to look around. When I go up to Camp 3, I want it to be with a good deal of support and a realistic chance.'

It was all very sound reasoning, but still a surprise to hear, given their close relationship and recent success on Broad Peak. Marty seemed to be fully understanding and said something about everyone having to make their call. We chatted for a few minutes longer on weather forecasts, equipment and their detailed plans, whilst finishing our tea. Marty did most of the talking, Denali didn't say anything. They'd agreed a call roster of 8 a.m., 12 midday and 6 p.m. each day, and we said we'd look forward to hearing their progress. Finally, Al and myself got ourselves up and bade our farewells. Chris followed immediately after and all three of us descended to Base Camp.

We reached Base Camp speedily in fine weather, arriving at noon. As we approached our camp, Al's worst thoughts quickly became apparent. The Swiss has already left and the Spanish were packing their tents. Lakpa came over to me solemnly.

'Adrian ... err, not sure what to say, but we have more problem.'

'What's happening, Lakpa?' I questioned.

'I'm willing to go up, possibly Nurbu, but Mingma and Nima won't. They say too dangerous.'

'Look, we all know it's dangerous now, but we're talking in five days or a week!' I said in some distress. 'Let me speak to them.'

Al and myself went over to Mingma and Nima and calmly, but firmly, stated that it could easily be excellent conditions in five days. They wouldn't budge. We tried for a further ten minutes to get some positive response, but they were adamant. Muttering as I left in exasperation, I said to Lakpa that I would see if the Japanese were on and ran down to their camps. They had also decided to abort summit attempts, but would help the effort in any way they could with ropes and equipment. I ran back up to our camp and called everyone in – Lakpa, Al, Alex and Nico and their Sherpa Pasang, Macedonia and the Spanish team's two Sherpas, Jangbu and Mingma Dorji.

'Guys, the Japanese are off, so it's us lot here. Are you keen to try again?' I asked in increasing exasperation.

'Myself and Nico are,' Alex replied.

'Yes, I am if we can get the support,' Macedonia chipped in.

'Lakpa, how many Sherpas do we need to have enough support to fix lines?' Alex asked.

'We need four minimum,' Lakpa answered.

'Can we do with the eight of us? Five climbers and three Sherpas?'

'I don't think so. Too much lines to carry. Too much fixing. Too risky.'

There were seven Sherpas left – Mingma and Nima who'd declined all attempts to persuade them to climb, Lakpa and Nurbu, Pasang, the Greek's Sherpa, who was injured, and the Spanish team's two Sherpas, Mingma Dorji and Jangbu. As they weren't our Sherpas we had no real authority, and it became a matter of money and time. A heated discussion then followed between all of us, with Jangbu needing to know by 1 p.m. if we were going or not, as his team were leaving then. He wanted a high fee which caused a lot of debate. Al got angry. Voices were raised. It was a 'Chinese Parliament', with time running out and little semblance of order. (Chinese Parliament: a slang common among British Forces, meaning an informal discussion in the field where all ranks can join in.) Finally, Jangbu said he had to leave. Last desperate attempts to persuade him to stay were in vain and he bid his farewells.

'Okay guys, it's off!' I shouted in distress. 'It's off! Just go, and leave me some space.'

I wandered over and slumped down on a rock with my head in my hands, feeling totally gutted. I was angry at the Sherpas who'd let us down, dismayed at the responses, and in disbelief that it was all over without even giving it a shot. Eighteen months' preparation, planning, time and money, not to mention the emotional and physical commitment, and it all came down this. I don't fail these projects, I told myself. This simply wasn't in the script.

After a few minutes alone, Lakpa came over and offered his apologies, followed by Al.

'You know Adrian, maybe it's for the better. I don't want to go up with a half committed and under-strength team,' he said.

'I know, you're right. It's just the effort all gone to such a waste!' I exclaimed.

After he'd left, I looked up at K2, in perfect sunshine, and struggled to comprehend what this was all about. What was the reason behind this? Why had this happened? What was the universe saying? Questions which elicited no answers. Everything happens for a reason I told myself, but this reason just didn't make any sense at all. Anyone who hasn't set such huge goals may struggle to understand the devastation I felt. Training for a marathon for over three months is one thing. Preparing for an Ironman over six months is another. But K2 and similar are goals that climbers put their entire life into. The training, the preparation, the equipment, the sponsorships, the team liaisons, the risks, the self-focus, the pressure, the enormity of it all. And we never even attempted the summit. What a total waste. I spent the rest of the day in a dazed reflection of failure and dejection.

At 6 p.m. that evening I went up to Chris Warner's mess tent with Alex and Nico to hear the scheduled radio call from Marty and Denali. Chris called in a few times, but there wasn't any answer. At 6.40 p.m. the three of us went down to the Greeks' camp for supper. Chris joined us fifteen minutes later.

'I've just come off the line with Marty. They are safely at Camp 3. It took them nine hours ...' said Chris as he entered the tent.

'Nine hours! Whew!' commented Alex. The route would normally take five or six.

'Yes. Marty said the conditions on the Black Pyramid were very tough. He sounded tired and said Denali led most of the route,' Chris added.

'What are they going to do?' I asked, echoing the thoughts in Alex and Nico's minds.

'Marty wasn't sure. He said they'll have a look in the morning and make a call then,' Chis explained. 'It's a bit unlike Marty. He's normally very decisive,' he added.

We continued chatting over supper for a good hour and said we'd come up to Chris's camp in the morning in time for the 8 a.m. radio call. Saying good night, I relayed the information to Al and retreated to my tent. It had been a long and emotional day and I needed some processing time to make sense of it all. I was too tired and disappointed to write anything on my Facebook page or contact my team back in the UAE. That could wait until the morning.

The next morning, Saturday, 27 July 2013, I went up to Chris's tent at 7.55 a.m. with Al, joining Alex and Nico there. At exactly 8 a.m. Chris turned on the radio to make the routine call.

'Camp 3. Calling Camp 3. This is Base Camp. Do you copy? Over,' Chris calmly spoke into the radio.

'Camp 3. Calling Camp 3. This is Base Camp. Do you copy? Over,' he repeated.

Silence. Just the crackles of the radio.

'Calling Camp 3. Camp 3. This is Base Camp. Do you read? Over.'

The same crackles greeted his calls. After five minutes of trying, to no avail, Chris turned to us.

'That's unusual for Marty. He's normally totally diligent on radio calls,' he said.

'Well, it could be anything. They could have had an early start to Camp 4,' Al suggested.

'Or on their way back down the Black Pyramid,' I offered.

Chris tried every five minutes over the course of the next forty minutes, with the same result – an eerie silence. He said he'd try again at the midday call and we returned to our respective camps. Not long after, we were all disturbed by the deafening sounds of a huge avalanche. Rushing out of our tents, the avalanche and its associated fog of snow and ice thundered down the Cesen route and right across the path to ABC, just 500 metres from camp. It was mesmerizing, and I managed to catch a photograph of the power of nature right in front of our eyes. Other avalanches were also seen on the surrounding peaks, the inevitable result of hot weather following a prolonged period of heavy snow.

I felt it was beyond time that those back home, in a far greater sense of worry in the unknown compared to us in the 'known', needed an update on our status and penned the following post on my Facebook page:

EXPEDITION ABANDONED
SATURDAY, 27 JULY 2013

I am extremely disappointed to write that our summit attempt on K2 has been abandoned along with all of the other teams at Base Camp.

The snow conditions encountered en route to Camp 3 were deep, impassable and dangerous, and a decision was made to return

*to Base Camp on Friday, 26th. Today a collective and reluctant
further decision was made to abandon summit plans for K2 this
season. Only the Kiwi duo, who went up to Camp 3 when the
other teams returned to BC, remain on the mountain as yet
another avalanche (pictured) thundered down the mountain
and across the glacier 500 metres from Base Camp at lunchtime.
Success on K2 is never guaranteed, this time the mountain has
had its say ...*

The post was responded to by many hundreds of
acknowledgements, comments, or messages from people all
over the world. All inevitably praised the decision, saying the
mountain would be there for the next time, praying for our safe
passage home and mentioning their best wishes for the Kiwis. It
gave me a degree of comfort that so many people were following
the expedition.

At 12 midday, we went up to Chris's tent to hear the response
to the call. Again, all we heard was silence. Chris tried to call on
satellite phones in addition, but the response was negative.

'This is strange,' Chris said with concern in his voice.

'It is ...' someone added. 'Maybe batteries are dead?'

'They have spare and even the satphone is off, so that's unlikely
to be the answer.'

'Well, if they are moving, then tonight will be the key.'

'Yeah, they'll either have reached Camp 4 or they'll be walking
into Base Camp.'

'Either way, we should either see them or receive a call,' Chris
reaffirmed.

Although I never said anything to the others, the first gut
instincts hit me that this was a cause for concern and that something
may have happened. I wondered how many of the others were
thinking the same. 'Something may have happened' could still be
relatively okay however – a fall resulting in a damaged phone; a
small avalanche burying a pack; a rock fall causing some injury or
so on. Many options and explanations could still account for the
lack of contact.

For the rest of the day all of us were secretly hoping we would
hear a booming 'Hey guys!' from Marty and Denali's cheerful
voices, as they bounded into Base Camp, explaining that they'd

lost their packs in a small avalanche or something, but were fine. No such greetings came. At 6 p.m. all of us went back to Chris's camp for the vital call.

'Marty and Denali. Calling Marty and Denali. This is Base Camp. Do you read? Over ...'

'Camp 3. Calling Camp 3. This is Base Camp. Do you copy? Over.'

The same eerie silence of radio crackles on the line was all that was heard. Chis tried for twenty more minutes to no avail. We all contemplated our thoughts. No one admitted it, but I believe that we all knew deep inside not that 'something may have happened', but that 'something had happened' and that 'thing' was serious.

On Sunday 28 July, three of us gathered for the 8 a.m. scheduled call. No response again. Chris said he would undertake a recce a few hundred metres past ABC to see if he could spot anything looking up to Camp 3. Then another idea arose. Our Sherpas were about to head up the mountain on a recovery operation for the equipment left at the cache halfway up to Camp 3, as well as from Camps 2 and 1. Chris asked me if I thought they might be willing to go up to Camp 3 to see what may have happened.

'They might do – but it would need to be worth their while if you know what I mean,' I replied, making a money sign with my hands.

'Yes, I realize that. What do you think it will take?'

'Well it will need a few hundred dollars; would that be possible?'

'I was going to suggest 300 dollars each.'

'That could work. Let's give it a go.'

We both walked down to our camp and repeated the conversation to Lakpa. He spoke to Minga and Nurbu, who didn't look too enthused, but the offer of 300 dollars each persuaded them. It was agreed they would try and reach Camp 3 that evening and they left shortly after, with empty packs ready to carry some heavy loads back down to Base Camp.

The rest of the day was spent in a state of heightened concern. Although none of us were expecting anything, I still showed up to offer some support for the 12 midday call, which resulted in the same silence. Warner then left for his recce to 200–300 metres past ABC. It was a remote possibility that he'd see anything but it had to be ruled out. His return a few hours later, with no trace or sight of equipment or life, only added to the suspense.

Meanwhile, on the mountain, Mingma and Nurbu reported their location regularly – within four hours they had reached Camp 1, within another three hours Camp 2 and by 4 p.m. were climbing the Black Pyramid to Camp 3. With an immense distance and height gain to cover in one day, their speed was astonishing, testimony to the amazing abilities Sherpas possess at altitude.

Those of us left at Base Camp all gathered in our tent from early evening to hear Mingma and Nurbu's final progress up the Black Pyramid and a hopeful answer to our worries. Lakpa relayed the radio messages in English as they came in – at the cache; on the second half; heading final stretch to Camp 3; nearing Camp 3… The suspense was profound. At 7.30 p.m. he came in to our tent:

'My Sherpa there. I think it's sad news for everybody,' he said.

'He say big avalanche in Camp 3. There's one tent, but only half. Some rope outside tent. He take picture.'

Questions fired back from all of us.

'Which direction avalanche?'

'Two tents or one tent?'

'Rope scattered?'

'How big the avalanche?'

And many more, which Lakpa tried to answer as best he could. Mingma then called through again at 7.35 p.m.:

'100 per cent *mareko cha*,' Mingma's voice on the radio said. I knew immediately what he meant.

'100 per cent die,' Lakpa relayed, with a torn look on his face.

'Two Black Diamond ice axes outside. One crampon outside,' he relayed.

The conversation continued in Nepali before Lakpa thanked Mingma and told him to come down safely.

'So finally he prove,' he said turning to us. 'Two ice axe scattered, one crampon. Tent in half. They have no chance. I'm sorry.'

There was a period of silence.

'Whew …'

'Rest in peace guys.'

'What we all feared …'

'Please thank them, Lakpa.'

'Chris, we are so sorry ...'

'It must have happened that night.'

'I prayed it wouldn't be, but somehow I felt this would end in tragedy.'

'He never misses a call. I felt something was wrong.'

'What a loss – Marty and Denali; utterly tragic.'

'That bloody camp is notorious.'

'K2 rears its tragic head yet again.'

'It could have been all of us ...'

Despite this being the outcome we all feared, all of us were in shock. Marty and Denali were dead? Marty Schmidt of all people? And Denali? After a while Chris started to ask some further questions of Lakpa. They wouldn't help much, but it was the inevitable response – wanting whatever detail we could find. Questions on the ice axe they had found, the crampons, where the camp was in relation to Camp 3, and so on. Lakpa did the best he could to answer, but we knew the full answers would only come once Mingma and Nurbu had returned to Base Camp. Lakpa left us on our own as a sign of respect.

We continued conversing for a long time into the night – as in all cases involving a tragedy, a close community providing a source of comfort, support and understanding. Five climbers and five Sherpas united in a profound loss and trying to find some explanation.

At approximately 9.30 p.m. Lakpa came into the tent to say Mingma and Nurbu were safely at Camp 2. The heated discussions of a couple of days earlier were completely forgotten, and Mingma and Nurbu had more than made up for their actions of then.

'That was incredible. Lakpa, please give them our huge thanks.'

'Outstanding effort.'

'Amazing.'

After many hours talking and conversing, whilst drinking copious amounts of hot chocolate, we gradually decided to call it a night.

'I'm not going to do anything tonight. I'll sleep on it and decide which way we inform the family tomorrow,' Chris added. 'It isn't going to be easy.'

'Anything we can do to help we will,' Nico responded, which was echoed by everyone.

I ventured outside into the moon filled night. K2 was again glistening in its magnificence and I went over to sit on the same rock I had two days earlier, then in distress at the enforced abandoning of the expedition. I gazed up at Camp 3, my thoughts on a father and son, buried together in a tent under a few feet of snow. Yes, deaths happen all the time on high mountains – seven in the past few weeks on the nearby peaks alone. But a *father and son* was tragic beyond any comprehension.

I reflected back two days earlier when I struggled to understand what this was all about. It hadn't made sense then. Now it all made sense. The gut instinct I'd felt the entire journey that 'something wasn't right' had proved itself the case in the most extreme of outcomes. That's what this was all about, I said to myself. Everything happens for a reason. And it does. We may not understand that reason for a day, a week, a month, a year or ten years, but at some time in the future, most of what befalls us will all find a meaning. In this case, two days later, the decision not to go up to Camp 3 and the abandoning of the expedition all made sense… Not for the first time in my life, I had escaped a tragedy through good fortune, gut instinct or an invisible hand. Though that did nothing to lessen the sadness for the Schmidts, it was something that none of us could ignore. I stayed in contemplation for over twenty minutes, the bitter cold being lost amidst my thoughts. 'Rest in peace, my K2 brothers,' I finally said quietly and retreated to my frozen tent.

CHAPTER NINE

REQUIEM

THE MOUNTAINS WILL ALWAYS
BE THERE; THE TRICK IS TO
MAKE SURE YOU ARE TOO.

- HERVEY VOGE

ON MONDAY, 29 JULY, on another warm and sunny morning, Al, Alex, Nico and myself joined Chris in his tent. He was preparing a series of calls he needed to make to the Schmidt family, having held off for as long as he could.

'This is going to be extremely hard,' he said. 'I'm going to have to really compose myself to make these calls.'

'Yes, the hardest call to ever make,' I responded.

'In particular Sequoia – she is a tough and assertive woman; a bit like her father,' he added.

'We'll leave you in private,' Al said.

Sequoia Schmidt was Marty's daughter and Denali's sister who lived in Houston and, aged only 22, was already a successful book publisher in the US. Chris told us that she'd had a troubled relationship with her father, not speaking to him for several years, but was extremely close to her brother. He also enlightened us as to further rifts in the family between Sequoia and Denali and Marty's second wife, Giovannina Cantale, whom he married in 2007 and with whom he lived in Christchurch, New Zealand.

Chris thought it best to call Lance Machovsky first, an old and extremely close friend of the family who was like an uncle to Denali and Sequoia. Machovsky, he felt, would be in a better position to inform Sequoia and Larissa Minerva, Denali's long-time girlfriend. He then called Cantale. After he'd made the calls, he met up with us, looking strained. It had obviously been a traumatic experience.

The exhausted Sherpas returned to Base Camp in the afternoon and, after being given some tea and food, quickly elaborated in full what they had seen. Most importantly, they showed the photographs they had taken of the ice axe and crampons scattered on the debris. It was sobering to see the pictures. We all thanked them profusely.

I was the only one left at Base Camp who was blogging and posting on my website and Facebook pages and, since confirming our expedition abandonment two days earlier, I'd continued to receive numerous messages or comments asking how we were and for any news or update on the Schmidts. I said to Chris that we owed everyone an update and couldn't deny or delay the truth. He agreed and suggested we post the news via my website and Facebook page. After carefully drafting the post and sharing it with Chris, I pressed the 'post' button that lunchtime.

TRAGEDY DISCOVERED AT CAMP 3

AS AVALANCHE KILLS NEW ZEALANDERS

MONDAY, 29 JULY 2013

Our fears on the fate of New Zealand mountain guide Marty Schmidt (53) and his son Denali (25) – who climbed up from Camp 2 to Camp 3 last Friday as we all returned to Base Camp due to the dangerous snow conditions – was sadly confirmed last night when two of our Sherpas reached Camp 3 to find it wiped out by an avalanche. As Marty's last radio communication took place Friday night from the camp, the avalanche almost certainly occurred that night as they slept in their tent.

The deaths of a father and son is a tragedy in itself but compounded even further by the fact that Marty and Denali – who were great people that we all got to know very well in the close-knit community of K2 Base Camp – were very well known, highly experienced and extremely strong mountaineers, the last people many would expect to be killed on a mountain.

Sadly, at times the mountains do not differentiate between ability and experience, least of all K2. The poignancy of the tragedy is not lost in that, had the rest of us not turned back that day – including Marty and Denali's Australian teammate Chris Warner – we also all would have been sleeping at Camp 3 when the avalanche struck.

In mountaineering, there is often a very thin line between life and death and here was yet one more occasion. 6 teams came down and are alive and well, one team went up and are tragically dead. On behalf of all of us remaining at Base Camp, our sincerest condolences to their family and may Marty and Denali rest in peace. Posted with the full cooperation and agreement of Chris Warner.

Without expecting it, I was about to become intimately involved with the entire Schmidts' tragedy... Within thirty minutes the post had caused hundreds of responses in the form of condolences, sympathies, sadness, questions and demands for more information. I received many direct messages in addition; replying to all as carefully as I could, but suggesting some could only be answered by Chris – who, unfortunately, was not on any social media channels. Some wanted assurances we were 100 per cent certain of the tragedy and even the New Zealand Embassy in Islamabad wrote that 'it was premature to report that the Schmidts had been killed', for which I was compelled to state to all those doubting that their reports were sadly wrong. It all became a frantic wave of communication for the rest of the day.

At the same time, Sequoia also published her official confirmation in the form of the following Twitter post:

It is with great sorrow that I confirm the tragic death of my brother and father, Denali and Marty Schmidt. May their spirits rest at K2. RIP

— SEQUOIA DI ANGELO
(@SEQUOIADIANGELO)
29 JULY 2013

News of the deaths was soon carried by networks across the world, with most major news agencies reprinting parts of my post. Within a few hours, many were contacting my team in UAE, or me directly through my website, for further information and quotes. Although I tried to refer most to Chris, it was easier to reach me with my communication systems and so I took many of the calls and responded as best I could.

Chris had to stay on another two days to organize recovery of Marty and Denali's equipment left at Camps 2, 1 and ABC and, in particular, to sort out all of their personal kit at Base Camp. It was a thankless task but, as their teammate, he was the only one who could do it. For the rest of us, it was time to pack up and head off. As guilty as we felt about leaving Chris at Base Camp, we had now been there four days since returning from Camp 2 and had our own loved ones to return to.

There was one last action for us to perform – to return to the Gilkey Memorial to lay a commemorative plaque for Marty and Denali, which Chris had his Base Camp staff engrave a tray with their names on. On Tuesday, 30 July, all of us remaining – Chris, Alex, Nico, the full Japanese team of eight, Al and myself and some of the Base Camp staff – trekked solemnly up to the rocky outcrop. With the warm sun shining on the memorial, he unveiled it and slowly fixed it to the rocks. The words read:

THE KIWI'S
MARTY SCHMIDT 53 YRS
DENALI SCHMIDT 25 YRS
FATHER AND SON
27-7-2013 K2 CAMP 3

As warm as the day was, I felt a chill reading the words as he attached the simple plaque. With the many different cultures and beliefs, it probably didn't feel appropriate for Chris to say any words and he was probably struggling to find them in any case. I felt it needed something, however, so stepped up.

'Can I suggest we have two minutes' silence as a sign of respect?'

The seventeen of us consequently locked ourselves in our own deepest thoughts. Some stared at the plaque, others bowed their heads. I looked up to K2, as I had so many times over the past few weeks, in silent contemplation. The calmness and beauty of the day was at odds with the terror and brutality that we were recording. All of us were hardened mountaineers who had seen and experienced tragedies before, and there was no show of emotion, just intense sadness. After twenty minutes at the Memorial we retreated to Base Camp.

Bidding our farewells to Chris and the staff remaining at camp, the mass army of porters and remaining climbers departed for the long trek back to Askole. I walked alone to Concordia along the broken and shifting moraines. I wanted to be on my own again, as I had at the beginning of the journey, to focus my thoughts, contemplate the meaning of it all and to hopefully gain some universal learning and wisdom. Thoughts of the Schmidts, thoughts of our own escape, thoughts of what this all meant infused my head. In those precious few hours I seemingly entered a different mindset, a different frequency, and an altered vibration. K2 kept begging me to look back, which I did every twenty minutes or so. Several times I stood for five minutes staring up at its icy summit. It was still, majestic and monumental. A cloud hung over its summit like a halo, which I couldn't take my eyes off. As strange as it may read, I felt as if I was in a relationship with this mountain, a profound sense of connection and understanding. It felt as if K2 was telling me that it would never be tamed. That it would allow selective visitors a brief glimpse of it sacred summit on its terms and no one else's. It emitted an indescribable connection of nature, the cosmos and consciousness. In my heightened state, it seemed to ask me to return …

'It's not about the destination; it's about the journey,' is an oft used, possibly overused, quote. But, for much of my life, that mantra has been vividly evident. On all my adventures, whilst the summit, pole or finish point have obviously stood out, there have been many other moments on journeys which have had the greatest impact. For K2, these few hours were one of the most enlightening, deepest and profound parts of the journey experienced.

I eventually reached Concordia Camp, well over an hour behind everyone else. There we met up with other climbers returning from the Gasherbrums and shared the stories of our respective failures and tragedies. The porters and Sherpas were happy, however. Home was in reach. It took a further six days to reach Askole. The trek was long, hot and tough. There were none of the normal feelings on a homeward trek of accomplishment or exultation, just reflection and realization. And fatigue and

illness. As we progressed further down the Baltoro, the dry
gullies we'd crossed on the way in were now awash with the
raging torrents of mountain rivers. In many places, we had to
wade waist deep across these fast-flowing streams cascading
down the mountains that weren't even there six weeks prior. On
the 4WD journey from Askole back to Skardu, rivers of water
had washed away the mountain road in many places, resulting
in our having to leap across rocks in the ravines to join a different
set of trucks on the other side of the hazard. On one washed
away section of the road, Aziz, the cook, admirably showed his
engineering credentials by single-handedly moving rocks and
creating a flat base whilst tied by a rope in a waist-deep torrent
of fast-flowing water. Seeing these old trucks drive across such
deep and unstable water was an amazing sight.

When we reached Skardu, I turned my normal smartphone on
for the first time in six weeks – until then I'd only been using my
satellite phone and computer – and called several people whilst I
checked the hundreds or thousands of routine work emails, texts,
WhatsApp and other messages. One message, from my good friend
David Thomson of support sponsors JA Resorts, stood out like a
beacon. It said 'Are you okay? I've just had a huge sense of you.
It felt like there was a real problem.' The date of the message was
very early morning in Dubai on 27 July. Reading it sent a shiver
down my spine. I called him and, after he offered his condolences
on what had happened and his best wishes for our safe return,
explained that he was in a 'right state' that morning, convinced
that a terrible accident had happened and that he'd told his wife
that he thought I might have died. He sent the message not even
thinking that I didn't have any reception on my phone. David's
wife, Deborah, would later tell me how affected he was and that
he was walking in a daze. It wasn't the first time he'd had strange
visions, but premonition, foreboding, my being kissed by death or
the energy we are all part of, this was uncanny. At some time prior
to 8 a.m. on 27 July, Marty and Denali were killed …

In Skardu I also took a prearranged call from Sequoia and
Lance. Whilst Lance tried to speak calmly and measured, Sequoia
was angry, direct and demanding of answers. I was ill and fatigued.
It wasn't the easiest of conversations.

'Why did they go up?'

'Tell me now and don't bullshit me here. Did my father make the call to go up?'

'What did Denali say when you saw him in the tent?'

And many hard-hitting questions, natural from anyone bereaved, wanting answers. She'd lost her father and her brother, half of her family, and was furious as well as in grief. I tried to answer her as best I could, being careful to distinguish between what was fact and what was my opinion.

Which brings me to the one question she asked above all; the question which countless people would ask me thereafter. The why. The how and why such an experienced mountaineer and his son went against the opinion of the eighteen other foreign climbers and five Sherpas to head up when all others came down. We will never fully know their motives but, in my opinion, there were several factors playing out that caused their decision.

The first was the highly negative atmosphere prevailing at Camp 2 on 25 July 2013, with the Swiss already cancelling their expedition and the Spanish and the Sherpas considering it. It wasn't the call to go down which seemed to rile Marty but these murmurs to quit K2 for this year. I wrote earlier of his, 'when it snows, you get snow!' and 'all this bullshit about quitting,' comments to us. Lakpa mentioned Marty said similar the night before, with a 'Fuck, we're going up.' There was thus a definite dismissiveness to these feelings of quitting and, I believe, they were trying to inject some positivity into this very negative atmosphere, with a very action-orientated response.

Secondly, they were experienced, ready and strong. Very strong. Fully acclimatized and fit from their Broad Peak success, they didn't need any more time, like many of us, to reach their fullest fitness levels. They may have felt there wouldn't be another opportunity and that there was nothing to lose by heading up then in the rapidly improving weather.

Thirdly, they had high stakes. It was Marty's third attempt on the mountain and, as history has demonstrated in many theatres of play, repeated failures can lead to errors in judgement when desperation comes into play, however mild. They were also trying to be the first father and son ever to climb K2, a massive accomplishment without doubt, which might not be possible again if Denali moved to pursue his art career. The accolade had 'significance' written all over it. And, as I wrote before, the drive for significance can lead even the most experienced of athletes to make a wrong call.

And fourthly, was the character of Marty Schmidt. That independent mindedness, assertiveness and all-important self-belief which defined who he was. A guy who I liked immensely, but someone who was opinionated and whom I believe would have upset one or more people in his lifetime. A man who was not going to take someone else's word for what it was like on the slopes to Camp 3 and would push on regardless. I write all of this about Marty of course, for whilst it was a joint decision – something that Chris Warner was always at pains to stress – it was undoubtedly Marty's views which carried sway. Denali, although extremely strong and skilled, was much less experienced and would have looked to his father for guidance. His saying nothing in the conversation at their tent on 26 July probably wasn't just coincidental.

As a coach, the defining factor was that of self-belief – one of the most powerful of weapons all of us hold. Virtually every successful leader, sportsperson, entrepreneur or business person will often say it is *the* critical element that determined their success. It drives us, propels us, energizes us, defines us. It is powerful beyond all measure. That self-belief, however, must be accompanied by 10–20 per cent of humility or humbleness to keep us grounded, balanced and in check. Without that balance, unchecked self-belief can lead to arrogance, and history is littered with examples of where leaders, politicians, generals, sportspersons and business persons started to believe they were more important than they really were – who overstepped the mark, and who eventually lost their followers, their empires, their conquests, their businesses and their status. From Alexander the Great to Napoleon, from Hitler to George W Bush, from Fred Goodwin (RBS) to Tiger Woods, all believed they were invincible, and that belief in their invincibility resulted in actions or behaviour ranging from the unwise to the cataclysmic. All eventually fell, sometimes with breathtaking speed.

Tragically Marty Schmidt could probably be added to that long list. A self-belief which was so powerful that he stopped listening to other climbers but, even more so, to the power of nature around him. Hindsight is easy of course and, had they made it to the top, they would have been heroes. But one matter all of us who came down agree on was that for two climbers, however strong, to manage to break trail over deep snow to K2's shoulder and then up the near vertical inclines of the final summit push, without any support, would have required an extraordinary effort. One that all of us deemed near impossible. This was K2, not Everest, a mountain that had beaten even the strongest and most skilled of climbers. High risk, high reward would have been one thing; this appeared to be high risk, low reward. As Chris Warner concluded, it was therefore just not worth going up to Camp 3 to 'check it out'. By coming down he survived and we all survived. Tragically, two fine climbers and two fine human beings – a father and husband, and a son and brother – were killed.

For my own escape, many people on the journey back to Islamabad and, as I would soon discover, in the UAE and UK would say comments such as: 'you are very lucky', 'thank God you all decided to come down', or 'had you gone up you would all have been killed,' and so on. But the simple, if stark, fact is that we didn't. We went down and survived. Two friends went up and were killed. And life is full of countless examples of where a second earlier or later, twelve inches to the left or right, a five-minute traffic jam, a last-minute diversion or a call was the difference between living and dying. Such is the fragility of life and the fine line between life and death.

The 2013 season was coming to a close in the Karakoram and, in addition to the eleven climbers killed at Nanga Parbat Base Camp, ten climbers had died on Broad Peak, G1 and K2. An eleventh would die on G1 on 9 August, making the total fatalities a tragic twenty-two – the deadliest year in Karakoram history (see Appendix C). The tragic expedition was over for all of us; it was time to go home. The personal reflection for me would only just be beginning, but, as I plugged in some music on the flight home from Islamabad, the beautiful and haunting song and words of Stevie Nicks' *Landslide* played in a synchronicity that perfectly fitted the moment, the season and the time:

I took my love, and I took it down
Climbed the mountain and I turned around
And I saw my reflection in the snow covered hills
Till the landslide brought me down

Oh, mirror in the sky, what is love?
Can the child within my heart rise above?
Can I sail through the changing ocean tides?
Can I handle the seasons of my life?

Well, I've been afraid of changing
'Cause I've built my life around you
But time makes you bolder
Children get older and I'm getting older too

Well, I've been afraid of changing
'Cause I've built my life around you
But time makes you bolder
Children get older and I'm getting older too
Oh, I'm getting older too

Take this love, take it down
If you climb a mountain and turn around
And if you see my reflection in the snow covered hills
Well, the landslide will bring it down

And if you see my reflection in the snow covered hills
Well, the landslide will bring it down
Oh, the landslide will bring it down

PART TWO

CHAPTER TEN

RE-ENTRY

THERE IS NOTHING LIKE
RETURNING TO A PLACE THAT
REMAINS UNCHANGED TO
FIND THE WAYS IN WHICH YOU
YOURSELF HAVE ALTERED.

– NELSON MANDELA

RETURNING FROM AN EXPEDITION into so-called 'normal life' can be tough. Very tough. It's the post-holiday blues magnified a hundred times. Something you've been planning, preparing and training for a year, two or more; a journey that is all consuming; and one which takes you to another world in our world, is a highly intense experience. After such an experience it can take time to adjust to shopping in supermarkets, watching *X Factor* or, above all, dealing with the mayhem of our communication overloaded world. Indeed, apart from the absence of family I sometimes question whether sitting around a campfire with close friends in the beauty of nature, sharing stories from the past, aspirations for the future and life in the present, isn't more of the real world than the one of materialism, technology and stress that we experience every day.

On all my major expeditions, the homecoming has followed an uncannily similar pattern. There is a short period of a few days of excitement, exhilaration even, of returning home and the joys of seeing loved ones, friends and family. With the flushes of success and the inevitable multitude of congratulations (all giving that feeling of significance) one would have to be a complete loner to not be uplifted. Everyone's pleased to see you, you're thrilled to see them, there's a lot of welcome, attention, communication and community. It feels good.

Then there is the come down. Everyone gets on with their own lives, their families, their priorities. And you, depending on your circumstances, are on your own. Even if you're with a partner and/or children, you can still be on your own. You play, laugh and joke, but it's not painting the true picture. Underneath it all, you're trying to adjust back to civilization. Trying to come to terms with this massive let down. And no-one understands what you've been through and what you're struggling with.

It's not just a mental challenge, but a physiological one too. Our incredible bodies adapt remarkably to their circumstances, but they only think one step ahead. When you go to altitude the body produces more red blood cells to carry oxygen to one's vital organs. It's not a priority that the sludge now flowing round your arteries may cause circulation to your toes to be cut off. Similarly, when one goes into regions of deep cold it diverts blood from the extremities to the vital core organs. It doesn't think that the fingers you could lose might be needed for typing on a keypad in a week's time. When you go into space for any length of time, the body actually starts to dissolve the bones in our legs, because legs have no purpose in zero gravity. It doesn't think that you might be walking on earth again in six months' time.

Scientists are discovering remarkably similar adaptions in our brains too. For thousands and thousands of years, our brains have largely focused on one thing at a time – the remarkable works of ancient civilizations have been attributed to the sheer time they had to contemplate, think and create. In the last twenty years, however, our brains have been under an onslaught like never before from information overload, coupled with electromagnetic assault from EMFs in mobile phones, Wi-Fi broadcast signals and brain-altering medications. The astounding result that scientists are discovering is that our brains are actually changing shape to cope with the bombardment – multitasking at the expense of critical thinking, contemplation, focus and strategizing. Some people may conclude that is evolution, but with children in particular showing major brain functioning alterations, distraction and behavioural difficulties like never before – greatly affected by the social media revolution - the implications are beyond anything we can contemplate. There is growing evidence that teenagers are in the grip of a mental health crisis, almost as if young people are turning in on themselves. In an article on our teenage mental-health crisis (*The Independent*, 27 February 2016), it was reported that rates of depression and anxiety amongst teenagers have increased by 70 per cent in twenty-five years. Numerous further studies are appearing all the time showing similar seismic shifts in our young people. That's the reality of our crazy lives today. Our bodies and brains, in existence for hundreds of thousands of years, were not designed for this sudden technological attack occurring in the past twenty years and are accelerating out of control.

When one goes on an expedition, that invasion of technology, radiation and distraction is largely subsided. You are back in a world where you can think, observe, feel, contemplate and focus. It takes a week or so to get into that 'zone' but, once there, it is a magical feeling akin, as I previously wrote, to operating on a different frequency.

All ventures to the extremes of our world or beyond, however, require some time to decompress or readapt. Decompression following a saturation dive can take weeks. Readapting after returning from space takes between six months and a year, both physiologically but also mentally. It shouldn't be a complete surprise, therefore, that returning from the extremes of latitude or altitude on earth requires readaption too. Apart from the huge time spent planning, preparing, training and executing that major goal, your mind is operating on that different level. And, no matter who you are with, when you come back to the unreal 'real world', our mind and body quite simply says, 'Help! Get me out of here! Get me back to the mountains and the ice!' That is the reality of re-entry.

Of all my expeditions, returning from the South Pole journey was the hardest and where this adaption proved most profound. Antarctica is the most incredible place on our planet, period. A pristine wilderness devoid of any life or influence of mankind. No animals, no birds, no insects live on the continent – all life is concentrated on the coasts and in the seas. No flowers, mosses or life forms of any kind exist on the ice. No aircraft fly across the sky. It literally is like being on another planet. And, as such, one's thoughts enter that different realm. A former colleague from the army – a tough and strapping Guards officer – who walked to the South Pole in 2005 told me he went into depression for a year after returning, which I found hard to believe. Until I returned myself.

Thrust straight back into the chaos just four days after I reached the Pole was all too much and I went into a downward spiral for many months.

Returning from K2 had some similar yet also different manifestations. With no success to share, there was no euphoria on returning. No feeling of a job well done. And no enthusiastic plaudits from those around me. I was also ill – something eaten on the return leg had given me acute diarrhoea and sickness. Having the runs for three days is normal in developing countries, but if it continues after five days it's generally something more serious. Flying straight back to the UK after a day in Dubai, I was feeling sick, listless and nauseous for a whole week, spending most of the time in bed. My haemorrhoids were also chronic. Finally seeing a doctor, he confirmed I'd picked up some unknown dysentery and put me on antibiotics and a host of other medicines.

Then, strangely, I experienced a period of complete presence and happiness, back in my home in the New Forest – a National Park and an oasis of beauty in southern England. A fantastic week spent with my daughter Charlotte, as ordered by a court in the ongoing proceedings, was the highlight and I gave her everything of my time. Another friend from overseas stayed for a week and, throughout, great friends surrounded me. K2 had failed, yes, but that uncertainty had gone. There was intense sadness for the Schmidts, but I was alive and there was gratitude for this. It was, surprisingly, a lovely summer of completely living in the present. K2 was put to the back of my mind and the past was, for these precious weeks, water under the bridge. The future, not least a return attempt on K2, could wait another day.

Ironically, all I was experiencing was what psychologists have found in relation to past-oriented people, future-looking people and present-living people with regard to the holy grail we all seek – happiness. The least happy people are past-lookers, because there is usually a sadness accompanying the fond memories, that things can never be the same. Future-oriented people can be happy but are often so busy planning and preparing for their goals that they can forget to enjoy the moment. The happiest, of course, are those who live in the present. As a generally future-oriented guy, the downsides stated above have been paramount through much of my life, although over the past ten years or more I have increasingly learned to savour the moment in addition. Here, however, in the summer of 2013 I was completely living in the present. And it was good.

Eventually I had to address both the past and the future, and K2 returned to the fore. A few publications approached my base team wanting articles or stories on the tragedy of K2, which I eventually got around to writing. My article 'The Fine Line between Life and Death', which detailed the events of the summer, the actions of the Schmidts and some of the reasonings and mental traits of climbers, was published in the *Huffington Post* and was carried in other newspapers across the world. Ironically and tragically, just a week later a good friend, Roy Nasr, was killed on his bike just a mile from my home in Dubai. I'd known Roy through fitness challenges, cycling and triathlons for eighteen years and we'd cycled the same stretch of road, part of the Friday morning group ride, every weekend when I was in the country. His death simply reinforced the title of my article and the fragility of life. Here I was, alive and well, having taken such high risks climbing such a notorious mountain, and yet my mate was dead after undertaking a low risk activity just a mile from my home. When your time's up, it's up.

I spoke to Sequoia Schmidt at length on Skype and felt her grief. To lose her father was bad enough. To lose her father and her brother, unfathomable. She told me of the difficult relationship she'd had with her father, not speaking to him for many years, and I sensed her deep regret. I also learned that Denali wasn't as gung-ho about mountaineering as his father or many others had assumed and was more interested in his art career. She told me of the devastation of his heartbroken girlfriend, Larissa, who he had lived with and to whom Denali had told, 'Our lives are just beginning and we will be together again before you know it,' on the morning he left for K2. It was all profoundly sad to hear and whatever words of comfort I tried to offer were in vain. She also desperately wanted me to return to K2 and succeed the following year, which was a generous act of kindness.

The next month I would also meet Joanne Munisteri, Marty's former wife and Denali's mother, when she transited through Dubai en route to Riyadh, Saudi Arabia, where she was teaching Foundation Science at the Princess Noura University. We spent four precious hours recollecting the events of the summer and her memories of Denali. There I witnessed in person the anguish and grief of a mother who had lost a beloved son, and her helplessness in the face of such a tragedy. Yet I was also struck by her enlightenment, wisdom and spirituality. I learned a great deal not of Denali the mountaineer, but Denali the artist, the man and the son. And, although understandably not all positive, more about Marty the man too. It was a powerful presence to meet her and to reinforce the growing bonds I was gaining to the family. The conflicts between the two sides of the family were also heard, but as I always do in family conflicts, I listened and didn't judge, while also attempting to reach out to Marty's wife, Giovannina Cantale.

In late September, I spoke to Al Hancock for the first time since we departed. There was no need to explain anything, both of us needed our own time to come back to reality.

'Hey, Adrian. How you doin' there, buddy?'

'Getting there mate. What about you?'

'Man, it's taken me two months to sort myself out, I'm still not there.'

'I understand totally …'

'So many people have told me we were SO lucky not going up to Camp 3 with poor Marty and Denali.'

'Oh yes, but as I have said to many, the stark facts for us are we didn't.'

'And I remind myself it's the fourth time I have escaped death by a short whisker.'

In addition to evading the massacre on a bus on the Karakoram Highway in 2012, Al had a lucky escape on Manaslu, the 8,163-metre, eighth highest mountain in the world, the same year. On 22 September 2012, he was at Camp 2 on a second rotation and about to head up to Camp 3 for the night. He and some others decided to head down to Base Camp for a rest and get ready for a possible summit push, whilst other climbers moved up. The next morning a huge ice serac collapsed, causing a large avalanche which destroyed Camps 3 and 2, killing eleven climbers and injuring sixteen.

On an earlier Broad Peak expedition also, he had a negative feeling about leaving for a summit attempt, after it had snowed all night with precipitation that was heavy with moisture. He stayed behind while others went up. Several hours later there was an avalanche, which killed a Pakistani HAP with whom Al had been

Camp 4 (7,800m)

Camp 3 (7,300m)

Camp 2 (6,700m)

Camp 1 (6,100m)

K2 from Concordia showing the Abruzzi Spur route and camp locations.

Al Hancock and Adrian Hayes at Base Camp after the Puja.

Adrian Hayes on the
Abruzzi Spur.
(Photo: Al Hancock)

Camp 2 (6,700 metres)
– tents placed on built
up platforms of snow,
ice and debris.

Climbing to Camp 2.

Marty Schmidt.

Chris Warner,
Denali Schmidt and
Marty Schmidt.
(Photo: Al Hancock)

Denali Schmidt climbing
to Camp 2.

Avalanche just above Base Camp.

The Gilkey Memorial overlooking K2 Base Camp.

Al Hancock and porter on the trek to Base Camp in 2014.

The 2014 extended team at Base Camp.

Crossing the glacier below ABC.

Camp 1 (6,100 metres).

Adrian Hayes at the Puja.

Camp 2 (6,700 metres) looking down on the Baltoro Glacier.

Tamara Lunger climbing the Black Pyramid to Camp 3 (7,300 metres).
(Photo: Al Hancock)

Ascending the steep ice wall after the traverse on the 2014 summit push (8,400 metres).

Sunrise over China at 8,400 metres.

Adrian Hayes on the summit of K2 at 3:20 p.m. on 26 July 2014.

drinking tea earlier and injuring several others. They never found the body of the Pakistani, only a blood trail and, in the search, narrowly missed two other avalanches.

'You're a lucky charm, Hancock. That's why I'm sticking with you, despite you being the ugliest climber I've ever shared a tent with,' I responded, injecting some needed lightness into the chat.

'Yer so kind!' he laughed. 'It's a deal. How you looking for next year?'

'Oh, I'm on but there's got to be some changes,' I responded. 'Did you see my ExplorersWeb interview?' I asked. 'I've written even more to Pakistan and Nepal. Will send you the letters.'

The adventure world had contacted me wanting my views on the tragedy and also on K2 and the Pakistan climbing scene. Returning with some existing doubts strongly reinforced, I was very keen to have these thoughts recorded. ExplorersWeb carried a major Q and A article, which was repeated in various publications, and I also wrote in full to the Pakistan Alpine Association, NSE and SST with my feedback on what I believed was so flawed with the Karakoram present practices. It was direct and, in places, hard-hitting.

The first one was the critical matter of K2 expedition timeframes. I carried out a full trawl of K2 summits statistics over the previous thirty years, which gave a clear picture that, in years where there had been successes, the vast majority of summits had taken place in the last ten days of July. As such, the standard practices of arriving in Pakistan in late June, allowing less than four weeks for inevitable Islamabad administration, flights (often delayed) to Skardu, the long trek to Base Camp, fixing lines, establishing camps up the mountain and the all too critical acclimatization, was pitifully short for the world's second highest mountain. Even if it was managed, the overtly tight timelines would likely give a single shot at the summit at the end of the season in a hoped-for weather window arriving at the same time. Unfortunately, nature doesn't always fit into man's timeframes. A lengthy period of excellent weather in early July, and another golden window of fine weather and far better snow conditions in mid-July, were ripe for summit attempts, but neither were remotely possible because we weren't even in Base Camp for the first, and hadn't even completed a single rotation for the second. The entire practice seemed to be one dictated by commercial considerations and I was heavily critical about it. There was a logical reason why Everest expeditions lasted two months and no logical reason whatsoever why K2 expeditions lasted five weeks.

The second doubt was on the regular practice of doubling Broad Peak with K2. The traditional rationale was that, by summiting the much easier Broad Peak first, climbers would be fully acclimatized to attempt the far more difficult K2 after. Yet with an already condensed climbing period and the unpredictable Karakoram climate giving even shorter and sparser weather windows, it was inordinately tight to fit even one 8,000-metre peak in, let alone two – one of them being the mighty K2. In addition, there was a mistaken assumption that Broad Peak was one of the 'easy' eight-thousanders. From the statistics and failures of the past few years, there seemed to be nothing easy about the mountain at all, and to regard it as a 'warm up' for K2 was highly flawed. I also trawled the statistics to find that numerous climbers had failed to summit one or even both due to attempting the double, and couldn't easily find the last time anyone had managed it. So, along with the delayed starting dates, the whole concept again seemed to be one based on commercial considerations rather than practicality. The only way I deemed it feasible was by commencing a Broad Peak expedition in late May or early June for a summit attempt in early July – which was exactly what the successful Austrian team on Broad Peak did in 2013. Had they wanted to attempt K2 in addition, they would have had sufficient time and been in a position to set up camps on the latter.

Which brought me onto the third point, which was the idea of trying to attempt K2 alpine style. Fabrice and others on the 2012 success said that, without a strong team of Sherpas on the expedition, summiting would have been extremely difficult due to the deep snow conditions experienced at higher elevations. It seemed that snow conditions were an even greater problem on K2 than the weather. That was an issue which required numbers to counter. In cycling, the practice of drafting (riding behind another cyclist) saves 30 per cent in energy output, which is why a two-man breakaway invariably gets caught by a twenty or thirty-strong peloton. Breaking trail in deep snow requires similar numbers – our small team wouldn't have been enough, the two-man Schmidts would have found it near impossible.

Furthermore, the Schmidts' intention of climbing K2 in a one-push alpine style attempt with all their kit made that near impossibility appear even more unlikely. Breaking trail with a light pack is exhausting; doing so with a heavy pack containing lines, ropes, ice screws and bolts even more daunting. Undoubtedly, in good snow conditions, some of the world's strongest climbers could probably manage it, but it was telling that the Swiss team – three highly competent mountaineers – whilst eschewing fixed lines still undertook a rotation to stock camps on the mountain. Again, starting the whole expedition much earlier, be it Broad Peak and K2 combined or K2 only, would allow that to happen.

Although I repeated, in my letters and articles, my intense respect for those climbing without oxygen, alpine style and without Sherpas in support, and was careful to refrain from any 'summit at all costs' insinuation, failures in four of the past five years didn't exactly lend support to current practices working. And it seemed that if a serious attempt was going to be made on K2 in 2014, then it required a strong team to be assembled, a much earlier start and focusing on K2 only. To their credit, all of the organizations appeared to listen and agree, promising to enact major changes for 2014.

The one area where I had some hesitation was on the Abruzzi Spur. Camp 3 had again reared its ugly head with its avalanche-prone location and killed two fine climbers. I wondered again whether the Cesen might be an option. What struck me, having seen the route, was how much more direct and clean a line it was right up to the shoulder. It was also much closer to Base Camp than the Abruzzi, which would allow for far quicker and easier access with more rotation opportunities. Above all, having witnessed the problems of not knowing what had happened to or the location of missing climbers on Broad Peak and K2 this season, the fact that the whole of the Cesen was completely visible from Base Camp seemed to be a huge advantage that was largely overlooked. The Cesen versus Abruzzi wasn't critical at this stage, however, and was parked for another day.

Aside from all the big picture items above, I also questioned, in private, my own preparation and practices. Foremost was that of my fitness. Yes, there had been unforeseen delays; I had suffered a chronic chest infection for weeks; and we only had the time for one rotation. Yet none of these reasons entirely convinced me that, despite training frenetically since the beginning of 2013, I was fit enough to conquer K2. I reflected on whether, by any remote chance, I had a slight degree of complacency after the successes of 2012, and my own track record of achievements.

I also never got fully into 'the zone' which I had on all previous major projects of recent years. One prime reason for that was the major distraction, time and strain in my personal life which, critically, took my eye off the ball. I wasn't in that place of total and utter focus so required in tackling these major goals. I even wondered how I would have fared higher up had we been able to get there.

I didn't know the answers to all of these doubts, but what I did know was what my gut instinct was telling me throughout the expedition that it 'didn't quite feel right'. And, although of no consolation to the Schmidts, for myself maybe the 'everything happens for a reason' actually had a purpose behind it. I vowed that, in the following year, no distractions could be allowed to take my mind off that goal. It wasn't so much selfish, but rather self-survival and self-preservation. Little did I know then that this would be tested to the full a few months later.

With these matters out of the way, I then started to experience a delayed 'low'. Undoubtedly, the combined failure of K2 in the summer and the entire uncertainty over 2014 started to have its effect. Thuraya and ZSI Trading / Marmot organized seminars where I spoke about the expedition but, whilst all allowed some processing and were evidently powerful stories, they were ultimately tragic and didn't create a great sense of well-being. I was alive, yes, but we 'failed'. Two friends were dead, their bodies lying for eternity at extreme altitude on a mountain in the middle of nowhere. K2 had only been successfully climbed from Pakistan one year in the past five. There was no guarantee of success the following year.

Coupled with these combined emotions of sadness and uncertainty over K2 was the even greater sadness and uncertainty concerning my children – an utterly emotional and debilitating effect of ongoing, countless and ultimately needless court cases and all that went with it. For K2, only those who had also put themselves through such an intense and risky experience could fully understand the effects. And, for the debacle of the UK's family law system, only those who had also been through the life-diminishing pressures of struggling to see their children could truly understand that too.

The combined worry, stress and emotions sent me into a deep low for the rest of the year and into 2014. There was little escape and little solace. It was a period of struggle and darkness. In the past, where there was the love, the light and the laughter, was now an aching hollowness. Every day I greeted the sun like a climber greets their rope, fingers holding on fast despite the pain and sadness. It was like a cold, flowing glacial river, washing all the goodness out of me. That sadness flowed through my veins and deadened the mind. It smothered my mojo, cowered my spirit.

The despair subsequently clouded the future. I well knew that uncertainty and expectation were, and are, part and parcel of life. Mountaineers live with it all the time. Security can be an insipid thing – the only thing that can make life possible is permanent, intolerable insecurity and not knowing what comes next. Yet the intrinsic human need for certainty was aching in my joints, and certainty in my life felt as far away as life on Mars.

As I teach in my development work with leaders, teams and executives, there is always a learning in the darkness, and I knew there would be from this. The most basic driver for all of humankind, however, is to avoid pain. And I was no different. Denial or not, the reality was too uncertain and too distressing.

One day I watched the film *Seven Years in Tibet*, starring Brad Pitt, which depicts the life of Austrian climber, Heinrich Harrer. Watching the account of an assertive and carefree Pitt being away from his family for many months to climb Nanga Parbat, I felt a certain resemblance to my own life. How easy it was for both Harrer and myself to be as free as a bird and venture to the extremes of the planet, carefree and with only one goal on our mind. And how difficult it was for those left behind. When those months turned into years, although in entirely different circumstances, the film started to resonate even more. It was the film's portrayal of Pitt's struggle to see his young son on his return, however, that inevitably hit me the hardest. The final scene, where Pitt was seen climbing an Alpine peak with his then assumed 18–20-year-old son, in an obviously extremely close bond, made my eyes well up. Hope, as always, providing a light at the end of the tunnel.

CHAPTER ELEVEN

IN THE ZONE

SUCCESS IN LIFE IS THE
RESULT OF GOOD JUDGEMENT.
GOOD JUDGEMENT IS USUALLY
THE RESULT OF EXPERIENCE.
EXPERIENCE IS USUALLY THE
RESULT OF BAD JUDGEMENT.

– TONY ROBBINS

AS 2014 TURNED THE CORNER, I started to get my head around preparing for my second attempt on K2. 2014 was the sixtieth anniversary of the first ascent and there were indications of many teams assembling to attempt the mountain, in particular a Pakistani team of HAPs, with some Italian attachments, commemorating the cooperation of the two countries displayed in 1954. Aside from Al Hancock and myself, there were also some highly-experienced climbers coming together under the SST umbrella, one or two of whom Al had been with on previous peaks.

With my own 'debrief' of fitness and preparation completed months earlier, I turned my attention to the plan ahead. On the fitness side, with just over five months to go, it was time to get into focused training. The two physical components which would determine my performance for K2, above all, were my legs and my lungs. Although there was plenty of serious and technical ice and rock climbing, it was severe climbing at between 5,300 to 8,611 metres elevation with a heavy pack, ice axe and crampons I needed, not an overhanging ultra-extreme rock climb at sea level wearing shorts and a bare top. I therefore put pure rock climbing training on hold in favour of specific training that would propel my legs and lungs to their highest possible level of fitness.

Legs, of course, contain numerous muscle groups but it was critical to focus on those which would be used primarily, namely the quadriceps and the calf muscles. I often get asked by beginners attempting a large mountain for the first time, such as Kilimanjaro, for advice on training. Some tell me with pride of how much they are walking with ski poles, running, cycling, using an elliptical trainer or StairMaster in the gym. When I ask how much mountain hiking they've done, however, sometimes I receive a blank look. As written before, fitness is largely sports specific – you don't train for a marathon by running 100-metre sprints; you won't complete a triathlon by doing CrossFit; and you won't climb a mountain by training on an elliptical trainer. All these other exercises are great for supporting work, but the key activity must be to do what you are going to be doing.

Mountaineering also involves two very different sets of muscle movement. Hiking uphill (or upstairs) involves the use of concentric movement, or muscle shortening exercises – flexing a bicep is the most obvious visual example. The quadriceps in your thighs uses concentric movement to propel, push or accelerate you from point A to point B. Hiking downhill, meanwhile, uses eccentric or muscle lengthening movement. This action results in your muscles working against the pull of gravity – muscles which are helping you slow down or stop. This deceleration is why hiking downhill can be so strenuous for our muscles and why we tend to feel pains never felt before, i.e. in the hamstrings and the muscles around your knees and hips. We don't use these muscles as often and there is no training exercise in a gym or anywhere, even stair descending, which will prepare them. Many guests on our UAE hikes end up walking like Bambi by the end, such is the shock to their system.

For K2 2014 conditioning therefore, when I was in Dubai it was back to the UAE and Oman mountains for this focused training involving hard weekend hikes with my friends, plus my own training hike in the week. I also joined another group of women friends trekking on Wednesday mornings. It was the 2013 regime stepped up a large gear. It also had its joys – camping at weekends, sitting around a roaring fire and chatting with close mates, sometimes with a guitar and usually with suitable liquid lubrication, was and is one of the great joys of living in the UAE in the winter months. We were a very close-knit crowd of climbers and hikers, all far away from our home countries, but sharing the great outdoors hiking, scrambling and climbing in the stark and rugged UAE and Oman mountains. With little chance of rainfall, I used to sleep in the open, falling asleep under the canopy of stars where my thoughts could roam a million miles.

There were some other amusing incidents also. On one weekend sojourn, I joined a climbing friend, Aiden Laffey – an Irishman who was the best heavyweight climber I've ever been on a mountain with – on a long, technical and exposed mountaineering route called Snake Charmer. At over 2,000 metres in height it was excellent training and just the type of route I needed outside of pure hiking. The downward trail followed the broken terrain of the descent route of the well-known 'Stairway to Heaven' hike, and, on the way down, we encountered what appeared to be two Pakistani labourers digging a one-metre pathway up the route.

'Holy cow! Whaat the heck is dat?' Laffey uttered.

'They can't be serious – a road?' I responded.

'Oi don't believe it! Two poor fellas alone building a frigging motorway 2,000 metres up t' frigging mountain?'

'Yeah, I think it used to be called slavery?'

'Oi tink we should give em a tip for their work. Whatcha tink?'

'Sure. What? Fifty dirhams?' (Approximately fourteen dollars.)

'Oh noo! We're gonna be using dis trackh a lot; oi tink we should give them 100 each!'

'Okay ... their eyes are going to drop to the floor!'

We arrived at the raggedly dressed men and gave them 100 dirhams each (approximately twenty-seven dollars). Their eyes did indeed drop to their shovels, pickaxes and rakes.

'Zank you, zank you,' they uttered, clasping our hands in gratitude.

'K2,' I said in half jest. '*M'aloum* K2 (do you know K2)?'

'K2 Pakistan!' one said or asked, I couldn't be sure.

'Yes, K2!' I answered making a sign of climbing with my hands.

'Good, good. K2 big!' he responded.

'Yes, it sure is – big, bold, bad and dangerous!' I replied, knowing they wouldn't understand a thing, but sharing some good-natured camaraderie all the same.

Moving onwards we bade our farewells to the two lone souls, with Laffey slapping his hands together feeling good with himself for his contribution to workers' rights. Until we turned a bend in the track. In front of us were three more labourers toiling away. Thirty metres behind them were four more, then another four and so on. The entire mountain was crawling with Pakistani labourers building a one-metre-wide walking track up the mountain.

'Oh fock! Dat's done it!' Laffey uttered. 'We'll have the whole frigging mountain now demandin a tip!'

'Yeah – all wanting to be the front diggers for the two dumb tourists handing out money!'

▲ ▲ ▲

In February 2014, the emotional toll and struggle to see my children that had lasted twenty months was partially, although far from fully, resolved. Whilst knowing that there could be future issues, it did allow me to focus on the goal ahead that, rightly or wrongly, I'd completely committed to.

At the same time, however, another momentous event of a different kind happened in my life. My American girlfriend, a woman I'd known for a couple of years and had been seeing for a year, became pregnant. As with Alex and Charlotte, I will keep the circumstances private but include the effects and implications. And they were seismic. All I will say is that the combined pressures of a long-distance relationship, K2 and now a pregnancy on top became an intolerable strain. It was impossible to manage all three. Something would buckle under the pressure ...

Readers may, firstly, well wonder by now whether there is a penchant in mountaineers for one, and myself for two, in looking for trouble, secretly searching for drama, lurching from one crisis to another. And there may be an element of truth in this. Marty Schmidt was a high-energy, full-drama, full-stoke, full-tilt, full-on guy. From rescuing nine people from a hotel fire in the Philippines when he was a pararescue jumper; participating in rescues on Denali, Aconcagua, Makalu and Everest; being involved in the infamous altercation between Sherpas and climbers on Everest in April 2013 (receiving a rock to his head in the process); to having a daughter who didn't speak to him for years, there was never a dull moment with Marty. Al Hancock was similar. And, for myself, I guess, although a different character to both Marty and Al, the same could be levelled. The boy of 12 who wrote down that he wanted to 'experience everything possible in life' had and was experiencing just that. It was called living on the edge. It was exciting, exhausting and often very difficult, but it was never dull. Be careful what you ask for …

Secondly, there will undoubtedly be those who feel I should have abandoned K2 to be with my pregnant girlfriend. And I respect that viewpoint. Instead, at the time, I made a call that some may see as selfish, but I saw as self-survival and self-preservation. As I found the previous year, K2 was simply too dangerous to even attempt with any distraction, crisis or chaos in one's life. It was too critical to be relegated to a part-time preparation. It had to have a full on, totally focused and entirely blinkered mindset. It was all or nothing. Only time would tell if it was the right one.

With March 2014 now upon me, I entered the critical three-month period prior to the expedition. I stepped up the treks in the UAE and Oman and was now wearing ankle weights and a pack weighing twenty kilos or more. As the heat became fiercer, I switched to night hikes and enlisted a surprising number of moon-loving friends to join me, which always made the treks more enjoyable. Aiden Laffey, myself and others also attempted other long technical routes, ending up being benighted on one. Sleeping out in the warm Emirates nights was and is never any reason to panic, although the air services are regularly called out to rescue lost hikers who do just that every few weeks.

I wore the same ankle weights in the week to run up and down the emergency stairs of one of Dubai's tallest buildings – in which, for several years, I'd managed to find an unguarded access. At 5 a.m. or 6 a.m. in the mornings, I wasn't likely to be disturbed for the ninety minutes I was pounding up and down the stairs and there was a surprisingly innate feeling of comfort every time I entered 'my stairway'.

Six weeks out from departure, the run-in on preparations began. SST and NSE had all agreed on my insistence to commence K2 earlier, with 16 June earmarked for arrival in Islamabad – still later than desired due to administrative hold ups, but a week earlier than in 2013. Our eight-person SST team was looking very promising, with five ultra-experienced female climbers coming together with Al and myself, including three Sherpa women trying to be the first Nepali women to summit K2. We would have a full team of Sherpas in support, equalling the number of climbers in the team.

I laid all my kit out on my Dubai living room floor to check, re-check and check it again. Clothing and equipment needing small repairs or reinforcements were taken to a local tailor. Dewald van der Wath, of support sponsors ZSI Trading and Marmot, supplied me with some new Marmot gear which would be fully utilized in Pakistan. Hans Kruijt, from support sponsors and satellite communication distributors Xtra-Link, supplied me with the Thuraya XT satellite phone and Thuraya IP Plus data transmission system which I would again use to send back videos, pictures and voice messages from K2. Hans also assisted with our registering on a third weather forecast channel, with which I could compare forecasts with my existing two channels. Greg Boucher, of MEFITPRO, supplied me with a host of nutritional supplements to take on the expedition. A local baker in the New Forest, Lisa Read, who had become a friend, made me some special high-fat fudge and brownies for the trip. All of this planning and preparation was carried out with meticulous detail.

Four weeks out from departure, I erected my oxygen tent in my bedroom, which I'd owned for many years and used for most previous high-altitude climbs, including K2 in 2013. The methodology was to sleep in the tent for seven to eight hours every night at steadily decreasing oxygen levels. The purpose, of course, was pre-acclimatization for altitude and limitation of the possibility of altitude sickness.

Altitude sickness is caused by the lack of oxygen in the air, although the precise reason this factor creates physiological symptoms in the body is not fully understood by scientists. One theory is that the lack of oxygen causes brains to swell and therefore increases pressure in the skull, leading to the various symptoms. There are three main forms. Mild altitude sickness is called acute mountain sickness (AMS) and is quite similar to a hangover – it causes headache, nausea and fatigue. The severity of symptoms can vary greatly, however, with some people only slightly affected, others feeling awful. Vomiting may accompany AMS in severe cases.

The second form is high-altitude pulmonary oedema (HAPE), which occurs when excess fluid has developed in the lungs and can be fatal. In addition to showing symptoms of AMS, sufferers will display breathlessness (compared to others) and often have a persistent cough, producing white or pink frothy sputum. It can be easy to confuse symptoms of HAPE with a chest infection but, unchecked, the breathlessness will even be noticed at rest and lips may turn blue.

The third form is high-altitude cerebral oedema (HACE) which is a build-up of fluid in the brain. It is thought to be an extreme form of AMS, where a severe headache, vomiting and lethargy will progress to unsteadiness, confusion, drowsiness and ultimately a coma. HACE can kill in a few hours.

Although serious and debilitating, altitude sickness is actually welcomed. For, if it didn't occur, we would have roads, helicopter pads, cable cars and hotels blighting the wonderful mountains in our world. Sickness is nature's way of saying 'Bug off; you don't belong here,' and the only immediate remedy to all forms is rapid descent. Some drugs can help also – acetazolamide (also known as Diamox) reduces symptoms of AMS and, for HAPE, nifedipine is a drug which helps to open up the blood vessels in the lungs. In severe cases of HAPE or HACE, dexamethasone (known as Dexi) is used. Descent remains the key action, however.

Whether or not someone gets altitude sickness will depend on four matters – the overall altitude, the speed of ascent, the vigorousness of exercise and their individual physiological make-up. Concerning the latter, altitude is the great leveller. It has no respect for fitness, ability, experience, skills, age, gender or anything. Some people suffer at altitude, others don't – a chain smoker may notice little at 6,000 metres while an Olympic athlete might struggle at 3,000 metres.

Unfortunately, I get it – indeed can get it bad. And I know my body well enough that, without any pre-acclimatization, severe headaches will descend on me when I reach 3,000–3,200 metres in elevation. If I ascend more than 500 metres in one day, I will suffer them also. And if I climb 1,000 metres in one day, I will invariably vomit.

Readers may be interested to hear of one experience I had when I led a group of nineteen novices on a charity trek to climb

Kilimanjaro. I don't lead many groups, preferring to do my own projects once a year, but this was for the Gulf for Good Charity, for which I am an ambassador, and was a good opportunity in a quiet summer. Having briefed and trained the members in mountain geology, glaciers, physical fitness, equipment, medicine, safety and altitude, along with delivering a personal development 'lesson' each evening of the trek, I managed to get seventeen members to the top, two within a few hundred metres, with only one guy failing miserably to even get above the final Kibo hut. That guy was yours truly, by then vomiting every three minutes or so, caused by the altitude. I had previously expressed concern over the elevation gains on the popular Marangu route, but the 'it's only Kilimanjaro' mindset blinded me. It reinforced my suspicion that the Marangu was and is a brutal commercial operation of a conveyor belt, pushing people up the mountain way too fast for the elevation gains involved. And that, if people want to actually enjoy the climb, they need to take seven days' minimum rather than the Marangu's enforced five or six day schedules.

Apparently, I wasn't alone in being an Everest summiteer who had failed Kili, but I hadn't heard of any K2 summiteer failing it! What I had experienced in previous years, however, was that, once acclimatized, I seemed to be very strong at the highest elevations.

My oxygen tent largely alleviated the possibility of AMS by preconditioning my body to produce more red blood cells to carry oxygen. The 'train low, sleep high' philosophy was also used by many Olympic athletes and professional sportspeople, where the purpose was for enhanced performance by having these greater number of red blood cells to carry oxygen. The drug EPO does exactly the same, but with some side effects. EPO is illegal of course, but using oxygen tents – which merely mirrors the effects of training or sleeping at altitude – entirely legal. With a generator pumping oxygen-depleted air into the tent through a small tube, it got hot by the morning and the mix of hypoxic air, carbon dioxide and, yes, a fair dose of methane, meant it wasn't the most enticing bedroom on the planet. Indeed, in addition to AMS, HAPE and HACE, there is fourth high-altitude condition called HAFE – high altitude flatus expulsion. If readers think I'm joking, I'm not – I'm being serious! The difference in atmospheric pressure in the air at altitude and the gases in our bodies causes an uncontrollable urge to, well, fart! I first got to witness this condition during a mountain climb in Nepal many years ago, with long-time friend and regular mountaineering colleague, John Young, who tended to suffer HAFE more than most people I know in the mountains. Although it isn't anywhere near as serious as HAPE and HACE, it can kill all-known life forms in the immediate vicinity!

The other form of artificial altitude training was to train in a hypoxic gymnasium, which I also did on occasions. As opposed to the 'sleep high, train low' philosophy of hypoxic oxygen tents, the practice here was to simply 'train high'. It wasn't intended to increase red blood cells, but merely to get one's body used to physical exertion at altitude. I also used a breathing mask on hikes, which restricted my intake of air, causing my lungs to work more effectively for the same purpose. The best training aid I used, however, was a power breath device which was similar to an asthmatic inhaler. Connected to a computer, the device trained your lungs to both inhale more air and strengthen the muscle functioning behind it. It was a gem of a device and I would use this throughout the upcoming expedition.

In between the stair climbing and hiking, I carried on running, swimming, weight training, circuit training and cycling during the week – my local cycling club, Dubai Roadsters, had a superb Sunday and Tuesday evening session, which was fast and furious, averaging forty kilometres per hour over ninety minutes. My power output on a bike, enhanced by the rest of my training, had never been greater.

The final training element was one of the very best. My friend, Kevin West, had located a steep sand dune forty-five minutes out of Dubai and we drove there, sometimes with other friends, every week or more in the three months prior to departure, to trek, climb and crawl up this dune. With one foot up, two feet down, on the soft sand, it was similar to climbing on snow and the ultimate in total masochism. Physically exhausting, it was an incredible means to murder oneself in the pursuit of supreme fitness.

With these superb natural and artificial facilities in the Emirates – and top-class colleagues to train with – I probably had the best training regime I could possibly ask for, and there was no advantage in heading anywhere else. The intense and quality training mix of night hiking, stair climbing and dune climbing, coupled with cycling, running, circuits and weight training in between, was reaching a crescendo. I was in a state of peak mental and physical fitness and, for the first time in many years, totally 'in the zone.'

Other than professional athletes, few people reading this book may have experienced the feeling of being 'in the zone' but, when you are there, it is profound. It's been described many ways but I can best define it as a state of flow – a linking of mind, body and spirit comprising complete absorption in the activity, merging action and awareness in total concentration and focus, and being completely in control. It is not a target that one tracks progress on or can set a goal of when you want to reach it; but a state that, once you are there, you know and feel it in every part of your physical, mental and spiritual true self.

The interesting part is it's not always guaranteed. I can recall having it in my SAS selection days, pre-Everest in 2006 and in the last third of my South Pole journey in 2007. Critically, the elevated mental and physical state I was now in made me recognize that I wasn't in it the year before – indeed, probably some way off it. A year on, nothing else mattered, nothing else existed, it was obsession, yes, but a necessary one.

A reporter from a leading newspaper in the UAE came to join Kevin and myself on my last sand dune session before leaving for Pakistan, to write an article on this crazy training regime. Collapsing with lactic acid overdose and bursting lungs 100 metres up the slope, he gasped that we were utterly bonkers. He was probably right. Then, as we departed a couple of hours later, an entertaining incident occurred which he would include in his feature. Opening a tin of almonds, I offered him some and he proceeded to move his hand to the tin to scoop some nuts up.

'Whoa ... hold out your hand, I'll tip some out,' I said, pulling the can away from his tentacles.

'Aha! You don't want my possibly dirty mitts in your tin?' He responded, with laughter in his voice.

'Sorry, but yes. Just can't afford to get an infection!'

'Fascinating!'

The above exchange became the opening sentences of his feature. I recall the word 'obsession' accompanying it also, in a humorous, but positive anecdote. Of course, he was largely correct.

Despite the positive arrangements, I thought it might be wise to update my Will and get some proper medical insurance. I guess it reflected my willingness to take risks more than many that I hadn't bothered to do so for most of my expeditions, preferring to take my chances and relish bluffing my way out of any situation I should find myself in. Thus my insurance was a basic travel insurance which covered, amongst other things, winter sports and walking holidays. Winter sports? Yeah, we'd be on snow and ice, good enough. Walking holiday? Yes, too – it didn't say anything about the maximum angle we'd be 'walking' at. However, in 2014, I felt it best to get some full insurance. The problem is barely anyone offered it. The erstwhile British Mountaineering Council thankfully provided the stated cover. Writing a Will is something many people find awkward and put off, but I didn't have a great problem with it. What it does do, however, is focus your thoughts on the one subject which everyone is in denial about – death. No need to go overboard about a Will, however, by contracting an overpriced solicitor charging 1,000 dollars or more – a simple online version costing fifty dollars served exactly the same purpose.

The day before I left, I went to see Dr Charles Jones of California Chiropractic and Sports Medicine Centre in Dubai, for a pre-expedition alignment. Charles, a leading sports medicine expert, had been treating and keeping me going for many years – my injury list over twenty years read like an encyclopedia of the musculoskeletal system. He was a generous supporter of my work, to whom, as with all my support sponsors, I was highly indebted. At my appointment, he had a visiting chiropractor over from the US and they both carried out a thorough check on me. Charles later told me that, after I'd left, he'd had a chat with his colleague. It included some profound words which exemplified what being in the zone presented.

'In all the years I've known Adrian, I have never seen him so determined, so focused and so fit. I think he's going to do it!'

16 June 2014 was departure day. Driven to Abu Dhabi airport, I checked in very early for the 1.55 p.m. flight to Islamabad. With visas all in order, finally I could relax and I allowed my mind to exit out of the 'zone' onto thoughts of my family. I thought of Alex, whom I hadn't seen for two years. He was a 13-year-old boy when I last saw him; now he would be a 15-year-old growing

teenager entering manhood. My heart filled with sadness. I thought of Charlotte, whom, since the court order of February, I had spent some precious time with, though there were already cracks appearing in the arrangements which would have to wait. Her dancing and singing lifted the feelings I was having. And I thought of my unborn son, as I now knew that he was – a feeling of uncertainty, yet something I couldn't put my finger on. He too, and all the huge implications, would have to wait.

They were the deeper, emotional thoughts that I had compartmentalized for many months, but it was the right time to let them come out now, with just a few hours before I returned to Pakistan. For, regardless of the zone I was in, I was about to embark on a highly risky venture which, for every four climbers who'd reached the summit, one had died trying. One that had killed our two teammates a year ago. One which had allowed success just once in the last five years.

The gremlins had returned to me at times in the previous few months, but the visits were less frequent and only ever at night. I'd worked out the way to melt them, if not extinguish them. Now I allowed them back in, to get that sense of reality. It took me down an old familiar path. I wanted to resist the walk, but I let myself edge down it. The sense of guilt, remorse and worry. The fire starting to burn in my mind and throat. The daggers being aimed from the crowd. The pictures of my children emblazoned across the underside of my eyelids as I closed my eyes to feel the sensation.

Then I tapped into my values. My true self. My very essence. Instead of looking at fear as a brick wall, I envisaged it as a doorway. Stepping through that doorway to the higher sense of being, learning and life itself. The guilt melted away, the remorse subsided, the worry disappeared. I felt it, sensed it and owned it and let it ignite my thoughts.

The thoughts consumed me for well over an hour and, for reasons that felt right, I expressed them publicly in a Facebook and website post along with a picture of Alex, Charlotte and myself taken on the last occasion we were together two years prior. Aside from the message to friends and family, it was a message, above all, to my two children, who I hoped would somehow see it. And, although nothing was clear at that stage, it was also a subconscious message to my unborn son. Vulnerability, transparency and honesty. And, above all, love. Godspeed and bon voyage.

PERSONAL THOUGHTS

MONDAY, 16 JUNE 2014

K2 2014. I rarely, if ever, post anything of a personal nature or my personal life – including its own 'Everests' – on Facebook, but as I head off to K2 perhaps am justified to put just this one …

Which is that no matter how big the goal, my focus, drive and determination, my thoughts will always be on my two children, Alexander and Charlotte. As any parent will resonate, they are more important to me than any mountain, any challenge, any job or, indeed, anything else in life. And they will never be far from my mind as I embark on what is one of the most difficult challenges on the whole planet.

There are some who probably feel attempting K2 is selfish. I agree. As I wrote on my website blog 'Preparing for K2: the Mental' – it is a necessary requirement to get into the total mental zone required to attempt such a feat. Without putting the blinkers on and getting into complete and utter focus in the 4–6 weeks before today, I wouldn't even be here.

But I do these things because, apart from savouring being in the wildernesses of the world away from all the crap and information overload we have to face on a daily basis; apart from being a goal driven guy who's always attempted big challenges; apart from the huge learnings I gain every time I step outside of my comfort zone; and apart from wanting to see how far and how much I can achieve in this one hat of my work that I wear, there is something else.

And that is that these challenges bring out the very best in me; they are my truth and that oft quoted 'being true to oneself'. And they make me come alive. And if anyone is questioning where they are, what they are doing and what is

*their purpose in this manic life, perhaps you can ask yourself
a similar question, namely:*

*'Don't ask yourself what the world needs, but ask yourself
what makes you come alive and go and do that. For what the
world needs is people who come alive'.*

*I approach K2 in the peak of physical fitness and fully 'in
the zone' but, critically, in a humble manner – particularly
in respect for our friends lost last year – and with full and
total respect for, and even a relationship with, nature. Nature
provides the answer to most things in life and we ignore it
at our peril. Or alternatively 'The Mountains will always be
there, the secret is to make sure you are too'.*

*To my family and all my many great friends, acquaintances
and those who don't know me but follow, your support and
messages are truly appreciated.*

*To Alex and Charlotte, I love you both and you will never be
far from my mind over the next two months.*

ALL IN THE TEAM

TALENT WINS GAMES, BUT
TEAMWORK AND INTELLIGENCE
WINS CHAMPIONSHIPS.

– MICHAEL JORDAN

MY FLIGHT TO ISLAMABAD TOUCHED DOWN at 6 p.m. on 16 June 2014 and the NSE team transported me to our hotel. Aside from comprehensive feedback on climbing matters, both Al Hancock and I had also told NSE and SST that we wouldn't be staying at the 'Intercontinental' again in our lifetimes, and insisted on a decent hotel. I'm fine sleeping in the roughest of places most of the time, but there's something about commencing an expedition in relative comfort. On driving up outside the JW Marriott, our message had evidently been heeded. After checking in, the first person I saw was Al.

'Alhancockdotcom!' I exclaimed, using the nickname I'd given him in 2013, as we greeted each other.

'Adrian Hayes! Must say looking very dapper there!' he responded, with a favourite saying of his.

'I think our messages on hotels got through – this is total luxury!'

'We have indeed, buddy: fine restaurants, a bar, even a masseur – and she's quite a cutie!'

'I'm sure she thought you were too. Right, first question – have you got a damn proper size pee bottle this year?'

'Indeed I have, right here!' he said, pulling out a shiny, brand new Nalgene bottle ten inches in length.

'My, wow! That's very impressive, Hancock – just a pity you've got such small equipment to fill it with.'

'Let me assure you there's been no complaints on that front for the past thirty years,' he laughed.

Good old banter. No one taking anything personally. It was great to see him again. He had formally announced he was aiming for the fourteen eight-thousanders, attempting to become the first Canadian to complete the feat. The quest is the ultimate in high-altitude mountaineering, first achieved by the legendary Italian climber, Reinhold Messner, who between 1970 and 1986, summited all fourteen without supplementary oxygen, many by new routes. The feat is considered so difficult that, as the 2014 Karakoram season got under way, only thirty-two people in total had accomplished it. Aside from the physical extremes and challenges, it is a long, costly and highly dangerous quest, with no guarantees on any of the mountains, and increasingly inflicted with political issues on some peaks, such as Nanga Parbat in Pakistan and Cho Oyu in Tibet. And with the shortest time anyone has taken to complete the quest being well over seven years, the sacrifice it requires is a sobering reality. Al was entirely capable and driven enough to achieve the feat with a tail wind, but nailing K2 was key. Failing the first time was entirely normal. Failing a second, very common. Failing three times would be very painful, as Marty Schmidt had experienced. For myself, there was no intention of ever going for the fourteen, preferring instead to concentrate on all-round adventuring goals, particularly in the polar world which I so loved. And with so many different hats in my life, dedicating seven full years on the eight-thousanders would be nearly impossible. My focus was solely on K2.

Dawa Sherpa of SST appeared as I met Al, having taken on the role of organizing our Sherpa team himself this year, with Lakpa and Nurbu back from 2013.

'Namaste Dawa. *Kusto hunu huncha, jati nei cha*?' I greeted him.

'Namaste Adrian sahib. Welcome to Pakistan.'

'Dawa, I'm impressed – a hotel without mosquitos or ants! And even the a/c works?'

'Yes, this is the second-best hotel in Islamabad!'

'What? Only the second!'

Dawa had retired from high-altitude mountaineering after completing the fourteen eight-thousanders and had no incentive to return, stating that he had been very lucky, but with no desire to push that luck. After we'd chatted for half an hour he headed off and Al and I had a bite in the fine restaurant. Anticipating flying to Skardu the next morning, we chatted for a few hours on climbing news, Karakoram updates and friends we were likely to see in a few days' time. Unfortunately, bad weather in the mountains two days running and an aircraft breakdown on another, resulted in us returning from the airport to the Marriott each day – an intensely frustrating experience, although not uncommon. On top of that, I ate something in the hotel one evening which resulted in vomiting and diarrhoea that night; I could accept such incidents in places of low hygiene, but to get it at the Marriott infuriated me.

We eventually flew to Skardu on Friday, 20 June, but had to wait there for another four days for the three Nepali 'Sherpanis', as they would come to be known, and the Chinese climber, Luo Jing, to arrive from Nepal before we could proceed. This would have been more frustrating and annoying given that Al and myself had been determined on arriving and getting moving quickly, but, fortunately or unfortunately, I couldn't go anywhere – my food poisoning had become increasingly worse. With my losing a ton of body fluids, Sher Ali, the Concordia Hotel owner, eventually took me to hospital to get a drip put up. Not a great start to any expedition, but better to have this now than later. Al conducted the Ministry of Tourism briefing and documentation procedures along with our liaison officer for 2014, Lieutenant Syed Inamullah, who arrived on 24 June.

On the morning of 25 June, the four women finally arrived, after driving two days from Islamabad, and we met them in the Concordia Hotel. The three Sherpanis, Maya Sherpa, Pasang Lhamu Sherpa and Dawa Yangzum Sherpa, were on a mission to expand the boundaries of Sherpa women in the world of mountaineering, so long a domain of their men folk. It was a bold quest. Sherpa women were expected to marry young, have babies and spend their lives in the home, raising children and farming crops whilst their husbands, fathers and sons used their renowned talents as climbing Sherpas. They, along with all Nepali women, faced a lot of social constraints and had virtually no voice in the political, social or domestic spheres. The three had already broken many barriers in recent years. Maya, from Okhaldhunga and the oldest of the three, was the first Nepalese woman to summit Cho

Oyu, the sixth highest mountain in the world and had summited Everest in 2006. Married to Dutchman Arnold Coster, whom we'd got to know very well the previous year; they had a young daughter. Pasang Lhamu, from Lukla, was one of the first graduates from the Khumbu Climbing Centre set up by renowned American alpinist, Conrad Anker and his wife, Jennifer Lowe-Anker, and had become Nepal's first female mountaineering instructor at the age of 21. She had summited Everest in 2007 and, married to a non-climbing supportive husband, spent her time guiding both in Nepal and elsewhere around the world. Dawa Yangzum, from Dolakha, the youngest of the threesome, had also graduated from the same climbing school and was a mountaineering guide along with her husband. She had summited Everest in 2012.

Undoubtedly, as with the rest of us, significance was their main objective, but they were also joining forces to promote women in adventure and to send the message that women could be married, have families and still climb. Additionally, they were also claiming to climb to raise awareness on climate change, the shrinking glaciers in Nepal and the effects on mountain communities.

'You look just like Daniel Craig!' Maya exclaimed when introduced to Al Hancock, referring to the famous James Bond actor.

'Well, that's a fine compliment there young Maya, I think Daniel Craig would be flattered,' Al replied to laughter around the room.

'I hope you treat us ladies like James Bond would!' Dawa said innocently, causing me to splutter into my tea.

'I'm not saying a thing!' I added to more laughter.

'Now, now, there buddy. I'm a man on a mission.'

'Yeah, that's why they look so worried!'

'James Bond – we're calling you that from now on!' Maya concluded.

And that was it – for the rest of the expedition the Sherpanis would call Hancock 'James Bond'. With his piercing blue eyes and fair complexion, it was more than a passing likeness and he revelled in his new-found fame.

The fourth woman climber, Luo Jing, from central China's Hunan province, was a single mother with a 9-year-old son, who had started outdoor pursuits in 2002. Quitting her job in the IT industry, she had started climbing mountains, using her savings, in 2008, reaching the 8,000-metre peak level within several years. She had conquered six eight-thousanders prior to arriving at K2 and was on a fast track quest to complete all fourteen. With her limited English, communication sometimes proved difficult, but some of our Sherpas, whose own language (as opposed to Nepali) was similar to Tibetan, managed to speak adequately in Mandarin.

After the combined delays from flight cancellations and late arrivals, we were at least six days behind schedule. Thus, despite their drive from Islamabad, after some breakfast and a wash, the four women had little choice but to join the eight-hour drive to Askole – our 'day one' of the journey to Base Camp. Knowing what to expect, and at least experiencing the drive recovered from sickness, at the best it wasn't as bad as the previous year. At the worst, it was still mind and bone-numbingly painful. It was also brutally hot.

With the mass army of porters allocated to a far bigger operation than in 2013, on 26 June 2014 we set off for the long trek to Base Camp with our first day's hike to Jola. As with the previous year, Al and myself agreed to walk on our own. It was good to finally get under way on foot. Good to finally breath the clear air. Good to be on my own again. Time again to think, to contemplate, to focus, and to appreciate the scenery unfolding before me. Jagged, white-topped mountains gradually appeared, rising razor-sharp into the clear, azure skies. The changing cloud patterns and sunlight created a moving canvas of shadow and hues across the rocky landscape, each moment a different view. The land around me undulated, wound untidily, folded between outcrops. Its beauty, peace and qualities of an earthly paradise, isolated from the outside world, pertinently mirrored the description of Shangri-La in James Hilton's novel. I passed sparse, low-growing vegetation of 'alpine-zone' grass, scrub, bushes and small deciduous trees. Bursts of colour sprang from the orange berries of the sea buckthorn, and bright vermillion Karakoram lilies perfumed the breeze at unexpected junctures. Delicate yellow corydalis flowers grew amongst the hard rock, while a rainbow of wild flowers in shades of reds, violets and blues were strewn across grassy stretches. And, beside me at varying distances, the raging Braldu River a constant companion, whose sheer volume and speed a magnet to transfix upon, a testimony to the power of nature.

All were aspects of beauty that I, and most people, would normally barely even notice. The things we fail to appreciate because we are all so busy in our lives – all so focused on or addicted to our screens and all too distracted by the clutter we face on a daily basis. All resulting in a feeling of being overwhelmed, stress, physical and mental illness, at the expense of awareness, mindfulness and happiness. Without the eyes, time or space to see it, perceive it or savour it, humankind is guilty of missing the most amazing things in the world, many of which are right before our eyes. Up here, however, with acres of time and every sense stimulated from the mental space I was in, my surroundings were fully appreciated and treasured. Everything around me had beauty, energy and life.

Askole to Jola was completed that day, and Jola to Pieu on day three, 27 June. There we were forced to spend a rest day, due to landslides obliterating the trail further up the glacier. The route from Pieu to Urdokas on 29 June was consequently an extremely long day's trek due to the many diversions created by these landslides. As always, the porters were the unsung heroes of the operation. Somehow finding and weaving a track through the moraine, the weights they carried were phenomenal, the speed they walked astounding, and the rags they wore sobering. Any of the hundreds of porters moving up and down the Baltoro could probably be a fell running champion in the Western world, such was their strength, stamina and ability moving over mountains.

In the evenings, I would often go over to give a simple 'Salaam w'Alaykum' as they huddled together in a makeshift shelter of stones and plastic, eating their *khubz* (unleavened bread) cooked on an open fire. Many times, they would offer me the rough but tasty bread which, braving the risk of eating food contaminated by dirty hands, I accepted albeit tearing off my own piece as opposed to being passed some. I'd previously been astonished seeing them regularly drink water from the turbulent and muddy waters of the Braldu – purifying water systems were totally alien to such hardy men. It was the same with sleeping. Whilst at each camp, we would sleep in our high-tech tents in modern sleeping bags, they would assemble in a group of twelve or more huddled under a plastic sheet. They weren't immune to illness or injuries, however. One day I brought out my medical pack to treat a porter with severely cracked heels – an affliction in which the pain is far worse than it looks. Within minutes I was quickly surrounded by hordes of young men with cracks on their feet which resembled small crevasses, some of which were so bad I wondered how they could even walk. Others begged me for medicines for headaches, eye infections, ear infections and sickness, and Al and myself ended setting up a mini field clinic. Their supplies were non-existent and we did our best to patch them up as best as we could.

They weren't immune to tragedy either. At Urdokas, a beautiful campsite on a grass bank at the side of the 6,500-metre mountain, twelve porters had been killed two years earlier by a huge boulder falling away from the grassy hills and crushing them as they slept at night. The makeshift memorial stones placed on a wall as we left the campsite, most with emotional personal messages from their colleagues, showed that death was equally mourned, and life valued, amongst these hardened men of the Karakoram. The later documentary, *K2 and the Invisible Footman* (20 April 2015), directed by Lara Lee and filmed during the summer, was a fitting tribute to their incredible attributes and contribution to the mountaineering efforts of Pakistan.

From Urdokas we proceeded onto the glacier moraine proper for the trek to Goro II on 30 June. Karakoram in Turkish means 'black rubble' and aptly described the moraine's gravel plains of rock, boulders and powdery ash-like earth, broken and pounded by the glacier's journey across the mountains over millennia. There, the high temperatures we'd experienced so far plummeted in the ice-cooled atmosphere of night. On the way to Goro II we caught sight of Broad Peak, named as such by British explorer Martin Conway in 1892, due to its vast volume in area – its summit stretches to over 1.5 kilometres in length.

On 1 July, we trekked from Urdokas along the glacier to Concordia. The vastly changed route from 2013 caused us to wade through fast-flowing glacial streams on occasions, testimony to the tough trek that K2 Base Camp entailed. No teahouses, no signs and no real trails, this was the Karakoram in all its wild and untamed beauty.

On reaching Concordia, as in 2013, I decided to defer looking at K2 until it was completely in view to fully record the moment. As I turned and my eyes met the great mountain looming up ahead of me, thoughts swirled around my mind as the winds swirled around its jagged walls of ice. It lingered silently at the head of the valley, a silence that was all the more powerful given its mighty presence. I felt small and insignificant compared to such magnitude and continued looking in silence, distilling my thoughts, before I finally spoke.

'Yep, it looks just as steep as last year … it's an impressive sight,' I uttered, as I contemplated the immensity of the mountain before me. 'You know, last year there was a lot of "Oh my God" and joking. This year we know what to expect. This year, we know what it's like climbing up those steep sides and I'm here, we're here, with a job to do. We're totally focused, totally determined to get up that mountain this year.'

My unscripted and honest words said it all. The previous year had been a combination of shock and awe, fun and laughter. This was now serious. It was known. It would be physically, technically and mentally demanding beyond almost anything experienced. And it would be highly dangerous – two of our friends lay buried on the mountain, along with eighty or so more frozen corpses who were foolish enough to attempt it. Something else hit me in those five minutes of contemplation – it felt at that moment that this was it for me – if K2 didn't allow me to reach its summit this year, then that would probably be it. I had no desire to return for a third year in succession. No desire to write off yet another glorious British summer in pursuit of a near unattainable goal. No desire to face the pain of such sacrifice for nothing but memories. That didn't mean summiting at all costs, but it did mean complete and utter focus on giving it my very best this last year.

We trekked on to Broad Peak Base Camp where we met up with Chris Jensen Burke and her boyfriend, Lakpa Sherpa (not to be confused with the other Lakpa Sherpa), who were part of our team, but had arrived much earlier in order to attempt Broad Peak first. Chris and I had corresponded a few times and, as we sat down to share some tea and food, it was good to finally meet her and Lakpa. A lawyer born in New Zealand, but now living in Sydney, with dual New Zealand-Australian citizenship, Chris was another climber aiming to summit all fourteen eight-thousanders. If successful, it would make her the first New Zealand or Australian woman to complete the feat. She had climbed seven to date, including Makalu, the fifth highest, just a month earlier and was planning to tackle Cho Oyu, the sixth highest, in autumn. She was also the first New Zealand or Australian woman to complete the Seven Summits (Carstensz Pyramid list), which she did as a tribute to one of her siblings, who passed away only months after her 2011 Mount Everest summit.

Her boyfriend, Lakpa Sherpa, from Sankhuwasabha in the Makalu region of Nepal, was a director of his own guiding company, Himalayan Ascent. He had also climbed seven eight-thousanders, with multiple ascents of Everest and Cho Oyu, and held the record for the most summits of 6,850-metre Ama Dablan, the sheer faced 'guardian of the Khumbu' which Sir Edmund Hillary once deemed unclimbable. His extensive experience would prove invaluable in weeks to come.

As there were some other climbers Al knew at Broad Peak, he decided to spend the night there, as did the Sherpanis and Luo. There were calls for the entire party to stay, but I was having none of it – we were already delayed and I was on a mission to get to K2 as soon as possible. There was no disagreement or fall outs, it was my choice and preference. Nurbu Sherpa, assistant cook Sikander and myself trekked on to K2 Base Camp that evening and found a location for our camp.

With it being the sixtieth anniversary year, as expected there was a lot of activity when I arrived. After dumping my bags, I walked along the moraine for a short 'meet and greet' of teams at camp to see who was here – as always, some easier to communicate with than others. The large Pakistan HAP team greeted me warmly, together with their three Italian advisers, aiming to become the first Pakistan team to conquer the mountain. Historically outshone by the phenomenal ability of Sherpas at altitude, the HAPs were nevertheless extremely strong, skilled and competent and many had excelled in previous expeditions. What they didn't have was strength in depth – their numbers were tiny in comparison to the Sherpa community. Ten climbers from Pakistan had summited K2 over the years, but all as individuals or duos in national or international teams and no full Pakistani team had ever been formed for the same purpose.

Another highly experienced Italian trio of Giuseppe Pompili, Tamara Lunger and Nikolaus Gruber from the German speaking province of Bolzano, made up a second Italian contingent. Two Spaniards, Ferran Latorre and Miguel Alvarez comprised a Spanish team – Ferran, on his eleventh eight-thousander without oxygen, hoping to become the first Catalan to complete the feat. Czech climber Radek Jaros, who would shortly arrive in Base Camp with two Czech teammates, Petr Masek and Jan Travnicek, and a film crew, was hoping to conquer his last 8,000-metre peak, having achieved his first eight-thousander, Mount Everest, in 1998. All the thirty-two mountaineers who had achieved the fourteen did so in varying orders, but it was interesting to see Radek had left the hardest until last.

Apart from Al and myself, only two other climbers were returning from 2013. Alex Aravidis from Greece was back with a new teammate, Panos Athanasiadis, a top technical alpinist attempting his first eight-thousander, as the Greek team. It was great to see Alex again and, as in 2013, we would be located next to each other at Base Camp, spending a lot of time in each other's camps. Macedonia – Zdravko Dejanovic – was also returning in a second international team's K2 2014 expedition, comprising members from Finland, Iran, Turkey and Singapore. The experience of the four of us from 2013 would later prove invaluable and was taken in thoroughly.

A Polish team were on K2, primarily to recce the mountain for a possible winter ascent. Winter ascents and the Poles go hand in hand – no other country has achieved so much in Himalayan winter mountaineering. An independent American woman climber, Cleo Weidlich, together with four Sherpas, were at Base Camp attempting the Cesen route, the only team who would end up attempting the route that year.

Finally, there was the American Madison Mountaineering team of guide Garrett Madison and clients Alan Arnette, Matthew (Matt) Du Puy and Rick Sylvester, who were a week behind us and yet to arrive. Sharing transport, logistics and cooking facilities from NSE and SST, they would be co-located with us at Base Camp, although with a separate mess tent, and we would be spending much time together.

That left our SST team of eight, in reality an umbrella team grouping four parties who would climb on their own schedules – Al and myself, the three Sherpanis, Chris Burke and Lakpa Sherpa, and Luo Jing, who would work with one of our climbing Sherpas.

I have often been asked about the personality traits of those attempting K2 and all I can say is that, whilst everyone in both 2013 and 2014 showed completely different characteristics, there were many commonalities – a love of nature, a propensity to take risks above 99 per cent of the general population and a large degree of nonconformity. With just seven women on the mountain, five in our team, the vast majority were, as expected, men. Any doubts on the abilities of most of the women would soon be blown away; the six women with us on the Abruzzi Spur would prove to be outstanding.

Three characteristic traits stood out, however. Everyone was highly experienced and the fitness levels phenomenal – it was a long way from the, sometimes falsely overstated, situation of inexperienced climbers attempting Everest. Secondly, aside from Alan Arnette and the Sherpanis, no one was climbing K2 claiming to do it for any cause, only for the sake of climbing it – an integrity and honesty which was refreshing. And, thirdly and above all, for the male climbers there didn't seem to be one happily married, 2.4 kids, 'normal' family man attempting the mountain. Many seemed to have girlfriends, although just as many appeared to be 'free agents'. Many were separated or divorced; many had children and there was more than one love child scattered around the world, but I would not hear one climber referring to their wife the entire summer. Or indeed, for that matter, did I hear the previous year, with the exception of Mike Horn, who had told us he once spent just nine days in two years with his wife when he traversed the equator. I guess that marriage and K2 were not natural bedfellows; happy families and K2 even less so, and it would take a very understanding spouse, or a 'different' type of marriage, to give a blessing to such a dangerous quest. And that was the same with the women climbers. Amongst the very few happily married climbers there, men or women, Pasang and Dawa had said their husbands were against K2.

With a strong contingent of Sherpas supporting many expeditions, the experience at Base Camp meant that K2 2014 had an extremely competent and skilled collection of teams, including some of the very best in their sport, on the mountain this year. All told, there were in excess of fifty climbers in these ten teams attempting to conquer the 'Savage Mountain.'

Numbers were a double-edged sword, however. We needed strength in numbers to have the support and manpower to share fixing lines and trail breaking on the mountain. On the other hand, too many climbers would present huge problems with the limited spaces at Camps 1 and 2. As always, the weather would provide the answers or problems – few periods of good weather would mean all teams being on the mountain at the same time and subsequent crowding problems. Good weather would enable spreading out of rotations and, ideally but unlikely, for a summit push itself.

Although arriving at Base Camp on 1 July was later than I had wanted, there was still time for two effective rotations up the mountain to be completed before a possible summit attempt towards the end of the month. All we needed was good weather, good conditions and an absence of any incidents. That was something which only luck could provide …

CHAPTER THIRTEEN

MIND, BODY AND SPIRIT

WHEN I LET GO OF WHAT I AM,
I BECOME WHAT I MIGHT BE.

– LAO-TZU

ON ARRIVAL AT BASE CAMP on the evening of 1 July, we barely had time to find a spare and suitably-sized location for our large team, level a small area, erect a few tents and set up a small kitchen before darkness fell. A basic meal was miraculously cooked by Sikander, and I retreated early for a sleep. It felt good to reach here a day before anyone else; the extra few hundred metres elevation gain from Broad Peak giving the red blood cell production factory in my body an extra boost in preparation for the steep altitude gains to come.

The next morning, we all staked out our full area, which ironically was virtually the same location we'd camped at in 2013. Like all moraines, however, the ground had moved, shifted, ebbed and collapsed greatly since the previous year and it was hard to distinguish any of the areas from where we had been in 2013. Once locations were all marked, as in 2013 I set my tent up at the top of our perimeter, as far away as possible from the hub, next to a giant rock with a flat top which I thought could be useful for drying clothes, camera work and even lying on when it was warm.

Digging and levelling my tent platform into the moraine rock with a shovel and pickaxe, my thoughts drifted back to the building sites I'd toiled on with the same implements for four years after leaving school, in between travelling the world, climbing and adventuring. The memories came flooding back to a time where my dreams were formed and manifested in an environment that one couldn't help but get toughened up in. 'Dig the sides; the bottom takes care of itself', the words of Brian Standfield, my boss over most of those years, came back into my ears, causing a ripple of smiles across my face. A few years later, when I commenced officer training at the Royal Military Academy Sandhurst, the advice and experience would prove invaluable when I'd manage to dig a trench five feet deep before most cadets had barely scratched the topsoil. The 'University of Life', as opposed to the university, or indeed sixth form college, neither of which I attended, definitely had its uses and was proving so again now.

Although we would be sleeping on an air mattress, the base needed to be as flat as possible to prevent rocks digging through the tent base into your spine. By the time we would leave in early August, it would also have melted greatly, so large boulders were piled up around the platform to limit the melt as much as possible. On erecting my tent after an hour or so's work, I sat back on the large rock and admired my handiwork, my 'home' for the next month.

The Sherpanis, Luo, Al, most of our Sherpa team, the full cook party and our mass army of porters arrived late morning on 2 July; Chris and Lakpa remaining at Broad Peak on their own timeframes. We spent the entire day digging tent platforms, erecting tents, constructing the toilet tents, unpacking bags, sorting out equipment and all the normal activities of a first day's arrival at a Base Camp. Then, that night, the snows arrived. After the glorious weather of the entire trek in and the first day at Base Camp, allowing us to set up our tents in fine conditions, the timing was uncanny. The heavy snows lasted three nights and two days.

We spent the days acclimatizing, eating, drinking, socializing, refining equipment and pouring over weather forecasts. Al and myself also had a thorough recap of our team agreements and ground rules. We knew and understood each other impeccably by now, but it was still invaluable to revisit everything laid out the previous year as well as a few new matters, so no stone was left unturned. On the Mars One Project, the one-way mission to Mars which I would shortly become an adviser on, one of their mantras is 'We are not selecting individuals, we are selecting teams'. As with K2, but even more so, teamwork is fundamental to having the best possible chance of success on their mission. One valuable practice Mars One discusses fully is that of annoyances or irritating behaviour. If someone (e.g. Person A) in a four-person team in the selection process finds an aspect of another team member's (e.g. Person D) behaviour, habits, or actions annoying, however mild, then the issue is openly brought to the table and discussed with full transparency – a practice in itself that is missing from 99 percent of team programmes. What then happens is that Person D (the so-called 'offender') either changes his or her behaviour/habits/actions or Person A moves to another team. There is no question of giving Person A the usual advice of 'acceptance', 'respect for differences', 'not getting hung up', 'letting it rest', or so on. No way. Because if the action is not corrected, that annoyance will fester over time until it becomes intolerable. And once on a long voyage to Mars, there is nowhere else to go. You are stuck with a teammate who annoys you. Perhaps if more couples in the world – also intending to be on a lifelong 'mission' together – had this open conversation at the start of their relationship then there wouldn't be such record numbers of break-ups. For in a relationship too, unless annoying behaviours are corrected by the 'culprit' then they will also fester, and the effects multiply over time.

Hancock and myself weren't on a lifetime together but the stakes were as high, or even higher, and thus we also had this open discussion. And with the small number of issues which each of us consequently learned annoyed the other, agreed to change them. As always, open, honest and transparent communication, with neither of us taking anything personally, was vital. Something which our corporate teams, as well as relationships, can learn from.

For the rest of the wider team, there were only a few small but critical things we needed to agree on. The most important displayed itself the very same evening when one of our extended teammates coughed openly over the food. Al and I shot each other a glance simultaneously across the table; we both knew instantly what the other was thinking.

'We need to get these ladies on the same track if you know what I mean,' he commented after dinner.

'Oh, I sure do,' I replied. 'Let's do a basic agreements session with them all tomorrow.'

With Chris and Lakpa coming over to Base Camp from Broad Peak in the poor weather, we gathered everyone after lunch, including the other Lakpa Sherpa, who was organizing the Sherpa team prior to Dawa Sherpa and the others' arrival, and Farmanullah Baig, the head cook.

'Guys, can we go through some basic agreements around health and hygiene?' I asked. 'Just to make sure we are all on the same page.'

'We can't afford anyone to get sick from any carelessness,' Al added.

'Yes, of course,' Maya replied; we knew her husband, Arnold, was equally stringent on the subject.

Al and myself then went through the basics. Coughing was the main one. Throat infections and colds are rife in Nepal and Pakistan because nobody understands the distance germs travel when one coughs into the open. However, the British lesson taught to children for over 100 years or more to 'put your hand over your mouth' is total bunk, simply spreading those germs onto a hand ready to transmit to every spoon, fork, knife, plate or food one touches. The clear agreement on expeditions was to cough into one place and one place only – the crease in the elbow, a practice which is taught in American schools. We also attempted to get everyone's agreement on not passing food with hands, but offering the plate; passing cutlery by the end of the implement as opposed to the part you put in your mouth; the agreement of sanitizing hands prior to every meal and the importance of washing hands with soap and water as often as possible. Cultural practices and differences can take time to reinforce, however, and we had to revisit the hygiene matters a few times.

We were adamant on getting a first rotation in as soon as the weather cleared but the timing of the all-important puja was causing some issues. Lakpa wanted to wait until Dawa Sherpa, Garrett Madison and his team and their Sherpas all arrived to have one large puja for the full team. With the weather clearing on the morning of 5 July and good forecasts for the next six days, however, we set out our stall.

'Lakpa, we've got great weather. We're not waiting a day longer to get going on our first rotation,' Al said strongly.

'Can we get some tents, fuel and food sorted for ABC and Camp 1 at least?' I asked, in a more diplomatic way. 'Are you happy for us to climb to Camp 1 before a puja?' I added.

'Yes, yes. This no problem. We best have puja on tenth or eleventh when moon in right place,' he replied.

On 6 July, laden with heavy packs, Al, myself and two of our Sherpa team proceeded to trek to ABC, where we set up a couple of tents which would remain throughout the expedition. The Sherpas proceeded to climb up to Camp 1 and deposit a tent there prior to returning to Base Camp. With the Abruzzi Spur soaring up metres from our tent, Al and myself camped the night at ABC.

On 7 July, we climbed up to Camp 1 over six or so hours and spent two nights there in fine conditions. With several other teams also utilizing the good weather, space was even more limited than the previous year, with eight tents crammed together on the small ledge. The Italian trio were forced to dig a platform on an icy outcrop due to the lack of space.

'Oh man! Where are these teams going to sleep?' I expressed, echoing my exact words of a week earlier.

'Yep, I am envisaging big problems here buddy!' Al responded.

'There is not a single place left for one more tent!'

'And that's where the problems start. We'll have people sleeping in here, kit going missing, the lot.'

On 9 July, we ascended to Camp 2. I'd already noticed my far greater fitness levels climbing up to Camp 1 and, today, felt even stronger. The months and months of intense, frenetic and at times brutal training on mountains, stairs and sand dunes, with heavy packs, ankle weights and restricted breathing masks were paying dividends. Neither of us would ever be gazelles racing up mountains. We were both very strong but steady and, critically, with the ability to keep going for hours, days, weeks and sometimes months at a time.

That skill of ultra-endurance had first become evident to me in my SAS selection days, when I was always near the back of the field for the first few hours but, by the end, was up at the front and powering away. It had also manifested itself in my polar expeditions, where I always felt stronger at the end of the day than at the beginning, with the same result. There were thousands and thousands of better climbers than myself – 'better' meaning vastly superior technical operators on rock or ice and able to ascend at speed on the most demanding of climbs. Sometimes, however, it would all be about the sheer ability to keep going on a brute of a climb in gruelling conditions, physically exhausted, after no sleep and little food, for an extended time.

We reached Lower Camp 2 after climbing six hours and, approaching a level spot where we would have a short break, saw the crumpled remains of an orange tent.

'You know something?' I said as we collapsed on our packs. 'I think this could be Marty and Denali's tent …'

'I think you're right! It's exactly the same spot.'

'Let's have a check.'

We stood up and walked over to the fabric. It was piled into a ball shape, about a metre in diameter, with many parts ripped and loose ends and ropes flapping in the wind. We pulled the remains of the tent apart and our thoughts were sadly confirmed – Marty's oval shaped 'MSIG' logo and a website along the bottom, and 'Marty Schmidt Int. Guiding' along the top stared into our faces.

'Whew, it is.'

'Yes.'

'Shit.'

We both crouched down and didn't say a thing for several minutes. The events of one year ago flowed right back through our minds. Here, at this very spot, we'd sat down and had the last conversation anyone would ever have with our fallen colleagues. I recalled Marty's very words, defiant in his determination to head up to Camp 3 and his 'when it snows, you get snow' dismissiveness. I remembered Denali's warm demeanour in the back of the tent, nodding in agreement with his father. I reheard the hesitant words of Chris Warner saying he was also coming down. At this spot one year ago we had given an unknown final farewell to two enigmatic teammates who would perish less than twenty-four hours later, sleeping together in their tent up at Camp 3. It was a poignant moment of reflection, of loss, of memories and of what could have been. Al and myself were in our own worlds, oblivious to each other and to anything else.

'Rest in peace guys,' I said, breaking the silence after a few minutes.

'If only …' Al added.

'The fine line between life and death.'

'We best check inside. Sequoia asked me to bring back anything we might find.'

We pulled the tent apart further and unzipped what remained of its zip. Inside was merely some used and rusty gas canisters. All their equipment from 2013 would either be buried with them at Camp 3 or, anything left at Base Camp, shipped back by Chris Warner. It smelt musty, and only added to the depressive scene. Gone was the sight and sense of life, energy and future ambitions we'd encountered in 2013. Now it was replaced with the sight and sense of loss, decay and past memories. It was a sobering thirty minutes we spent in reflection.

After taking some photos of the scene and folding the tent back into a neat pile with some rocks on to keep it intact, we climbed up the vertical House Chimney and onto Camp 2 proper. Our aim wasn't to stay there but to merely 'touch' the camp and return to Camp 1, greatly aiding the all-important acclimatization process. We abseiled down to Camp 1 that night and, the following day, 10 July, to ABC. Leaving my Millet boots, ice axe, crampons and climbing harness there, we completed the sortie by trekking down to Base Camp. It had been an invaluable five days' rotation on K2 and I felt fit and highly satisfied to be fully on track as we entered camp.

Shortly after reaching the camp we met the American team of guide Garrett Madison and his clients Alan Arnette, Matt Du Puy and Rick Sylvester. Madison had been guiding professionally for fifteen years, including eight years guiding on Mount Everest, where he had led a total of forty-four climbers to the top. He had also guided expeditions on other 8,000-metre peaks, so, like most at Base Camp, was a highly experienced operator. Alan Arnette was a Colorado-based mountaineer and motivational speaker who was well-known in the adventure world for his widely-read blogs together with his frequent newspaper, radio and television articles and appearances. A former executive in the technology industry, he had completed over twenty-five expeditions since taking up mountaineering at age 38. Following the death of his mother from Alzheimer's in 2009, he devoted all his expeditions to raise awareness and money for the disease and his integrity and passion for finding a cure was never in question.

Matt Du Puy was a long-time adventurer, mountaineer and software engineer from San Diego, who had climbed many mountains in his lifetime, including Everest in 2009. And finally, 72-year-old Rick Sylvester, a former stuntman and pioneering climber with many first ascents, was attempting to become the oldest American to summit K2. Unfortunately, he would shortly struggle on their first rotation and abort the attempt thereafter.

I was surprised they had left it so late to arrive at Base Camp, which would result in them being totally dependent on a reliable period of sustained good weather to be able to complete adequate rotations.

On Friday, 11 July, we held our auspicious puja ceremony. The Sherpas follow the Tibetan branch of Buddhism, incorporating much of the ancient Bon religion prevalent in Tibet before the Buddhist master, Padmasambhava (also known as Guru Rinpoche) introduced Buddhism there in the eighth century. The ceremony is considered an essential and sacred component of any expedition, the purpose of which is to ask the Mountain Gods for permission to climb, safety for the climbers and forgiveness for damaging the mountain. It comprises an absorbing ritual which brings a notable calming atmosphere to Base Camp and everyone usually attends.

The preparations for the ceremony had commenced days earlier with the Sherpas building a large stupa (a dome-shaped Buddhist shrine made out of rocks) at the most prominent location at our camp, which contained a small furnace for burning juniper and incense. It was the largest stupa I had experienced in any previous puja on a mountain, and marked our camp as the spiritual centre of K2 2014 Base Camp.

The day began early with the Sherpas unravelling Tibetan prayer flags attached to a large pole which would stretch to the furthest four corners of our camp. They then asked us to bring all of our climbing equipment to the stupa, as is normal protocol. As most of mine had been left at ABC, I brought my trekking boots, ski poles and anything else of importance to the shrine and carefully placed them against it. I placed the card that Lama Geshi had given me in 2013 in Nepal which would be in my pack if I was fortunate enough to summit. I also placed a picture of Alex and Charlotte on the rocks, a picture I had looked at every night of the expedition to date.

The Sherpas conducting the puja were two of Garrett's climbing Sherpas whom he had used for many years on expeditions, Purba Sherpa and Kami Rita. We seemed to be in good hands. Purba had been a Buddhist monk for nineteen years and had summited Everest ten times, whilst Kami had been a monk for ten years and had summited Everest nineteen times. I thought if we couldn't get the Dalai Lama himself these two would be adequate replacements.

With all equipment, memorabilia, rice, water, food, pictures of the Dalai Lama and other artefacts placed on the stones, Purba and Kami began reciting and softly chanting mantras and passages from the 300-year-old Tibetan prayer book. They were assisted by our Lakpa Sherpa, who had also trained to be a lama. Mattresses and blankets were laid out on the ground and people sat down to observe. There wasn't a strict ritual however, and many stood to take pictures and videos. Other Sherpas talked and laughed – it was a serious and respectful, yet relaxed, ceremony.

The chanting built up, interspersed with periodic throwing of rice in the air from the lamas or instructions from Lakpa, and we settled down in a quiet reverence, absorbed by the centuries-old traditions. The weather was sublime, with bright sunshine and little wind. K2 provided a monumental, inspiring and fearsome backdrop. The burning juniper and incense filled the air with a fragrant haze. Everyone was locked in their own inner world of mind, body, spirit and soul. The chanting of the lamas took me into a reflective place where I remembered the tragedy of last year, my lifelong dreams and plans, my values, core self and my purpose. I thought of my children intensely, gazing at the small picture on the altar through the haze of smoke. And I reflected upon the coming challenge.

As the ceremony reached its climax, the Sherpas moved with precision to erect a long pole on the puja platform, carefully built to enable it to be inserted into a stable platform. It soared high into the air, lifting the multicoloured Tibetan prayer flags attached to it from the corners of Base Camp like spokes of a wheel, all of them soon fluttering in the light breeze. Each flag had a different meaning: yellow meant earth; green represented water; red was fire; white equalled air; and blue meant space.

We all stood up as Sherpas passed around rice into our hands and, on a signal from the lamas, threw the rice into the air three times, each time to the collective chant of *lakalu*, which means 'victory to the Gods'. This symbolized the warding-off of evil spirits and that, as opposed to conquering K2, we would be allowed to climb it only with the permission of the Mountain Gods. Kami and Purba walked around the watching party, tying a sacred thread and a *kharta* around our necks. Other Sherpas then proceeded to spread *sampa* (a barley flour) on all of our faces to represent a grey beard and a long life. Nuts, bread, sweet milk tea and *chang* (a potent rice wine) were also passed around. I took a sip, but at this altitude a mug of *chang* would have seen me horizontal for days. With flour everywhere and alcohol flowing, smiles and laughter soon filled the air as cameras clicked. The ceremony concluded, and everyone retreated to the mess tent or their own tents.

I'd participated in many pujas over the years, but this one stood out for many reasons. The size of the stupa and the span of our flags was one; a perfect day of clear skies and gentle winds was another; the conducting of the ritual by Purba and Kami another. Above all, however, was the symbolism of K2 watching over us – the mountain which had claimed so many lives in its turbulent history. Whatever everyone's spiritual beliefs, we all knew that reaching the top of K2 and surviving its icy slopes was largely dependent upon forces beyond our control, and the puja gave an opportunity to reflect upon this. It also provided the greatest opportunity to share the strong bond between climbers and Sherpas, so long an integral part of most Himalayan expeditions. The puja was about connection, sharing, camaraderie and support; to commit ourselves to each other, and to be there for each other if the time came.

The puja platform would remain until we left Base Camp at the end of the expedition and each morning some juniper leaves would be lit to symbolize an offering to the Mountain Gods.

CHAPTER FOURTEEN

ONE STEP AT A TIME

WHEN YOU DANCE, YOUR
PURPOSE IS NOT TO GET TO
A CERTAIN PLACE ON THE
FLOOR. IT'S TO ENJOY EACH
STEP ALONG THE WAY.

- WAYNE DYER

WITH A REASONABLE, if not perfect, forecast of weather for the coming few days, Garrett and his cohorts left that afternoon for their first rotation up the mountain, and Al and myself, meanwhile, prepared ourselves for our second rotation beginning the following day.

On Friday, 11 July, we again trekked from Base Camp to ABC and up to Camp 1 (6,100 metres). The next day we climbed up to Camp 2, passing Lower Camp 2 again, where three new tents occupied the space where the Schmidts' tent had been. The remains of their tent had been thrown to the side and was now lying crumpled up on some rocks a few metres away. It seemed an undignified end to their tent, but the new climbers camping there wouldn't have known the significance or the memories it held. Sequoia had also confirmed that there was no need to bring back what amounted to shredded nylon.

Ascending to 'proper' Camp 2, we encountered a sobering sight of numerous tents clinging to the mountain in close proximity. Compared to our experience in 2013, our tent was relatively comfortable but, as with Camp 1, I was becoming increasingly concerned about the limited space available. Tents were placed on the most unstable looking platforms, built up with ice, snow and debris in a futile attempt to create a horizontal base. Rubbish and human waste again littered the site. Faeces were impossible to avoid, but rubbish could be dealt with, and I fumed at the carelessness exercised by one or two of our climbing colleagues. We spent that night, the following day and following night camped at the 6,700-metre camp in slowly deteriorating weather, solely for acclimatization and preparing for the next big push on the mountain – the climb up the Black Pyramid to Camp 3.

On Tuesday, 15 July, we rose early to strengthening winds and intense cold. One team had managed to fix lines on the route to an elevation close to Camp 3 the day before, but no one had reached the camp yet. Our aim was merely to touch Camp 3 and return to Camp 2 that evening. As previously mentioned, reaching Camp 3 and retreating was now a normal practice for those who would be climbing with oxygen on their summit pushes. And being such a notoriously dangerous camp, which had claimed the lives of the Schmidts the year before, the less time we spent there the better.

The Black Pyramid was the main challenge facing the ascent up to Camp 3 – a renowned 400-metre climb at seventy to ninety degree steepness over rock and ice and dangerously exposed. We soon experienced why it had gained such a fearsome reputation – sustained technical climbing over many hundreds of metres. The howling winds and cold temperatures made it an even more intense experience. Al aptly summed up the climb on a dispatch that he recorded on a voice recorder when we eventually returned to Camp 2:

Today I was in a dicey section in a near vertical rock band, I slid my ice axe sideways between my body and backpack. I needed both of my hands free to climb. I inhaled deeply and then slowly, slowly exhaled. I am committed, I look up and see a rock protruding. I reach for it with my right hand. I test it. No movement. I do the same with my left hand. Looking down I see space. Nothing but space. Then my eyes catch movement – it's the wings of a bird far below.

Before my mind can register what is happening, my body is in fluid motion moving upwards one movement at a time and then – bam! I cannot move. The rope is tangled with my ice

*axe. My heart starts to beat faster. I say to myself relax …
relax … breathe. I release my right hand balancing on my
front points and holding on with my left hand. Ever so slowly
with my right hand I untangle the rope from my ice axe and
continue climbing.*

The wind became ever stronger. Our eyes were feeling the
effects of the assault. Cold permeated our core and, despite our
gloves, our fingers were freezing. The sky was thickening with
black clouds. It began to snow. Conditions were far from safe and
looking decidedly unstable.

'Adrian …! I think …!' he bellowed five metres ahead of me,
his words drowned out in the storm.

'What? I can't hear you! Hold on!' I shouted back, not
understanding anything he'd said.

'Climb up!'

'Let's get out of the wind! Behind those rocks!'

'Watch your step. This is really dangerous!'

'I think … I think … we should call it a day,' he repeated
his earlier words, the wind howling around us, providing little
protection.

'I think you're right. What are we at? Mine says 7,050 metres,'
I panted. 'What you got?'

'About the same.'

'Okay, I'd love to go higher, but this is crazy.'

We thus took the joint decision to return to Camp 2. As it was
only a foray to Camp 3, as opposed to a night stop, the benefits of a
few hundred metres acclimatization were sacrificed for the safety
of retreating. We might have reached Camp 3, but descending
back to Camp 2 would be increasingly dangerous in the rapidly
deteriorating conditions. And, with no sleeping bags, which were
left at Camp 2, sleeping at Camp 3 wasn't an option.

The descent was indeed precarious and took nearly as long as
it had taken to ascend. Each step, each lowering down vertical
rock bands, and each clip onto a fixed line was carried out with
the utmost caution. Yet, speed was also paramount. We descended
together, being careful to allow the first climber to clear the pitch
before joining him. Rock fall was a constant hazard.

We finally reached Camp 2 late afternoon and dived into the tent to escape the wind. As we'd experienced in 2013, Camp 2 is one hell of a windy location, the estimated sixty-kilometre-per-hour winds channelling through the gap between Broad Peak and K2 with an unimaginable ferocity.

'Base Camp, calling Base Camp. This is Camp 2, do you read; over?' I relayed on the radio. 'Base Camp. This is Camp 2. Do you read, over?'

'Hello Camp 2. This is Base Camp. We hear you,' came the response.

'Is that Dawa, over?'

'Yes, Dawa here. Where are you, over?'

'We are back in Camp 2. Conditions too dangerous. Over.'

'Yes, weather show bad storm coming. Strong wind. Most climbers back Base Camp.'

'We descend tomorrow. See you then. Out.'

In the night, the wind became so strong that, at times, we wondered if our tent would hold onto its tethers. The sides were caving in under the onslaught and snow was blowing through the hatches. It was a night of little sleep.

'Whoa, whoa!' Al shouted in the night. 'The tent just lifted up!'

'I felt it!' I stuttered in concern. 'It should be okay. There's more tethers on this tent than the Golden Gate Bridge,' I added as we settled back down. 'Lucky you're such a fat oaf – it would take 500-kilometre-per-hour winds to blow this tent off the mountain,' I mumbled as I put my head down on the makeshift 'pillow' of my backpack.

'Ninety-five kilos of pure muscle, I will have you know; former bodybuilding champion, Western Province!' came the response through the walls of his sleeping bag.

'Well, James Bond, if we do blow off I expect you to call in your helicopter to pluck us off!'

'Only if a Pussy Galore lookalike is the pilot!'

'More like Ali Baba with a thick moustache. You're welcome to him, Bond.'

'Let's get back to sleep.'

With little sleep managed in the howling storm, we awoke bleary-eyed at dawn. Leaving a large stuff sack full of stoves, canisters, some food and high-altitude clothing, the descent to

Camp 1 was equally serious. Several times on the descent huge rocks came hurtling by us. The wind showed no signs of abating. Depositing sleeping bags, food and equipment in another large stuff sack at Camp 1, we descended to ABC and Base Camp on Thursday, 17 July, arriving exhausted.

Despite the onslaught, we'd largely achieved what I was determined to accomplish after the issues of last year – two long rotations, each of five days' duration, reaching progressively higher elevations. I was as fit as I could be and now fully acclimatized, with our failure to reach Camp 3 the only hitch in our plans. In the wider scheme of things, a few hundred metres missed wouldn't make too much difference, but being stranded at Camp 2 for four days in a storm would. Heavy snows and strong winds had arrived. Now all we could do was wait for the all-important summit weather window.

Base Camp life took on a relatively relaxed routine. Chris and Lakpa had come over from Broad Peak, having abandoned their attempt on the world's twelfth highest mountain after an unsuccessful summit push, in order not to miss a summit attempt on K2. Our cook party of head cook Farmanullah Baig, assistant cook Sikander, and kitchen boys Karim and our dear friend Ali, back again at our insistence, produced some increasingly special dishes to savour. It was quantity and (relative) quality that we devoured; appearance didn't matter two hoots up here and, for all we cared, the nouvelle cuisine and dainty arrangements of MasterChef and so-called celebrity chefs could be shoved where the sun doesn't shine. We even had films – Garrett and his team inviting us in every evening after dinner to watch a Hollywood blockbuster. With freezing feet in the minus fifteen degrees Celsius temperature, we would watch films which would take us into a different world. Two James Bond movies were watched, of course reinforcing the thoughts of Maya weeks before that Al was indeed Daniel Craig, or at least his elder brother. We even watched *Vertical Limit*, the appalling 1993 film supposedly located on K2, which caused guffaws around the mess tent. Retreating to our tents and climbing into frozen sleeping bags with frozen limbs every night, two Nalgene bottles filled with hot water provided the most exquisite of sensations. As always, the simple things in life were all that mattered.

I had some great chats most days with Garrett, Alan and Matt, all of them the best of Americans, being intelligent, thoughtful and, above all, quieter than many of their compatriots. Rich, deep conversations, drinking tea around a table, on anything from Alzheimer's disease to the state of the world today; the environment to the American dream. Long conversations that are part of the enriched experience of expeditions, yet which are increasingly difficult in the frenetic society we live in today. Alex and Panos, the Greeks, were regular visitors and vice versa and we shared many meals together. We also saw other climbers frequently, such as Italian, Tamara Lunger, Spaniard, Ferran Latorre and a few of the second international team, such as Sami Mansikka, the President of the Finnish Alpine Club, on his ninth eight-thousander.

Our own wider team of Maya, Pasang and Dawa, Chris and Lakpa, and Luo were also gelling well, along with our Sherpa team. It was a close-knit extended team. And, for two of them, even more close-knit than I had imagined …

'Well now buddy, I do believe we have an amorous liaison going on in Base Camp!' Al exclaimed with an excited look on his face as he walked into our mess tent one day.

'What?' I looked up from my book. 'Who, what, when, where and how?'

'Well, I was reading in my tent and heard someone walk up and stop,' he explained.

'I peered out and young Nurbu was standing outside Luo's tent. He was looking left and right, back and front, up and down, like a thief about to rob a bank!'

'No! You serious?' I laughed.

'I sure am buddy, and there's more – before I could spell "K2" he was gone; disappeared right into Luo's tent!'

'No! The little rascal!'

'Oh yes, and he was in there for well over an hour. I can safely assume he wasn't in there to learn Chinese!'

We had a good laugh at the circumstances. Luo and Nurbu! Whatever next! Romances weren't uncommon at high altitudes of course, but this was an amusing distraction from Base Camp routines.

'Well, that brings a whole new meaning to Chinese-Nepalese relations and the Friendship Bridge!' I laughed, referring to the famous bridge which links Nepal to Tibet.

'Oh yes. We can be sure there was a lot of bridging – and other manoeuvres, going on!'

An hour or so later Nurbu popped into the mess tent to retrieve an electric device charging on our batteries. Glancing smiles with Al, I nodded and we decided to have a little play with him, each interchanging some banter.

'Hey Nurbu, how you doin son?' Al started. 'Come on in, have a seat, sit down, relax,' he added, as the Sherpa shot a sideways look in suspicion at the unusual suggestions.

'You're looking at little hot Nurbu. You feelin' okay?'

'Tell me, how's the Chinese lessons going?'

'Good good,' came his reply, looking like a boy who'd just been caught kissing a girl behind the bike shed.

'Well, now I don't wish to pry into anything personal, but I just happened to see you go into young Luo's tent quicker than an avalanche thundering down the Cesen. And you seemed to be in there for some time. In fact, I made it well over an hour.'

'Yes, yes, we were just checking some equipment!'

'I have no doubt she was doing a thorough check of your equipment, Nurbu. Maybe a little jiggy-jiggy too?'

We all burst into laughter, Nurbu included, albeit with embarrassment. We reassured him that it was all okay, that we wouldn't say a word to anyone; and wished him the best of luck for future 'excursions'.

'Al, Al, you have condom?' he asked Hancock the next day, as he rushed into the mess tent in a hurry.

'Well, now Nurbu, there's some things that are useful in certain places, but a condom on K2 is about as good as a fishing rod in the Sahara.'

'Sorry!'

'I've got a ziplock bag you can fold in five if you're desperate?'

As the snows cleared and good weather returned on 20 July, all the teams at camp started to witness something unprecedented on our weather forecasting channels. An excellent weather window was appearing, not just for a few days, but an extended period of at least ten days into August. We checked, double checked and tripled checked with every forecast online, but they all showed the same, fine, stable weather and low winds, even at the highest altitudes. On K2, even getting a weather window was far from assured and, for many years, never even arrived. When they did occur, they might be for four or five days' maximum and rarely ideal. Ten days was unheard of, however. The excitement was palpable, a plan was about to be set.

With the unprecedented weather window upon us, we still faced at least five major hurdles and decisions to make in our quest to summit K2. That was: snow and ice conditions, which could still be a showstopper high up on the mountain; rock fall dangers which we couldn't control; avalanche threats which we could only partially mitigate against; the steepness and technical demands of the summit push which we could hopefully tackle; and overcrowding which was somewhat in our control. With all this considered, a first summit date was set, from which we would work everything backwards.

As the team with the largest Sherpa support who would be fixing lines from Camp 3 onwards, we took the decision to go for a summit day of Saturday, 26 July 2014. That would mean leaving Base Camp for Camp 1 on Tuesday, 22 July; Camp 1 to Camp 2 on Wednesday, 23 July; Camp 2 to Camp 3 on Thursday, 24 July; Camp 3 to Camp 4 on Friday, 25 July; leaving Camp 4 that evening to enable reaching the summit around lunchtime on Saturday, 26 July; and back to Camp 4 by darkness the same day. This schedule would allow the two full days of recent snowfall to consolidate in the hot sun, something that we had miscalculated in 2013. All the other teams at camp agreed with our planned timetable and first summit date.

The issue of avoiding overcrowding as much as possible was then discussed with the teams. In many eight-thousanders, most notoriously on Everest, there is always a needless rush to attempt a summit at the first opportunity of the first weather window of the season, causing the now notorious queues some years. On K2, we only had one weather window, but severe limitations on space and even more severe technical hurdles to overcome. It needed some diplomacy, liaison and common sense. Thankfully we managed it to a degree. With our team on the first summit push, the Americans offered to go one day later which would cut down numbers to start with. The Pakistani team were very keen to be on the first push given the historical significance of the occasion, so that was agreed. The three Italians and the two Greeks also decided to join us on the first push, with the second international team joining Garrett's team in aiming for a 27 July summit. The small Czech, Spanish and Polish teams said they would check conditions in another day or two. Thus, although top heavy on the first summit day with the large SST and Pakistani teams, we had some semblance of spreading the assault. Space in the limited real estate of Camps 1 and 2 would still be an issue though. And how the relatively large number of climbers on the first wave would transpire on the final push from Camp 4 to the summit remained to be seen.

On the technical side, we all knew that this final push from Camp 4 to the top of K2 would be, by far, the most technically demanding day of the climb, notorious for the steepest sections of the climb on the mountain, the dangerous hazards and the unrelenting stresses of tackling these at high altitude. With our large contingent of Sherpas, it was agreed that Lakpa Sherpa would lead a rope fixing team leaving by 7 p.m. on Friday, 25 July, three hours before the rest of us left Camp 4. That would hopefully enable them to fix lines on the notorious near vertical ice. The other hurdles would largely be in the hands of the Mountain Gods.

With the plan set for leaving two days' hence, we began the all-important final preparations and run-in. Ropes, ice screws, oxygen systems, communications equipment, batteries, high-altitude clothing, tents, food and cooking equipment and other supplies were all checked, refined and, where applicable, given individual responsibilities. With our two efficient rotations completed, Al and myself had deposited equipment at ABC, Camp 1 and Camp 2, so we were in a good position logistically. Oxygen and tents, the two main large ticket items, would be carried by Sherpas for the higher camps.

As in all expeditions, it was the little things which could make a large difference to an outcome. The small stuff sack accessible at close hand with an ibuprofen container, sun cream, grease and zinc oxide tape. The larger, but still basic, medical pack that could be located quickly inside my pack. The clothing choices that, with ventilation systems, would cater for cold and possible heat – getting too hot would be detrimental to performance. And so on. Satellite telephones, the altimeter watch, compass, the all-important harness with ascending and descending equipment, plus emergency descent lines and screws. Everything was meticulously checked to ensure that it was necessary, accessible and working 100 per cent.

Critical for me was my nutrition. I'd brought my own ultra-high calorie freeze-dried meals from 'Be Well' nutritional products, which had proved highly successful on my recent polar expeditions. These were already cached at Camps 1 and 2 for the six days of the summit push. The snacks were the next most important item – my utilization of food containing fat, protein and carbs, as opposed to purely sugars, long testified to their effectiveness on endurance adventures. That meant almonds, macadamias and cashews in addition to chocolate; a special nutritional bar with all three nutritional ingredients; and fat-based gels as opposed to sugar gels. Added to this were all-important supplements – daily vitamin and mineral tablets amounting to fifteen tablets per day, with everything from antioxidants to amino acids to fish oils to Gingko Biloba. Supplements which I have been taking since I was 16, carefully prepared into small ziplock plastic bags for each day.

The final supplement I would carry was just one tablet. That tablet was a small blue tablet of the drug Viagra. A long-standing joke with those who know me, I'd first read of its possible benefits in mitigating against acute mountain sickness prior to my Everest ascent in 2006. The premise was that the drug helped prevent possible pulmonary oedema and cerebral oedema by increasing blood supply to all your vital organs – not just, men may agree, to your most vital organ! I used it on Everest to summit and on most peaks since. The jokes of hoping to get laid on the summit, whether I was excited when I reached the top, or whether I used it to give me a spare ice axe, are aired each time the story comes up. As is the true story of Pfizer, the makers of Viagra, calling me one year wanting me to feature in an advertising campaign on the benefits of the drug! 'We wanna show Viagra's for everyone,' the American Marketing VP for the Middle East had drawled on the phone. 'Sexual dysfunction, peak performance, reach the highest of the high, we think yer'll be a great role model!' Wonders never cease – a giant billboard of me atop some mountain adorning the main highway running through Dubai, loudly proclaiming, 'Adrian Hayes uses Viagra!' My credibility punctured at a stroke.

It was the mental preparation, too, that became equally as important. Getting that all important mindset in the best possible mental frame. It was the 100-metre sprinter visualizing his race, the rugby player preparing to enter the war zone of a match, and the soldier preparing to launch into battle, combined. That mental focus, discipline and visualization which would be critical in the huge challenges we faced.

Needing some quiet place and space to fully get into that zone, I trekked down to the Gilkey Memorial. Walking down the moraine and passing the last camp, the Pakistan team, on the way, I was soon on my own and savouring the solitude and space. I warily crossed the numerous glacial streams, edged across the boulder fields and climbed up the rocky outcrop as the plaques glistened in the sun. It was the first time I'd had the opportunity to visit it this season and, on arrival at the shrine, I collected my thoughts. Strolling around the plaques to remind myself of the sacrifices and price mountaineers had made and paid, I noticed that a new and more elaborate memorial plaque to the Schmidts had been attached to the rocks, to accompany the basic one Chris Warner had fashioned a year before. Evidently from Marty's side of the family, its words, in red and black, were simple and poignant, and I stood staring at the plaque in silent contemplation for a few minutes:

> *FATHER AND SON*
> *MARTY AND*
> *DENALI SCHMIDT*
> *DIED ON K2*
> *27 JULY 2013*
> *REST IN PEACE*
> *SCHMIDT*
> *FAMILY*

I then reflected on how different this and all my previous visits to the memorial had been, with each providing differing emotions and energies. The first visit, soon after our arrival in 2013, had been a sobering and stark reality check on the high risks and costs incurred in attempting the Karakoram giants. The second visit, to attach the plaque for the Schmidts, had been one of intense sadness and a subtle 'memorial ceremony' for our fallen friends.

My energy this time was different, however. Alongside this reflection was the determination to not have my name and memory join them in this lonely isolated post thousands of miles from anywhere. Sitting down alone in the warm sun, amongst the names of the fallen, I stared up at K2 for the umpteenth time on this and the previous year's trip. 'Safety is paramount. Don't make stupid mistakes. Focus, concentrate, *feel* the mountain,' I told myself in this heightened meditative state. Using visualization techniques, I zoned in on the upcoming climb – reaching Camp 1, Camp 2, Camp 3 and Camp 4, and then scaling the near-vertical walls of ice leading to the summit. Focus, concentration, awareness. I didn't ask to be spared the same outcomes of the 100 names besides me; I didn't ask to be one of the lucky few to reach the top; but reflected on how the universe seemed to have a plan for everyone and trusting that it would have the plan for me, for whatever reason.

I spent an hour and a half up on the rock, looking over the glacier, up at the mountains and up to the skies above. It was the silence, stillness and space that I needed. I was ready to commit, ready to launch, ready to go.

CHAPTER FIFTEEN

OVERCOMING THE ODDS

THE EDGE … THERE IS NO
HONEST WAY TO EXPLAIN IT
BECAUSE THE ONLY PEOPLE
WHO REALLY KNOW WHERE IT
IS ARE THE ONES WHO HAVE
GONE OVER.

– HUNTER S. THOMPSON

I AWOKE AT 4 A.M. after a restless night's sleep. My mind was too active to sleep properly, but getting up in the early hours on little sleep is all part of expedition life – it's a sport for larks, not owls. Everything was packed and ready to go, and I quickly got dressed in the minus-fifteen-degree-Celsius temperatures. Before leaving my tent, there was one important task to do. The night before I had penned two handwritten letters to my children, Alex and Charlotte and another to my unborn son, and placed them in sealed envelopes with their respective addresses. These were the letters which I hoped they would never read. For if they did it would mean that I wasn't coming back. It was an acceptance of vulnerability, humility and humbleness, similar to when I posted the personal message on Facebook the day I left for K2, which I allowed to soften the complete focus I was in. They were three very deep and personal letters and, as they were never opened, I will keep their contents private. All I will say is that when one confronts one's own death, the priorities of life are starkly revealed.

I then took a last look at my picture of Alex and Charlotte, which I had carried with me through the journey and placed on the puja stupa weeks before.

'I love you both so much,' I whispered quietly, giving it a kiss before placing it, along with the letters, in a ziplock bag. 'I promise I'll be back soon and if for some reason I don't, just know that you mean the world to me and I will be with you forever in spirit. Take care of yourselves and look after Mummy.'

Giving the bag a final hug close to my chest, I placed it on top of my sleeping bag, closed the tent, put on my pack and stood outside. It was a short opportunity to marvel at my surroundings and see a far greater picture. Approaching the new moon, the ocean of blackness in the clear skies above was illuminated by a canopy of billions of stars flickering in the darkness, as vast as any eye could wander. The foamy white mist of the Milky Way, containing 100 billion stars alone, stretched across the horizons, as clear as I had ever witnessed it, giving an incomprehensible glimpse into hundreds of thousands of years of time. The glacier glistened in the stillness, silently creaking under the strain of its enormous weight. The surrounding mountains lay in a long line like the spine of the land, providing a barrier and a guard to the great mountain by our side. K2 soared menacingly above us, seemingly wanting to challenge the skies itself as if determined to kiss the heavens. It emitted a paradoxical energy of power, peace, magnificence and danger. The stillness was absorbing, the connection with the universe mesmerizing, and time stood still for an all too brief moment.

After ten minutes I met Al, Chris, Lakpa, Maya, Pasang, Dawa and Luo in the mess tent, where we devoured a hastily prepared breakfast of eggs and toast, picked up some food for lunch and stood to leave. All the cooks came to give us a hug, handshake and prayers for our safety. We joined the six Sherpas who were accompanying us to Camp 1 and bade our farewells.

We had one more ritual to perform – to stop by the puja stupa. Our Sherpas bowed their heads and all of us joined in as a mark of respect, everyone locked once more into their inner world of deepest thoughts and contemplation. Then we each picked up a handful of rice from the shrine and threw it into the air. That was the signal to pass by the stupa, on the left-hand side as is the ritual, and begin the journey.

The stillness was soon punctuated by the crunching of feet into the hard snow as we started the trek. Passing quietly by the camps of sleeping teams, we left the Base Camp periphery and crossed the frozen glacial streams onto the ice. Head torches lighting our way, our party weaved its way up the glacier like a pilgrimage to the Indes. The glacier we had trekked so many times before fell away behind us, and I prayed that this would be the last time we had to ascend its broad reaches. The crevasses and tricky traverses of the head of the glacier were negotiated in the emerging dawn, as salmon and purple tones lit up the skies above.

Stopping at ABC to don our climbing boots, crampons, harnesses and ice axes, we stepped onto the ice slopes that marked the first pitch up the mountain. No ropes for the first 100 metres, just a steady traverse left and right up the fifty-degree slopes. Then the clip into the lines for the first long pitch up the eastern edge of the Abruzzi Spur, protected by the rocks to our left. Then the second, the third and so on. I knew every pitch of this climb to Camp 1 like the back of my hand; the snow slopes; the fixing points; the small rock protrusions to cross; the traverse into the gully; the steep final climb to Camp 1.

Despite the early start, the hot sun reflecting off the ice on a windless day became intense, and as always, I struggled greatly in the soon debilitating heat. An hour into the climb I had stripped down to my thermal inner shirt rolled up to my chest to expose my bare navel in an attempt to dissipate the furnace inside my body. My climbing trousers were unzipped at the sides to provide some additional ventilation. The effects of the sun and heat rapidly changed the constitution of the ice to soft, deep and sugary snow. It was an exhausting day, and I was relieved when we finally reached Camp 1, which was indeed busy but manageable. 1,100 metres of the total 3,600-metre ascent from Base Camp were ticked off.

The following day, 23 July, we started the 600-metre climb to Camp 2, a steadily increasing climb up the mixed rock and ice slopes of the Abruzzi, with far more rock to cover than the climb to Camp 1. Again, the sections of the climb were, by now, vividly remembered. We ascended the first section of rock and ice of reasonable steepness in the company of other climbers. The snow and ice conditions were much better than the previous day and, with a light breeze, conditions were far more comfortable. We reached the first of the many vertical rock bands, where the sound of steel crampons against rock provided an unmistakable screeching and scraping at complete odds with the peace of our surroundings. Brute strength aided the effort to haul ourselves up each band. We ascended and traversed a nameless buttress. Stones and boulders flew down regularly, causing the shouts of 'ROCKS!' to echo down the mountain.

In the cooler air, I was feeling fit and strong. We stopped for some lunch below one steep ice section of the climb, a tiny perch of rock providing a small resting place to sit on our packs, drink some water and eat some food. We climbed on over five hours to reach Lower Camp 2 for the third time this season and stopped for another short break. Then it was onto the House Chimney, pulling, pushing and heaving ourselves up the near vertical ice-filled chimney, attaching ourselves to the safest line we could find. And then finally onto Camp 2. 1,700 metres of the 3,600-metre climb knocked off.

Camp 2 was exceedingly crowded and the limitations on space on the mountain laid bare, with tents being placed in innovative ways on the hastily erected piles of ice and debris. All the debris would be blown into China or buried at some stage, but still caused me to question the impact of climbers on such mountains. We slept miserably with five of us crowded into a three-man tent.

The next day, 24 July, we proceeded to tackle the challenging climb to Camp 3. In infinitely better conditions than the first time we'd attempted the Black Pyramid, we could at least concentrate on our feet and handholds, rather than protecting ourselves from the weather. Weaving in and out over the rock and ice, we climbed, manoeuvred and ascended the increasingly sharp terrain to the point we'd reached a week or so before. And then onto new ground where it became even more exposed. This was climbing at its most absorbing. I looked down on Tamara Lunger, ascending thirty metres below us. Thousands of metres below her, the avalanche splay from the Cesen route could clearly be seen as a stain across the Baltoro glacier. The sense of height was breathtaking.

Approaching Camp 3 for the first time starkly jolted my mind from its present focus to the events of the year before. We were about to reach the most dangerous camp on the mountain; one which was notorious for avalanches; one that was the last resting place of Marty and Denali Schmidt. We weren't sure what we would find but Sequoia had asked me that, if there was any sign or trace of their equipment or bodies, to send a picture to her rather than post anything public. That was the instruction I was ready to give to all the climbers arriving at the camp.

I've experienced many dead bodies in my paramedic training years before in hospitals, in the ambulance service and even in mortuaries, but this was different and there was a degree of unease as we moved over a crest and onto the thirty-degree slopes that marked the camp. As it happened there was nothing. No sign or trace of anything untoward ever occurring, just deep snow, smoothed across the landscape like icing on a cake. We couldn't even be sure where they had camped that fateful night a year earlier, such was the purity and virginity of the snow before us. And with the obvious regular onslaught of avalanches, their final resting place could have moved many tens, or even hundreds, of metres. This was the final unknown resting place settled which Sequoia, her and Denali's mother, Joanne, and Marty's wife Giovannina would have wanted. Their loved ones would remain buried for eternity under the depths of snow at 7,300 metres in one of the world's remotest places. No agonizing over equipment, personal possessions, or above, all their bodies would ever have to take place. A final closing of a tragic incident.

The depth of snow would become strikingly apparent as we created dugout bases for our tents. Instead of Camp 2's necessity to build up a platform of ice, snow and debris on the lower side of a tent facing down the mountain, at Camp 3 we simply used our lightweight shovels to carve into the upper slope. The shovels slid into the hard crust and soft snow like a knife into soft butter and, before long, we had fashioned a 1.5-metre vertical wall into the upper slope providing a two-metre wide notch of a level base for our tents. All the tent platforms were built into one long ledge running west to east along the site, with newcomers adding to the easternmost edge as they arrived. The weather was excellent, the views stunning and it was as relaxed a late afternoon and evening as anyone could possibly expect at such a location. 2,300 metres of the 3,600-metre climb from Base Camp completed.

I would be lying to say that I didn't have any concerns. The glaciers, snow and ice walls above Camp 3 could easily unleash their loads without notice. Our safety was only partly enhanced by the excellent snow conditions we were encountering, with at least four days of strong sunshine consolidating the previous days of precipitation. It was still Camp 3, however, and heading to sleep for the night, I allowed my mind to wander to all sorts of possibilities, ready to dive out of the tent at a second's notice.

On 25 July, we ascended the relatively short 500–600-metre climb from Camp 3 to Camp 4 at 7,800 metres – by now on the eastern side of the Abruzzi Spur, a section almost entirely on snow and ice. I wore my one-piece down suit (clothing that to most outsiders resembles a space suit) for the first time; it was barely required due to the increasing heat of the day. We climbed the precipitous walls of blue ice safely to reach Camp 4 and complete a total of 2,800 metres of our 3,600-metre climb.

Camp 4, located on the distinct 'shoulder' of K2, was the only camp and virtually the only place on the entire mountain, that wasn't situated on a steep ice, snow or a rock wall or slope, instead being a welcome near flat surface in an avalanche free area. Arriving after four hours in perfect weather, the atmosphere was, surprisingly, akin to a party as we reached the tents. Perhaps it was nerves and expectation displaying themselves in an outflowing of positivity, but bear hugs and slapping was happening all around as fellow climbers arrived and took pictures and film of each other.

The enormity of K2's climb from Camp 4 to the summit presented itself like a movie in an IMAX theatre. There before us, in clear view, we could see every section of the most technical, difficult and dangerous part of the entire climb. The first section was the easiest – the steadily elevating slopes to the start of the so-called Bottleneck. Then the Bottleneck – an eighty-degree narrow gully, approximately 100 metres in elevation, notable for the technicality that it presented. That led to the ice seracs, the notorious 150-metre walls of ice which had collapsed in 2008 causing the greatest tragedy in K2's history. The westerly traverse under the seracs, the steep ice climb to approximately 8,400 metres and then the slightly shallower final 200-metre climb to the summit followed. It was an awesome, mesmerizing and sobering sight.

As we settled down for the few hours rest before leaving for the summit, we all knew that the final fifteen-hours' ascent to the summit and back to Camp 4 would be the crux of the entire expedition. This was it. The gold medal race after all the qualifying, heats, quarters and semis. The *race* where anything could happen. Where we would be tested to the limits of our endurance, stamina and skills. Where things could easily go wrong. Where the possibilities of incidents or accidents were ever present.

As darkness fell and we rested, cooked up a meal and hydrated as much as possible, the possible problems soon presented themselves. The unexpected, last minute nausea of one of our rope fixing team, led by Lakpa Sherpa, caused some urgent discussions as a replacement was sought. Together with collating enough rope, their leaving time was delayed, giving me concerns on the lead they would have on us. It was agreed we would wait an hour longer. And then, just before our departure, I felt some unease in my bowels. A hasty visit to the toilet confirmed I had a bad bout of diarrhoea. 'Damn it!' I shouted to myself. Having the runs on the toughest night of the toughest mountain on earth was all I needed. I swallowed an Imodium tablet, but knew that the equivalent of shoving a cork up one's backside couldn't disguise the fact that my body wasn't functioning at its optimum and that I could have problems from here onwards. With the rope fixing team heading off as late as 8.30 p.m., we left at 10 p.m. for the climb.

'Best of luck, buddy,' Al said as we left our tent with Pemba and another Lakpa (3), the two of our Sherpa team we'd be climbing with.

'Let's give it horns.'

'Stay safe and sound.'

'See you at the top.'

With head torches on, we proceeded up the first section of the climb, now using oxygen. It took longer than planned to reach the Bottleneck. I looked down to see a trail of lights heading up the slopes below me. Above me all I could see was blackness.

A fixed line, set by our guys ahead, marked the start of the Bottleneck. It soon transformed from a snow slope to the eighty-degree ice slope I'd read so much about – sustained front point ice and rock climbing up a seemingly never-ending gully. The ice fell away beneath my feet into the darkness, but I couldn't see it at all. Probably just as well, for below me was nothing. All I had was the rock, ice or my ice axe to hold, one flimsy line, the wind and one heck of a long way down. The lack of sleep over the past three days could only be ignored. Focusing on the next hold; the delicate placing of ice axe and crampons; my lungs bursting to get air in, my quad muscles building with lactic acid, my calves screaming under the strain they were under.

Then we learned why the Bottleneck had obtained its name – we literally hit a bottleneck. My doubts on the limited gap between the advance party and the main body leaving were unfortunately warranted as we were left hanging on the sheer wall for over an hour whilst the fixing team struggled to find placements ahead. It was very cold, and it started to snow lightly. Wind was blowing spendthrift down the slopes. With my boots and crampons locked into the ice on their front points, any movement other than a shift of weight from one foot to the other was very difficult. Feet began to cramp up, ankles were in increasing pain.

'I've lost feeling in one foot,' Chris Burke groaned, hanging in the upper reaches of the gully next to me. 'I think I might go down.'

'I feared this might happen, but think we should stick it out,' I replied, as Lakpa arrived from below.

'Lakpa, I'm getting too cold, I think we should go down and try tomorrow. What do you think?'

'Yes, maybe we go down to Camp 4 and come back tomorrow,' he pondered. 'No, let me go up and have a look.'

Lakpa gallantly manoeuvred himself ahead of Chris, Al, the Sherpanis and myself and slowly disappeared into the forbidding darkness above. No stars could be seen in the sky in the direction we faced. Shouting could be heard from above and Al and myself both tried to relay some communication, but with the wind and being out of sight, blocking our voices, nothing got passed and confusion reigned. We'd ground to a standstill on a highly-exposed gully with only one thin line providing any semblance of safety.

After what seemed an eternity of delicate and exhausting holding and balancing in the couloir, we started to move.

Slowly inching up, we came to the top of the Bottleneck and over a clump onto a less steep section. We'd been climbing over six hours and were only just at the top of the Bottleneck. It wasn't a good start. As light slowly arrived, two things became apparent. Firstly, the hold-up appeared to be at the base of the ice seracs where the traverse commenced. And, secondly, the 150-metre vertical ice seracs weren't vertical at all.

'Shit! Those ice seracs are overhanging!' Al shouted to me.

'Just as well we couldn't see them!' I rasped back.

'Just stay in place, baby. Just hold it together now.'

'I wondered why I couldn't see any stars – it's a ceiling of ice!'

There are some occasions in one's life where having 'fingers crossed' is something of an understatement. This was one. An imposing cliff of blue ice sheared vertically and then overhanging as far as the eye could see. A sculpture of epic proportions whose crevassed walls seemed to sway like a giant curtain in the growing light. A tower of ice that guarded the access across its base as menacing as a team of heavyweight bouncers guarded a nightclub – one step wrong and you were thrown out or down; a large misfortune and their full weight would come crashing down on you. There was no way past them other than the route we were on. All we could do was to cross our fingers and trust that they held in place.

We reached the base of the seracs. After a short break, we traversed west. If we thought the Bottleneck was the crux, we were mistaken. Here the route traversed sixty metres or so across vertical ice along the base of the cliffs. Below us was a sheer drop thousands of metres into the abyss. I would later learn how close we were to having to abort the summit attempt at this point. The rope fixing team of four young Sherpas from SST had struggled to fix anchors to the traverse and were ready to give up and descend until Chris's Lakpa arrived from below. Picking up a rope on the upper stretch from a Pakistani HAP, who was too exhausted to carry the rope further, he joined SST's Lakpa Sherpa at the start of the traverse. The two Lakpas' then led across the sheer vertical ice, fixing lines as they climbed.

We edged along the traverse, focusing totally on each foot placement and ice axe hold. It was slow and all consuming as we edged along the seemingly never ending ledge. And then, with the traverse complete, we stopped for a break whilst the rope fixing team regrouped for the next section of the climb. We'd been climbing for nearly nine hours or more and I could feel the sun on my back. I turned around, rested against a clump of ice to see the view for the first time – such had been my focus on the entire climb so far, I hadn't managed to look around until this point. Now that I did, I realized how uniquely special this view was. The yellow sun hung in the sky above China, filling the air with amber and tinting the few clouds with endless rays of pink. Its hue illuminated the mountain tops of the Karakoram far below. The ice on the cliffs turned to blue. This was why we climbed. It was a view which so few people would or could ever see. Over 8,000 metres above the earth, it was a precious and mesmerizing sight.

We eventually climbed on. Once again, any thoughts that, after the Bottleneck and the traverse, things would finally settle down, were rudely dismissed. Once more, the slope was a sheer seventy-five to eighty degrees, often on blue ice, requiring all of us to be 100 per cent on our game as we front pointed and thrust our axes into the flaying ice. It took us many hours to move up the 300 or more metres elevation of snow and ice. By the time mid-morning arrived, the strength of sun rays in the rarefied air and the reflection off the snow, once again created a furnace of intolerable heat. As may be obvious reading this by now, after five cases of heat stroke or exhaustion in the previous six years, my internal thermometer had been thrown completely off-kilter and I simply cannot operate in heat. I thus dropped my back to the ice, carefully attached by a sling and karabiner and, again, dropped my one-piece down suit to my waist, tied it around, took off my second layer and climbed on in a single skin. Had I been able, and if it wasn't for the strength of the sun, I would have taken that off too and climbed bare-chested. It seemed completely ridiculous to be at 8,400 metres climbing in a T-shirt, but that was the reality of the situation.

I was also in considerable discomfort, and even pain, caused by an increasing desperation to relieve my bowels from the intense pressure of diarrhoea they were under. The problem was there was simply no place to go. Unzipping the special zip across the backside of my down suit wouldn't present the climber below me with the most aesthetic of views, and unleashing my innards all over his face would spoil even that. There was nothing to do but to hold it in, at times with a strain of epic proportions. As amusing as it might read now, I was in increasing distress and desperate for a solution. There wasn't one.

At around 1 p.m. on the Saturday afternoon, having been climbing intensely for around fourteen hours, we reached a ledge at the top of the ice section, at approximately 8,400 metres. A natural geological fault line leading to a rock pinnacle thirty metres or so off the route, it was the first place we could sit down and rest since leaving Camp 4. Above us the slope lessened to a reasonable forty-five to fifty degrees for the final 200 metres of the climb. It was an angle which all of us could ascend without lines, but it was the descent that would be the issue – a descent where a slip could easily happen with serious consequences. Unfortunately, we'd run out of rope and some frantic searching, together with calls on radios, would be made before reinforcements finally arrived from below.

Sitting down on my pack in considerable pain, I looked at the ledge leading to the rock pinnacle and wondered whether I could finally go to the toilet. It looked too exposed, however, and I started to consider something which was, frankly, ridiculous. An interesting fact that I'd read was that, for all its steepness, the summit of K2 was quite flat – about the size of a tennis court. I thus decided to hold my pain in until, hopefully, summiting K2 and having a crap on the top. If nothing else, it would be a third Guinness World Record for myself for the highest dump in human history.

Three minutes after I arrived, Al reached the ledge. I saw his face and he looked in distress. After two seasons climbing K2 together, I'd got to know his every emotion, pattern, and idiosyncrasies, including his bowel movements. 'I think he's desperate for a dump,' I said to myself as he slumped down.

'I'm desperate for a dump!' he gasped.

'I'm in agony, I've got to go somewhere!'

'Blimey! That's two of us!'

'No … if I don't go now I'm going to poo in my pants!'

'Well, there's this ledge. We can try.'

'I have to. Please, Pemba, Pemba, get some rope and lead me out,' he said to the young Sherpa.

'Yes, Lakpa fix rope to top. We wait for line to come,' Pemba replied in broken English.

'No, no, not rope to the summit. Rope for me. I need shit'

'Yes, we wait for line then you climb rope.'

'NO, NO! I need SHIT! POO POO! Tie your rope on me and lead me out!'

The exchange would have been hysterical if his situation wasn't so desperate. I quickly shouted to Pemba in Nepali that Al needed to go to the toilet urgently and to tie his short rope to his waist, although I couldn't remember what the word for poo was in Nepali. A quick squat and pointing to my backside completed the translation.

With Pemba finally understanding, he untied the short rope on his harness, gave an end to Al, who tied it around his waist in the quickest knot tie I have ever witnessed. As Pemba belayed him, Al scurried across the ledge for about four metres before squatting down. As he looked up, he saw twelve climbers gazing down at him.

'Oh, gawwd!' he groaned.

'Al's having … a shit,' I shouted. 'Amuse yourselves for ten seconds!'

Having unzipped the 'undercarriage' zip on his one-piece down suit and done his business, the wannabe James Bond then found his zip was stuck in the mayhem, requiring Pemba to inch along the ledge and zip up Hancock's backside as he bent over. With all this taking place at 8,400 metres on the world's most notorious mountain, you couldn't have made it up if you tried. Leaving a pile of turd standing proudly on the ledge, both men inched back to the rest of us.

'That … was so … close. I was … desperate!' He panted.

'I'm … sorry, but … it was hilarious!'

'So embarrassing!'

'Well … even James Bond goes to the toilet!'

'Not with M pulling up his pants!'

The ledge would thereafter be known amongst the SST team as 'Hancock Point'. We still await its official recognition alongside the House Chimney, Black Pyramid, the Bottleneck, and the Traverse as one of the defining locations of an ascent of K2.

Time was marching on as some of the Pakistani HAP team arrived with more rope. We still had 200 metres left to climb which would take between ninety minutes and two hours to complete. It was now 1.30 p.m. Climbers reading this will fully know the implications; for non-climbers, we were going beyond what would normally be considered a safe time to summit, i.e. summiting early enough in the day to enable a safe return to Camp 4 by last light. Most fatalities on eight-thousanders happen on the descent, when altitude, oxygen depletion, fatigue, exhaustion, deteriorating weather, visibility and darkness, combine to cause mistakes. Many incidents, such as the Everest 2006 disaster and the K2 2008 tragedies, were compounded by climbers summiting far too late in the day – on the latter, some reached the top at 6 p.m. A mid-afternoon summit was pushing it close but, understandably, in the fine conditions, few of us were going to retreat.

Chris and Lakpa and Luo and Nurbu pushed on up, using their own short ropes, whilst the other Lakpa and a second Sherpa climbed ahead of us with the newly arrived lines to perform a basic fix. Unlike the ascent until then, the snow was now soft, and some of these attachments were a mere ice axe placed in the snow. Waiting for Hancock to finish his ablutions, we left the ledge behind the others. More climbers were slowly arriving from behind.

This final 200 metre climb to the summit was technically easier than what we had encountered to date, but that was offset by the height we were now at and the duration of time we had been climbing. Looking to our west, I saw clouds building. I was still in considerable discomfort in my bowels. It was hard and slow going.

Placing one foot in front of the other we edged our way up the final slopes. We were now well into the 'death zone' – an elevation above 8,000 metres where humans cannot survive any length of time. It was a place and height we didn't belong. With the Everest season completed two months before, we were now the highest human beings on the entire planet. Below us, over seven billion people would be going about their normal day-to-day lives on a Saturday in late July. Many would be on summer vacations, sightseeing, enjoying sun, sand and sea, visiting friends or relatives, driving, or heading to airports for their holidays. All would be completely oblivious to what we were experiencing far above them.

Chris and Lakpa descended past us on the way, having summited and retreated immediately. Luo and Jing followed shortly after and, finally, Lakpa. He and Chris's Lakpa had been an immeasurable component of us getting to this height and I thanked him greatly.

The sky above was now a pure uninterrupted blue that stretched seamlessly across my field of vision. It was alive with crystals of light reflecting off the snow in an ambience of pure energy. In the valleys below, the dusky grey peaks revealed the jagged surface of earth. Broad Peak, our neighbouring 8,051-metre peak, kept an eye on us like a little brother looking up to his elder sibling. On the horizon, scudding clouds slewed colours of white, grey, blue and brown. Below my feet, the soft snow sunk on every step, emitting absorbing sounds every step I took. And, above me, the summit of K2 loomed ever closer. It was allowing us to pass to its sparsely visited summit, seemingly willing me to move every painful step. And as the clouds built up and mist appeared on its peak, warning us that it would give a brief glimpse only and that was all, I entered an ethereal connection of mind, body, spirit and mountain, my lungs gasping for oxygen, my legs fighting the lactic acid overload, my mind absorbing the pain in a higher state of vibration. We had seemingly moved beyond life itself and entered the heavenly spheres.

Just after 3 p.m., I turned a corner and saw the last fifty metres of shallow slope leading to the summit. It flattened out as I'd read. A gentle finish to such a brutal mountain. As I approached, I could see Maya, Pasang and Dawa celebrating together, having arrived a few minutes earlier. Tamara Lunger was there, as was Alex Aravidis and a couple of Sherpas. And, finally, at 3.20 p.m. on Saturday, 26 July 2014, I took my last few steps to join them. The ground fell away in all directions to the world below. Above me was only sky. I stood in awe looking over the elusive curvature of the earth. And, perhaps, glimpsed the curve of my own soul. I was on the summit of the mighty K2.

CHAPTER SIXTEEN

DESCENT TO SAFETY

GETTING TO THE TOP IS
OPTIONAL. GETTING DOWN IS
MANDATORY.

– ED VIESTURS

REACHING THE TOP of any 8,000-metre mountain is a surreal and sublime experience; one which is full of contradictory emotions. On the one hand, depending on the mountain, weather, time and other factors, you usually know half an hour, an hour or two prior that, bar any unforeseen incident, you are going to make it. There is, therefore, a gradually increasing expectation in contemplating the immense event. When you finally reach the summit, there is then a huge feeling of accomplishment and satisfaction on achieving a goal that may have been years in planning, and of overcoming the countless challenges on the way. There is a marvelling at being at the very top of nature's most awesome display of power in its armoury. And of looking down on the world below in one amazing view. There is the human interaction, and often emotion, with the teammates you have shared such pain with in reaching the hallowed place.

On the other hand, there is the stark realization that the climb isn't over yet and you are only halfway there; that you have to get down again: that descending is where even greater challenges might be faced. Celebrate, yes, but don't get carried away. The usual total exhaustion, chronic sleep deprivation and the debilitating effects of lack of oxygen mean getting 'carried away' is unlikely anyway. The warnings, however, do temper the celebrations.

Reaching the summit of K2 was very similar. On making those final few steps in sunshine, I reached the second highest point on earth, stood on the ice and raised my left arm and ice axe in victory. The wind whipped across my face as I briefly experienced the enormity of the moment, looking down at the dizzying drop on all sides. Nothing met my gaze apart from clouds, hiding the treasure of the landscape below. Then I received the congratulations, hugs and high fives of the seven or eight climbers already there. The Sherpanis – Maya, Pasang and Dawa – who had uniquely achieved their goal, were in tears. I gave a hug and high five to Alex Aravidis, our friend from last year, almost certainly Greece's most-accomplished high-altitude mountaineer. And then to Tamara Lunger, without doubt one of Italy's finest women mountaineers. Her wide goggles reflected my image starkly and I saw myself, for a brief moment, on top of the world.

'We did it!' I uttered.

'We did! Congratulations! Awesome!'

I gave a hug to the two Sherpas still there and Lakpa 3 who'd arrived behind me. It was a quick round of hugs and slaps for all of us savouring the experience and each other.

I then quickly scanned the view more thoroughly. The top was indeed an angled tennis court size area, though tailing off steeply at the edges. To the east and north, over China, I looked down at a sea of cloud; clouds of greys and whites heaped in chaotic ways like stones on a beach, stretched to the horizon and thickening. To the south I looked over the neighbouring peaks of the Karakoram; giants in themselves yet dwarfed from the viewpoint we were standing on. And to the west I saw ... little. Just mist rising close as the clouds rolled in below us and bubbled away like boiling water in a pan, threatening to overflow at any moment, which they had already in the previous thirty minutes. The sun's strong rays would beat them down regularly, but it was an uneven battle – for all its power, the sun was ninety-two million miles away; the clouds on the west were only hundreds of metres below us, encroaching up the mountain like an army about to overrun an enemy position.

The mist settled briefly and I looked over to the west. Ominous grey clouds were blowing in, rising visibly, and the build-up of cloud and strengthening winds was worrying. The mist rose again to block the view. Uncanny. It felt as if the mountain was again warning me that my time here was limited; to savour the experience, record it and then get down quickly. Any ideas of my world record-breaking ablutions were put firmly to bed. On such a precious piece of real estate, it didn't seem right in any case. I would suffer the pain for another five hours, or however long it took me to get down.

It was therefore time to get to 'work' – a call to my team, a few pictures and a brief video. I dialed up the mobile number of one of my team from Professional Sports Group in Abu Dhabi on my Thuraya XT and very briefly spoke to Jenny.

'Jen, we've reached the summit!' I gasped.

'Wow! Amazing! Congratulations!' came the reply.

'Can't talk; we've got to get down! Will message when back in Camp 4. Cheers.'

And that was it. There was no time for anything or anyone else. Jenny would immediately post something on my Facebook page and the many following could read it there. Although I'd only see it days later, this was the post:

> *Adrian Hayes*
> *26 July 2014*
> *#K2 2014 – Summit Push*
> *ADRIAN HAS SUCCESSFULLY REACHED THE SUMMIT OF K2!*
> *He reached the top at 15:20 local time.*
> *He is only halfway and we will report more when he returns safely to Camp 4.*
> *Posted by Professional Sports Group*

I pulled my camera back out of its pouch, moved away from the others a few metres and quickly recorded a selfie video and a few pictures. Passing the camera to Alex, he took a couple more, then Lakpa 3 some video, as I unrolled my Union Jack flag and held it high above me in triumph. I quickly took out my card from Lama Geshi and took another picture.

In between all this activity, I saw Al about five metres away, who'd evidently arrived a few minutes after me and was getting pictures taken. Spotting each other through the other climbers, I gave a thumbs up and he did the same. There was no need, or time, to exchange platitudes, felicitations or hugs. We'd achieved the goal that had been denied us the year before, and would save the congratulations until we'd returned to Camp 4.

All told, I was on the summit for not much more than five minutes. Five precious minutes on a small piece of flat ice which would be insignificant were it not a small piece of flat ice at the very top of the notorious, tragedy-filled and dangerous second highest mountain in the world. By the end of those minutes, the cloud and mist in the west blew up once more to smother the view and were threatening to envelop the entire mountain. I was lucky to have been able to take pictures and video in sunshine, but it was now time to go.

Knowing that I would never again return to this precious but inhospitable site which so few people in history had ever visited, I uttered a quiet farewell and appreciations to the mountain that had been so kind on this one day in time. I quickly donned my pack and led off ahead of the others, who followed in a line behind. Although I'm only a steady ascender, speed wise, on mountains, I'm a relatively fast descender, as well as seemingly able to operate better as time marches on – which was one reason for continuing the climb beyond what would normally be considered a safe turnaround time. I bounded down the upper slopes at relative speed, passing the ascending Pakistani team on the way. Then I clipped into the fragile attached lines as the slope steepened. No weight was placed on it, merely a safety line in case of a fall. The snow was soft and we'd created steps on the way up which aided the descent. We passed a few more ascending climbers, the last being Tamara's teammate, Klaus Gruber, fifty metres above the ledge we called Hancock Point. We'd quickly descended to this point. Then the clouds did what they'd been threatening to do all afternoon, which was to fully envelope the mountain. We found ourselves in a white-out as we reached Hancock Point, and it started to snow. At the place we were about to start the perilous descent of 300 metres of steep ice; the parlous 100-metre traverse under the ice seracs; and the precarious 100-metre climb down the Bottleneck, conditions were fraught. This was now serious.

Attaching an Italian hitch onto the line, which is quicker than using a Figure 8 device, I zipped down the first pitch. Then the second. These were moments where one's entire life depended on a single line and its attachment holding in place. One loose attachment, or one mistake, and I would fall over 3,000 metres down to the glacier below. It was focus, focus, focus in the increasingly jeopardous conditions as I abseiled down each line.

Then I hit a stall. A fellow climber, who I will not name for reasons which will later be clear, was moving very slowly descending the line below me. Painfully slowly. As he reached the bolt point, his switching over to the next line was even slower. He was suffering, perhaps even worse than that.

'Are you okay?' I bellowed to him from above. No answer.

'Are you okay? We have to get a move on!'

Still no answer. I descended to join him as he clipped into the next pitch and asked him to look at me. He didn't respond, merely slowly manoeuvered himself down the slope. He was incoherent, badly suffering the effects of altitude, possibly even suffering from cerebral oedema. All I could do was wait until he'd reached the next anchor point – two climbers on the same pitch of line was too dangerous.

'Hey buddy, what's going on?' Al shouted from above.

'We need move fast!' I heard another voice, I think Pasang's, above him.

'It's xxxxxxxx. He's suffering. Holding me up. Not responding!' I shouted back. 'Can't do anything yet!'

When he'd reached the next anchor point, I again abseiled quickly down to meet him.

'We've got to keep moving, mate!' I urged next to him. 'Are you okay? We've got a queue above, just keep putting one foot in front of the other! You can do it. Just don't stop; keep moving!'

Again, he didn't respond with anything. My memories briefly transformed back to my descent from Everest where, with a broken mask and no oxygen for sixteen hours of the eighteen-hour climb, I'd also ground to a near halt. I knew what he was suffering. Knew that he probably couldn't even make sense of what I was saying, if even hear me. Knew he was in his own world of utter turmoil, as I was eight years earlier. Yet stopping wasn't an option, keeping moving was essential.

There have been many criticisms over the years of climbers passing struggling or dying climbers on Everest, many of which have been scathing in their ferocity. Few, if any, of the protagonists, however, realize what it is like up there. The idea of putting a debilitated teammate over one's shoulder and helping him down is physically impossible when you're struggling to survive yourself. On the major rescues I've witnessed at high altitude, it's taken between twelve to seventeen Sherpas to carry one stricken climber down, such is the exhaustion of any physical exercise above 6,000 metres. Above 8,000, you are on your own – rarely can anyone move up to rescue you. Critics forget that no one has forced any of us to venture to such extreme heights; it's been a completely free choice we all make amidst all the dangers.

Suffering myself on the descent, in menacing conditions and on a threatening eighty-degree ice slope, all I could do was to urge him on, try and get through to him and, above all, keep him awake. That was all I could do. And hope he had his own mantra, motivation, God or reason to keep going. After all, when things get really, really, tough, there are only two choices. You either give up. Or you fight like hell. There was never a question of stopping until the 'finish line' was crossed. There is always a reserve if you're stubborn enough to demand it.

When we eventually reached the traverse, my suffering friend took a breather and, checking he was coherent enough to get down, I passed him. There would be many others climbing down, but, aside from the seven climbers who'd summited earlier, as the person at the front of the next batch of climbers I needed to keep going.

I crossed the traverse gingerly. This was the atrociously exposed traverse across a near-vertical ice wall with a drop thousands of metres below me. The ice fell away beneath my feet, as I dug my crampons into a wall I could barely see in the white-out conditions. My right foot crampon point slipped from the hard ice, my entire weight hanging on one inch of crampon of my left foot and an ice axe point thrust into the wall above me. I carefully placed the crampon again into the ice, sliding down the line a foot, before repeating the process. It was slow, delicate and formidable.

Eventually completing the traverse under the treacherous ice seracs, Al caught up with me for a minute. It was now getting dark. The blue walls of the ice creaked and groaned under the strain of their weight.

'How you … feeling?' I rasped, from nineteen hours of being on the move without a break.

'This is … by far … the most … dangerous … difficult … mountain I've ever … been on,' Al responded between his panting, his usually booming voice reduced to a whisper.

'It's … never-ending.'

'My brain … can barely … take any more.'

'I'm in agony … too; desperate … for a dump.'

'One more section … let's go.'

We scaled down below the ice seracs to the top of the Bottleneck. Weakened and drained and now in darkness, this was where we needed to be as alert as we'd been the entire climb. The adrenaline was coursing through my body unchecked, urging me to move when everything in me wanted to stop. I felt more awake than I'd ever been, but I knew that was a fake mask. We were totally frazzled, yet knew that we needed to 'give it our all' – meaning giving until you think you're spent and then finding more to give anyway. It was the kind of endurance that transcends the normal capabilities of a human body. One which demonstrated the immense reserves that our bodies can possess when crisis hits, and one that experience gives us the knowledge and skill to tap into, despite being completely debilitated.

I descended slowly, searching for hand holds. I knew they were there somewhere, I just couldn't see them. Then, by feel alone, the steep couloir appeared. Rappelling down slowly, it looked even steeper than when we ascended. It was an impending, deadly and unstable gully that we were in, descending in a vulnerable and perilous position, with rocks and ice sporadically raining down on us from above. Again, we prayed that the 150-metre-high ice seracs would hold.

After an hour's descent of the Bottleneck, we reached the last fixed line. All that was now required was the trek along the gradually reducing angle of the shoulder to Camp 4. The weather cleared somewhat and the head torches of the camp could be seen. At 7.30 p.m. Al and myself finally stumbled into Camp 4, dehydrated, cold, hungry and spent. We'd made it back from the summit alive, with just one final leg to complete to reach safety.

On arriving back at Camp 4, the first thing I did was dump my pack, rip off my harness and walk twenty metres to the side to squat down and relieve myself. After twenty-one hours of climbing in pain, without being able to perform a 'number two', the relief virtually made me cry. I will spare the reader any more details, but it wasn't pretty. I didn't care who was looking – privacy and morals went completely out of the window. Burying my effluence, I walked back to our tent and collapsed inside, Al arrived a minute or so after.

'That ... that was so lucky,' I croaked as he fell into the tent.

'We sure were,' came the reply.

'Adrian, Al, is that you?' Chris shouted weakly from the neighbouring tent.

'Yes, yes, we're here!' I retorted.

'We were very close to turning back.'

'We are very, very fortunate.'

We were too exhausted to say much else. With no sleep at all for two days and only fitful sleep for the previous three nights, the temptation to collapse immediately into a deep slumber was immensely powerful. However, we were also badly dehydrated from the extreme efforts exerted at these altitudes with little water and very hungry. It took an almighty effort to brew up some liquid and food. Then more problems were encountered.

'Hey, my mat's missing!' Al grunted in shock.

'What you mean?'

'I left it here with all my kit, and it's gone!'

'Serious?'

'FUCK!' he gasped, 'My spare oxygen bottle isn't here either!'

Al ventured outside searching in vain for his mattress and bottle, shouting out if anyone had been in our tent or had seen it. No one had. He was notably distressed as he fell back into the tent after five minutes.

'Someone's stolen it. It's the only explanation,' he groaned.

'I don't believe it,' I uttered, sadly believing it all.

'Another scar on the integrity of climbers.'

'Yes, it's going to be a cold night.'

With the small amount of oxygen in his summit bottle soon running out and no mat to sleep on, Hancock endured a bitterly cold night lying on the bare tent floor, despite being dressed in his entire collection of clothing. There was little I could do, exhausted as I was myself. After some food and drink and a quick call to my team in Abu Dhabi to let them know we were safely back in Camp 4, we fell into a fitful night's sleep. The mind acts in strange ways when deprived of oxygen and, as I had experienced before, my dreams were vivid and threatening. Parts of the climb were relived in my subconscious, danger abounded and disaster struck, causing me to wake up in shock on a few occasions. It was very sobering.

We awoke early the next morning to, thankfully, strong sunshine again, which slowly warmed our chilled bodies as we ventured outside the tents. Chris and Lakpa came outside and we gave each other a big hug. Chris alarmingly told us that they also had a bottle missing. I was furious that, even if it was just one culprit, such appalling conduct had found itself even onto the 'mountaineer's mountain'.

Looking up at K2 we saw the amazing sight of the second party of climbers ascending the steep ice after the traverse – the American team and the second international team, probably twelve to fifteen climbers in total. With lines in place, they were moving faster than we had and, barring any disaster, would also summit K2 – earlier than we had the previous day.

Other climbers emerged from their tents and we all shared our experiences and congratulations as we gazed up at our compatriots who would be enduring their own personal battles. There was no sign of Nurbu and Luo, who were still inside their tent – although it would have taken stamina beyond the norm for them to be having 'Chinese lessons' at this altitude.

It was tempting to sit and watch the panoramic scene unfold in front of us and rest our aching bodies, but we had a highly demanding descent to navigate down to Base Camp to follow. We were also still at nearly 8,000 metres, and the cells in our minds and bodies would be dying rapidly due to the lack of oxygen. Descent to lower altitudes was demanded and quickly. We loaded up our packs and descended to Camp 3. Although the shortest distance of any of the climbs between camps, I felt totally spent and took far longer to descend than I anticipated.

A brief brew and some food, as well as the lower altitude, perked me up slightly and we descended the dangerous slopes down to Camp 2. It was delicate and relatively slow, being so easy to make a mistake at this late stage. At Camp 2, we loaded more equipment onto our now-bulging back packs and climbed down to Camp 1. As with the descent to Camp 2, rocks were flying down regularly and it was a precarious descent – on one occasion a massive boulder, half a metre in diameter, came flying just two metres past us.

'ROCK!! HUGE ROCK!' I screamed as my voice echoed through the valley.

'Rocks!'

'Rocks!'

'Rocks, Rocks!' could be heard from above and below, and from my own echoed voice.

After a brief stop at Camp 1, we descended the ice and snow slopes to ABC. In the heat of the past few days the snow was now a deep, watery sludge with mountain streams being heard flowing rapidly under the ice. It was tricky and wet and I got thoroughly soaked on one slip into the slush.

At ABC, the entire Pakistani team gathered together to welcome their team down. They were thrilled, as we all were, and greetings cascaded between all of us – a fitting finale of camaraderie between locals and visitors. By this time, we'd been descending for over nine hours and darkness was approaching. Al and myself packed our final kit remaining at ABC and with a load now weighing a ton, slowly descended to Base Camp. On the glacier, Ali the cook-hand had trekked up with a hot flask of tea in his flip flops to meet us.

'Sir, sir, well done!' he said, with genuine emotion in his eyes.

'Ali, you are a star!' I weakly replied, as we guzzled the warm contents into our chilled core.

'We vote you President of Pakistan!' Al added, to warm gratitude from our Pakistani friend.

With Ali carrying our duffel bags, we trekked on to meet Dawa and some of the other Base Camp team meeting us on the moraine, with more hot drinks and food.

'Congratulations, Adrian! Congratulations, Al! This is fantastic!'

'Thanks Dawa for all your help. We are very privileged,' Al responded.

Then, finally, to yet another welcome from the cooks and those there, we entered Base Camp. I dropped my pack by my tent in the darkness and we walked down to the mess tent to be met by tea and a freshly made pizza.

'Al, congratulations, mate! We did it!' I said, as we finally embraced.

'Adrian, I am overwhelmed. Congratulations buddy. We were right to come back this year!' he responded.

It was a show of solidarity, trust, understanding, friendship and bonding forged over two very different expeditions on the mountain. We were finally at Base Camp, finally safe, finally secure. Only now could we relax and recognize the enormity of what we had achieved, our elation eclipsed only by exhaustion. We had summited K2. And, most importantly, got back down again.

CHAPTER SEVENTEEN

RETURN TO REALITY

FOR LIFE AND DEATH ARE ONE,
EVEN AS THE RIVER AND THE
SEA ARE ONE.

– KHALIL GIBRAN

MY FIRST SLEEP IN BASE CAMP, after returning from our epic six days' summit push, was long and deep. Physical and mental exhaustion, chronic sleep deprivation and the toil of focusing on a serious technical climb over the six previous days had left me utterly drained. Now my mind and body could finally quieten down and I slept longer than I had on any night of the previous seven weeks. It was heavenly.

Monday, 28 July felt like the day after the party the night before. It was a daze. The enormity had yet to sink in and mental and physical fatigue and exhaustion neutered any exhilaration or excitement to that of a deeply ingrained sense of satisfaction instead. It was of a job well done, but of being humbled rather than triumphant over it. I went onto my Facebook page and saw the many hundreds of congratulations and comments which made me feel even more humbled. I had no idea just how many people had been following, most of whom had been intensely worried. I posted some summit pictures, said we were now finally safe, and thanked everyone sincerely for their support. Throughout the day, interspersed with eating and sleeping, I couldn't take my eyes off K2.

At the end of the day, our American co-located team of Garrett Madison, Matt Du Puy and Alan Arnette returned to Base Camp, along with the second international team, after their successful summit the day after us. We heartily congratulated them all as they arrived at our mess tent. Alan, who had become the oldest American to summit the mountain, looked totally wiped out. After sharing our respective stories, challenges and struggles of line fixing, the Bottleneck, the ice seracs, traverse, vertical ice and the summit, I thought time was ripe to finish on a lighter topic.

'Did you see Al's legacy on the ledge?' I asked. 'His pile of manure!'

'Oh, that's who it was!' Matt replied. 'We saw this frozen turd and I walked over and kicked it into China!' he added to laughter around the tent.

'Kicking the shit into China – US-Sino relations plummet to an all-time low!'

'Yes, I can see a major diplomatic incident arising and ambassadors being expelled. We'll just blame the Canadians!'

'Man, I have never been so embarrassed in my entire life,' Al said. 'Twelve people looking straight at me having a dump and then having to get a Sherpa to do my zip up!' he added to roars of laughter.

'We've named the ledge Hancock Point!' Chris announced.

'Hancock Point, oh jeez!' Al sighed.

With over forty climbers managing to summit K2 on 26 and 27 July, and the Polish team, along with Bulgarian Boyan Petrov – who'd summited Broad Peak on 23 July – still on a late summit push, the 2014 season was heading to be one of the most successful years in K2's history. However, the mountain's dark side again revealed itself in two separate incidents.

The first involved the climber who I'd encountered struggling on the descent. The reason for keeping his name anonymous was due to his subsequent claim that he had summited the mountain.

'No, he didn't make the summit.' Al said to one of the climber's teammates, who asked us where we'd last seen him.

'Impossible.' I added. 'He was wearing the same red down suit as me and the first I saw of him was when we were descending the steep ice below the ledge. I was right behind him and he was struggling.'

'Yes, I know. No one saw him near the summit,' came the reply, with a distinct sigh.

Other climbers verified that he had probably turned back around Hancock Point at 8,400 metres. I felt sorry for the individual, who was a nice guy who had attempted the mountain before. However, the fact remained that he didn't summit, but claimed he did. It left an uneasy feeling in camp, particularly with his teammates, who said the atmosphere was tense. Panos Athanasiadis, the Greek climber who also turned back suffering from exhaustion, was particularly indignant, saying that honesty was paramount. He would later launch a formal procedure to refute the wrongdoer's summit claims. However, after gathering statements from many on the mountain, the miscreant's national Alpine body said that there was 'insufficient evidence' to strip the transgressor of his summit. Denial continuing amongst some organizations and so another 'disputed' summit was added to the growing list.

The second incident was tragically learned on the morning of 30 July, prior to our heading off from Base Camp on the long trek home. Miguel Alvarez, the second Spanish climber, was found dead in his tent at Camp 4. He had climbed with the first wave of summit attempts on the night of 25–26 July but also turned around 300 metres short of the summit and returned to Camp 4. He then launched a second attempt the following evening, 27 July, and reportedly made the summit on 28 July, although that was unsubstantiated. Alvarez was forced to spend that night in a bivouac above the Bottleneck on his descent and only made it down to Camp 4 on the morning of 29 July. According to American-Brazilian climber, Cleo Weidlich, who had arrived at Camp 4 with her Sherpa team via the Cesen route, he appeared okay and they spent the evening of 29 July talking, drinking and eating. However, by the morning, his four days in the 'death zone' had proved too much and his name was sadly added to the long list of experienced climbers killed on K2. Ferran Latorre, his teammate, was forced to spend several further days at Base Camp organizing retrieval of possessions and notifying relatives and the authorities. It was a sobering reality check on what we all thought would be a fatality free season on the mountain. As always, nature had the last word.

On an additional darker matter, Al, Lakpa and Chris confided in me with their suspicions of the reasons for their missing oxygen and mat. Desperation to summit can sometimes cause desperate actions …

    With the army of porters arriving on the morning of 30 July, most teams on K2 headed off towards Concordia. I was the last one to leave Base Camp as I wanted to perform one more ritual on my way. That was to pay my final visit to the Gilkey Memorial. As before, I needed some alone time to process the events of the past week, if not the past two years, and to pay my final respects to the fallen.

    Scrambling up to the rocks, I once more sat down in the warm sunshine and scanned the rows of plaques, plates and memorials which shone in the sun's strong rays. I wondered just how many, or how few, of their families or friends would ever make such an arduous trek to pay their last respects to their loved ones. They were the unlucky ones, I was fortunate. How cruel life was for these countless names before me, I wondered, as I touched the assortment of memorials with an involuntary gesture of caring and remembering. I spent several lost minutes looking at the plate for Marty and Denali Schmidt, and remembered the solemn events of a year before as we stood with our heads bowed at this very spot. Their tragic story had been a catalyst and offered insight into the futility of climbing and our failure in 2013. Yet they also provided an even greater insight into why mountaineers climb and our success of 2014. Neither they, nor any of their deceased companions at this lonely outpost, expected to die. Yet death smiles on all of us; all we can do is smile back. My mind flashed back to my childhood, to the 12-year-old boy who determined that only with the honest knowledge that one day I would also die, could I truly begin to live. What we did in life echoes in eternity. That's why my fallen friends here died; because they truly lived …

    After slowly descending the hill, I pulled on my pack which I had left at the bottom of the hill and continued alone on the two-hour trek to Concordia, a good two hours behind everyone else. It was what I wanted, a time of silent reflection, contemplation, remembrance and rumination. I was in a deeper zone than ever and, once again, I stopped frequently to look back on K2, lost in a different world.

    The moraine was shifting, the glacial streams were flowing rapidly; summer was again upon us in the high Karakoram as I approached Concordia, the junction of the Baltoro glacier which provided the first and last sight of K2. I stopped for five minutes to take a final gaze at the mountain. It was almost without doubt the last time I would ever set my eyes upon her. There would never be any sane reason to tackle K2 for a second time and I couldn't ever envisage returning to purely trek to Base Camp. The only other reason for revisiting Concordia would be for the purpose of climbing either Broad Peak, G1 or G2 – the respective twelfth, eleventh and thirteenth highest mountains in the world. If I was attempting any of these three giants, it would only be if I was aiming to climb all fourteen eight-thousanders – something I absolutely had no intention of doing. So, as K2 stood aloft in a brooding sense of serenity, calmness and placidity, it was a parting and a farewell. A final farewell to an iconic mountain; to a monument which embodied everything of humankind's striving to stretch the boundaries of possibility; and to a symbol that defined the limitless power of nature far and above mankind's futile attempts to tame it. It was also a farewell to the mountain that I had formed an even deeper and intimate relationship with than the previous year; one which had allowed me to reach her hallowed summit; and one that had spared me the fate of so many before me.

'Goodbye my friend.' I uttered quietly. 'And thank you.'

I walked on to some tents at Concordia, and sat down with some Sherpas and our Pakistani hosts to devour some lunch, before trekking on to Goro II. There I met up with the others. There was the emphatic closeness, bonding, laughter and fun of a team who had experienced success. From Goro II we trekked direct to Pieu on 31 July, bypassing Urdokas where we only stopped for lunch. On 1 August, we trekked from Pieu direct to Askole, stopping for lunch at Jola on the way. Fully acclimatized it thus took us just three days to trek from K2 Base Camp to Askole – a journey that had taken over twice that time on the way in. They were long and hard days, but all of us wanted to return home as soon as we could and it was measurably easier than the previous year. We were fatigued, yes, but with a spring in our step flushed from our success, we had time to cherish every moment, conversation and memory together, and to savour the magnificence of our surroundings, with every rock face, flower, insect and bird appreciated for its beauty and its life. Even the eight-hour drive from Askole to Skardu – which frequently required us to walk around, over and through washed-out roads and mountain rivers – didn't seem anywhere near the hardship experienced before.

We spent two nights and a day in Skardu and, on hearing that all flights to Islamabad were heavily overbooked for the next week, it was decided to organize a bus for the two-day drive to Islamabad. This would be along the infamous Karakoram Highway that passed through notable hotspots such as the town of Chilas. Any thoughts that a dozen Western climbers and the same number of Nepalese Sherpas would be transported incognito were dismissed as a large shining bus arrived at Hotel Concordia, emblazoned with 'K2 TOURS' on its side.

'Are they serious?' Matt Du Puy laughed.

'Not quite as inconspicuous as I'd imagined!' Alan Arnette chipped in.

'K2 Tours!'

'It's basically a giant sign saying, "Hello all you Taliban, here we are!"' I added.

We bade a fond farewell to the great team of Nazir Sabir Expeditions, who had efficiently and effectively organized a highly complicated logistical operation to enable us to complete our goal. We said farewell to the Concordia owner, Sher Ali, and to the town of Skardu, the Karakoram and the people of Baltistan. It truly was a beautiful landscape, and everything Pakistan needed to display to the world, rather than the dismal sights we normally saw on our screens. Perhaps I would indeed return again, I said to myself.

There was one man who Al and myself both wanted to help-Ali the cook-hand. He had been a gem throughout both years, a kind, thoughtful and immensely supportive man who would and did do anything for us. His wages would be sparse and so we both gave him a heavy tip which would enable him to support his family. He thanked us wholeheartedly with tears in his eyes. He was just one man of Baltistan, but a symbol of our appreciation to this entire region of Pakistan.

The journey to Islamabad passed through some further stunning scenery on the first day. We also drove passed Nanga Parbat, the scene of the massacre of a year before and, alone of the Pakistan eight-thousanders, devoid of any climbers in 2014 by government order. Interestingly, the famous sign, at a point on the highway which offered the best view of the ninth highest mountain in the world, had been amended. It now read:

> *Look to your left*
> *Nanga Parbat*
> *Height 8,126 metres*
> *26,660 feet*

Between 'Look to your left' and 'Nanga Parbat' a second line had been obscured by green paint. It used to state the words that the mountain was referred to – 'Killer Mountain'. Tragically, the 'Killer Mountain' had proved only too true on that fateful day of 23 July 2013, when the Taliban had murdered ten climbers and a cook in cold blood. Silence fell upon all of us as we gazed at the mountain with the now tarnished history.

With the heat steadily increasing in our painfully air-stifled bus, we endured the final eight hours drive into the furnace and smog-infested metropolis of Islamabad, arriving at 4 p.m. I had no intention of hanging around and sorted my equipment into two piles – one to go back to Kathmandu, where I store much of my high-altitude gear, and the other with me on my impending flight to the UAE. As I headed off with my loads, I gave a heartfelt hug and farewell to my extended teammates who had contributed so much to the expedition – the Americans, Garrett, Matt and Alan; the Sherpanis, Maya, Pasang and Dawa; Chris and Lakpa; and Luo Jing. Then to our Sherpa team whose efforts were fundamental to our triumph – Dawa, both the Lakpas, Nurbu, Pemba and the others, plus Purba and Kami, of Garrett's team, for their efforts and blessings with the puja. And, finally, to Al – my teammate, close companion and now lifelong friend, with our mutual trust largely beyond comparison. Unlike the mountain, I would undoubtedly see him and the others on future climbs – the world of high-altitude mountaineering is fairly close-knit – so it wasn't a final farewell, but a mere temporary departure.

I headed to the airport to catch my 7 p.m. flight to Abu Dhabi, arriving well after midnight. After a day sorting out stuff in Dubai, I flew to the UK on 4 August 2014 and had my beloved daughter, Charlotte, in my arms that afternoon.

'Charlotte!' I shouted as she was dropped off at Basingstoke station.

'Daddy!' she screamed in delight as she ran into my arms.

'I love you so much my Princess!'

'I love you so much Daddy. I missed you too much!'

'I'm back now sweetie and won't ever let you go …'

She was too young to understand the significance of the warmest, closest and longest hugs and kisses I had ever given her but loved the affection, as she always did. My gratitude for being able to hold her in my arms again affected me profoundly and my thoughts briefly ventured to those girls and women who would never have the chance to be held by their father, partner or brother again.

The slow readaption to so-called reality would take several weeks, if not months, and the other major issues in my life would need to be addressed in due course, but now wasn't the time. It was a time for gratitude for conquering a mighty goal; for being alive to tell the tale; for living in the present and to give the love, time and interest to what truly matters in life – our family, relationships and friends, all of whom had astonished me with their sincerest concerns, support and, yes, love. I would write or speak to the vast majority in the coming weeks, but, for now, my complete focus was on my adoring and adored daughter. I was finally home.

CHAPTER EIGHTEEN

THE LIVING YEARS

SOMETIMES YOU HAVE TO
GO UP REALLY HIGH TO
UNDERSTAND HOW SMALL YOU
REALLY ARE.

– FELIX BAUMGARTNER

IN CLIMBING TERMS, i.e. planning, preparing, training, failing and succeeding, my project to climb K2 took over two and a half years of my life. The lessons, ramifications and implications of K2, however, together with my accompanying personal journey, continue to this day. All the major quests in my life, not just expeditions, have been life changing experiences and the journey and aftermath of K2 has been one of the greatest. Challenges and pain are part of life and it's the challenges we face in life which define the person we become.

To mountaineering first. All told, a total of forty-eight climbers, plus one disputed, managed to summit K2 in the 2014 season on four separate days of 26, 27, 28 and 31 July. Although it wasn't the greatest number of climbers to summit in a single season – that honour goes to 2004 when fifty-one climbers summited over six separate summit pushes – the success of thirty-two confirmed climbers reaching the top on 26 July was the single highest total on any day in K2's history.

Inevitably, after such an accomplished season, there would be some feature articles in the climbing press, syndicated to some national papers in the following weeks and months, asking 'is K2 the next Everest?' The 'new Everest' question, however, is widely off the mark and, having summited both, I can reasonably conclude they are worlds apart. Some go even further: 'Everest and K2 aren't even the same sport,' says expedition guide Chris Szymiec in the trailer for the film *K2: Siren of the Himalayas* (directed by Dave Ohlson, released 20 February 2014).

Whilst extreme physical fitness, determination, ability at altitude, reaction to supplementary oxygen, good experience and a hefty bank balance will enable one to have a good chance of summiting Everest, the demands of K2 are extraordinary. As written, with its vicious and sustained steepness and technicality, those attempting K2 need to be highly competent ice and rock climbers with both ability and self-sufficiency, capable of moving quickly at extreme altitude with a heavy pack. The entire climb is inordinately difficult, greatly exposed and totally committing, with no quick and easy descents off the mountain. Add in the notoriously poor and unpredictable weather, the unstable and dangerous snow and ice conditions, and the constant rock fall and avalanche dangers and it makes for a gargantuan challenge. You have to be on your game 100 per cent, can't make any mistakes and the ordeal in attempting to reach the top is colossal. It doesn't end there – descending the 300-metre steep ice slope, the traverse above the eighty-to-ninety-degree ice wall and the dangerous Bottleneck couloir are desperate features for an exhausted climber to be encountering on their summit day, as history has only too frequently tragically demonstrated. We suffer alone up there, in a place we do not belong and our pain and turmoil is quite personal.

Only our fortuitous combination of great weather, excellent snow conditions, skilled climbers, adequate support and a lot of luck allowed us to achieve the ultimate goal in mountaineering, and the statistics speak for themselves. For myself, that achievement doesn't make me anywhere near being a great mountaineer – there are countless better climbers than I will ever be, who merely didn't have the opportunity, desire, acceptance of the risks or the conditions to either attempt or succeed on K2. Summiting the mountain changes little and, aside from the required attributes mentioned, all I brought to enable it to happen was a clear goal, without bluffing or denial; a clear reasoning and observation of risk and reward; a willingness to step into fear, and the fine line between self-belief and arrogance. Far from returning triumphant, I came back with humility and humbleness.

It is the deeper lessons learned from K2 that, to me, are more enlightening than the pure achievement. One of these was my connection to nature, which has never been more profound. Nature does not hurry, yet everything is accomplished. In every long walk in the wild we receive far more than we seek. It provides an answer to most of our issues in the world. Yet, under the onslaught of technology which I have referred to many times in despair, we are becoming increasingly divorced, to our peril, from our natural world.

On a city street, I am a walking wallet, a consumer and an object of the world's relentless need for economic growth. There are rules and regulations, laws and conduct, authority, rank and titles, to which we are expected to conform. In nature, I am just another organism, another animal salvaging food, water and shelter, connecting with my kindred spirit and free to run, hike, swim, climb or shout at the top of my voice, with an echo reverberating across a valley of hills. I am wild, untameable and a free spirit, yet one who lives in a tribe and a community. I have time to contemplate, to think and to just 'be'. It is fulfilling, it is liberating and it is the essence of freedom to bask in the new greenness of spring, the heat of a sultry summer, the brilliant shades of fall and the stark beauty of winter.

Although one can gain that connection in the woods, the magnitude, stature and power of K2 and the Karakoram, provided the most intimate connection with nature that, along with Antarctica, I have ever experienced. In both years, I felt my lungs inflate with the onrush of fresh air, trees, rivers, mountains, sky, sun, stars and people and thought 'this is what it is to be happy'. It was also a reminder that nature is not there for us, the world is not a gift to humanity. We are creatures of nature, just the same as any other, only with a few more toys and a bigger ego.

Along with this connection came the related matter of observation. That is having one's antennas fully extended to see, hear, listen, smell, feel or sense what is happening in the world around us. It is a sense that humans are also gradually losing as technology encroaches on every aspect of our lives, yet is fundamental to our very existence. And, again, my experience on K2 provided my observation and awareness muscles with far-reaching and astute development. My very life often depended on it and when life is stripped down to its bare essentials, it is astonishing what we can observe, both visually, auditorily and kinaesthetically. I returned from K2 with these antennas extended further than ever before, and the implications in so-called 'normal life' have been both advantageous and problematic. The benefits include such innate and varied matters as route finding, locating my car in a car park and always being the first to hear a speech starting at a function – when, invariably, I have to give the 'shhhh' to those around me continuing their conversations oblivious to what's happening on stage. On a more detrimental note, I wake up at night with the slightest sound, cough, dog barking or car moving and often have to sleep with a fan on to provide some 'white noise'.

Further related to both connection with nature and acute observation, came the no small matter of gut instinct. That feeling, knowing, listening and, if wise, acting on these stimuli, is also being lost amidst a flood of information, and we are losing touch with the natural world. I've increasingly developed and learned to listen to my gut instinct muscles in the past ten years and they came back stronger than ever before from K2. In 2013, it told me throughout that everything 'didn't feel right' but ego probably masked it for some of the time until the tragic events of 27 July that year. As a consequence, and having ventured into some further work on the subject, it was a deep-seated reason for my, thankfully successful, return in 2014. I now use gut instinct more than any copious SWOT analysis, risk assessments or due diligence reports in all walks of my life, and the results have been sagacious. Looking back on the past, I also recall the times that I allowed other emotions to override my gut instinct and the consequences usually proved profound.

All three of these deeper learnings are intrinsically linked and all connected with energy. Scientists are only just beginning to understand how our ancient civilizations, who, above all, had the time to think, connect and contemplate with this energy, used such enlightenment with unfathomable, mystifying and far reaching results.

On wider lessons learned, I have been lucky to have been able to look down on our planet from the top, bottom and roof of the world (Everest, South Pole and North Pole) and, on each of those journeys and occasions, the perception of our world and our lives on it was shifted. K2 added to this greatly. When one tackles death head on, when life is stripped to those bare elements and when one is in complete connection with rock, ice, sun, sky and stars, our priorities in life take on a whole new meaning. I look at materialism, consumerism, vast possessions and flash cars with amusement – even though I'm a 'petrol head' F1 fan. They mean nothing at 8,000 metres and, in reality, should mean little at sea level. None of them ever bring happiness or fulfilment and, indeed, merely add to the clutter and chaos of our lives.

I look at the world's incessant drive for economic growth at all costs, at the expense of our society and our environment, and its astronomical debt of over 230 trillion dollars with total disbelief. All of us – individuals, families, cities, governments, countries and the world are living completely beyond our means with such detrimental effects to our planet. It is a world in complete denial and the failure of governments, environmental groups and campaigners to even address the three greatest impacts on the environment – our unsustainable numbers on earth, economic growth and our consumption of animal products – are the height of naivety.

I look at conflict as something so utterly futile, whether it's a fall out over something someone says on social media, a divorce, a punch up in a street or a terrorist attempting to murder hundreds. On the latter, I'd love to take a moth-brained Taliban, Al Qaeda or Daesh terrorist up to 8,000 metres and see how he struggles. Be it any of those examples, or countless more, life since K2 simply feels too short, too precious and too beautiful to waste on such life-diminishing emotions and energies, or their manifestations of hate, bitterness or resentment. As Lao-tzu, the ancient Chinese philosopher, wrote in his timeless quote, 'If there is to be peace in the world …' it all eventually comes down to peace in the heart. Or, in other words, the 'stuff' that all of us carry from our childhood, from parents, siblings, order of birth, housing, environment, education, friendships and so on, but which many people won't or can't see, let alone address. Even to those who've transgressed me, I try to feel compassion, for if I retaliate, I haven't learnt anything.

There have, however, been negative implications on tackling both K2 and all the other extreme adventures I've embarked on.

One is the sacrifices I, and others like me, have had to make. Eugene Cernan, the last man to walk on the moon, who died on 16 January 2017, admitted he had been an absent husband and father, saying, 'We were so tunnel-visioned about going to the moon that we never had time to get off that big white horse we were riding until it was too late.' Marty Schmidt, were he alive, would probably say the same, as would most mountaineers, explorers and adventurers with families. I am no different. Like many, I deeply regret not spending more time with my children when they were young – although I am probably similar to many senior executives caught in the pressures of a high intensity job. That was only a part reason for the tumultuous personal circumstances I have found myself in but, as I wrote in my Facebook post prior to leaving for K2 in 2014, there is the matter of living your values, your truth and your purpose. The key with loved ones, when frequent absences are involved, is quality in the absence of quantity, and I have strived to give this to my fullest in the past few years.

I have noticed other, less critical but notable, implications from my two years attempting K2. On returning home, my free spirit, which has had to be muted at many stages in my life, seems to have been completely unleashed. It may have to be reined in for future circumstances, but it is part of my core values and my truth. Whilst that may sound positive, there are some negatives. One is an increasingly frequent disregard for rules and regulations – I realize they are important for an orderly society but they just don't seem so valid anymore. And I view authority, rank and titles with indifference. None of them mean anything above 8,000 metres either and, since returning, mean far less now. I've also come to look for, subconsciously and perhaps even relish, challenges and possibly even trouble. I guess it's called living on the edge. I arrive for many flights about an hour and fifteen minutes only prior to departure, and, yes, I've missed a couple in the past few years. On trying to find a parking space, I will often search in near glee for some back alley, waste ground or unmetered space to park my car – not to save a dollar, but purely for the challenge. And, yes, I get my fair share of parking tickets, but they don't really matter either. Or, on encountering a traffic jam, will search with similar zeal for any way I can overcome that obstacle, sometimes acting in, let's say, 'unusual' ways, for example, driving through a building site or over a grass bank in my 4WD to find an escape. I've not broken any law, but I guess it's beyond what most people would attempt. For all of these examples, and others; overcoming the challenges pushes a boundary line and gives an immense feeling of liberation.

On my personal challenges and struggles that were intertwined with K2, all I will write is that we all have our own 'Everests', even those who conquer mighty goals. The change over the last few years has been to try and see these challenges in the bigger picture. Not just the passive 'everything happens for a reason' mindset; rather the active 'things happen; it's up to us to find the reason'. Out of our deepest pain comes the greatest gifts, but only when we take control of the meaning. We can be a victim, a casualty or bury ourselves in self-pity, or we can find the greatest learnings of our lives. Life can only be understood backwards; but it must be lived forwards and there is a universal order that everything works out exactly how it was meant to.

I have noticed a distinct shift in my attitude to a subject which I've faced and mentioned many times, that of death. It is the one certainty in all of our lives and yet the least spoken of, with most of us preferring to live in denial. Without doubt the facing of death has made me more attuned to the priorities in life, to living fuller than ever before and, in all irony, to being more alive. That 'living on the edge'; the reminder that courage isn't the absence of fear, rather the willingness to face it; the appreciation of that which is around us and the gratitude for what we have, rather than what we don't have, are lessons for all and it doesn't take summiting K2 to find them. Death comes to everyone and, although I'd prefer it not to be for another sixty years or more – as I have so many things I still wish to do and because it's the only life I will ever have (on this earth at least) – I am not afraid of it. The universe seems to have a plan for all of us, and when my time's up, it's up. What facing death does do is to make one treasure one thing above all - our health. 'Without health, you have nothing!' my late father, Con Hayes, used to say. Whilst mentioning him, we will only ever have one father, one mother and one set of siblings and I celebrate the ancestry which he and my living mother, Linda, gave myself, my elder brother Damian and my younger brother Eugene.

The key nuggets that bind all these lessons together are consciousness, awareness and mindfulness, which are integral parts of my work and the reasons I do what I do. When we evolve, when we increase our consciousness and as we become ever more aware, the short-sighted issues we vainly and presently strive for, fight for and, often, die for, will fall into insignificance. K2 magnified all of this.

I look back on my journey on K2 with wisdom from the heartaches, lessons from the pain, accomplishment, joy, laughter and memories. I miss the wind across my face, ice in my beard, the struggle to breathe and the warmth in my minus-thirty-degree-Celsius sleeping bag whilst a storm howled outside. I fondly remember the simple joys of a hot bowl of soup at 6,000 metres, warming my frozen hands on a Nalgene bottle of boiling water, and the sharing of stories alone in a high-altitude camp. I miss marvelling at a hawk soaring in the lofty breeze above the rock pillars and buttresses, the essence of freedom that I forever aspire to. I miss marvelling at the morning and evening skies – an endless canvas of pinks, oranges and reds, reflecting off the clouds and filling the world with a haze of wonder. Or the day skies, where pure uninterrupted blue stretches seamlessly across my vision. And the night skies of clear air, a billion stars that are alive, constantly moving across our horizon, and the glowing moon on the ice, lighting our path. I miss looking at clouds ripped into scales by jet stream winds blowing across the mountains. I miss the smiling faces of the Balti and the beauty of the Karakoram; the bonding of our Sherpas and the laughter of my teammates. And I miss being on and part of the brilliance, power and eternity of the 'mountaineer's mountain'.

I look back at the total trust I shared with my teammate, Al Hancock, who will be a friend for life and who I would trust with my life in any circumstance. With him and the wider team, it was and is the camaraderie we shared, the spirit of our bond, the events that shaped our collective experiences and the tests that hardened our resolve which were and are so tangible. You cannot replicate that bond and it binds you forever. The respect, the commitment, the blood; you have been through them all with the guys you stand alongside.

I remember standing solemnly at the plaques of the fallen at the Gilkey Memorial, the countless names a stark lesson of the sacrifices we make. I remember the ebullience of Marty Schmidt and the warmth of Denali Schmidt, two lives who had so much more to offer, tragically cut short ahead of time. Perhaps we will all walk, trek or climb on diverging paths forever, onwards to new adventures.

Finally, I remember the heartache of writing farewell letters to my own beloved children and the unborn son who would never know me, and of kissing them goodbye. One day they will know how much they were, and indeed are, deeply loved.

K2 is behind me and part of my history now, but I still see its shadow in everything I do. It's a reminder of the dreams I set as a young boy and my future dreams, which I hold very tightly. It's a reminder of both sadness and joy, of a profound personal journey lasting over five years of my life. It's a reminder of the shortness and fragility of our lives here on earth and what truly matters in our lives. It's a reminder that some of our greatest battles will be fought within the silent chambers of our own soul. It's a reminder of being completely human ... And it exudes a glow in my mind, body and spirit whenever I think of it – an 'Everglow' perfectly captured in Coldplay's ballad of the same name, with which I complete this story.

Oh they say people come, say people go
This particular diamond was extra special
And though you might be gone, and the world may not know
Still I see you, celestial

Like a lion you ran, a goddess you rolled
Like an eagle you circled, in perfect purple
So how come things move on, how come cars don't slow
When it feels like the end of my world
When I should but I can't let you go?

When I'm cold, cold
Yeh, when I'm cold, cold
There's a light that you give me when I'm out in shadow
There's a feeling within me, an everglow

Like brothers in blood, sisters who ride
Yeh we swore on that night we'd be friends til we die
But the changing of winds, and the way waters flow
Life as short as the falling of snow
And now I'm gonna miss you I know

When I'm cold, cold
Yeh, water rolled, salt
I know that you're always with me and the way you will show
And you're with me wherever I go
Cos you give me this feeling, this everglow

What I wouldn't give for this moment to hold
Yeah I live for this feeling this everglow
So if you love someone, you should let them know
Oh the light that you give me will everglow

EPILOGUE

SUBSEQUENT SEASONS ON K2 continued the controversies of its past history. In early 2015, the Pakistan Government issued a ruling prohibiting the employment of any Nepalese Sherpas for mountaineering in the country. The move, designed to force expeditions to employ Pakistani HAP's instead of Sherpas, was greeted with large protests by both Pakistan expedition agencies and the climbing community. All pointed out that, despite their fine qualities, there wasn't anywhere near the strength in depth of HAP's – and that, far from creating employment, the move would likely lead to dwindling expedition numbers. It was subsequently watered down, allowing Sherpas to continue on a one to one basis with HAPs, i.e. for every Sherpa employed, an expedition needed to employ an equivalent HAP.

The consequence, aided by the successes of 2014, was a hefty increase in numbers attempting the mountain for the 2015 summer season, with around ninety climbers – foreign, Sherpas and HAPs – on various expeditions. This raised large concerns amongst K2 veterans on the limited space at Camps 1 and 2, crowding on the crux sections of the climb and subsequent safety. The mountain had its own response, with treacherous snow conditions, blue ice, avalanches and rockfalls, and all teams eventually abandoned their expeditions.

The 2015 season was remembered more, however, for a far greater controversy. Swiss climber Mike Horn, back attempting K2 with his same teammates from 2013, posted a short promotional video in July 2015 which included a deceased climber's skull. The image resulted in outrage in the mountaineering press, deriding the lack of sensitivity to dead climbers who had fallen on the mountain. Foremost of these was Sequoia Schmidt. For the head looked uncannily like Denali Schmidt.

Details emerged that the head was part of some severed body parts that had emerged at the foot of the Cesen route, located en route from K2 Base Camp to Advanced Base Camp. On several telephone calls and messages with Sequoia and Chris Burke, who was back in Pakistan attempting Broad Peak, we reassured her that it couldn't be her brother – had Marty or Denali's bodies emerged at the foot of the mountain it would have been past ABC on the Chinese border. Either way, however, it failed to dampen the controversy or the anger from Schmidt. In response, not least to a public letter from her on social media, Horn initially tried to defend his post, saying he had meant no disrespect; that Marty was a friend of his; that he (Horn) had a different perspective on death and wanted to show the 'Killer Mountain' in its true sense. Notwithstanding such viewpoints, it never explained why such a shot needed to be included in a corporate video and it was eventually taken down.

Sequoia then arranged a trip to K2 Base Camp within a week, despite having little trekking experience, to identify the body parts via DNA testing and to bury the remains. Confirming that they were not those of her brother or father, she has remained confidential as to their true identity. The remains were given a proper burial, prompting questions about why none of the ninety climbers on K2, who had passed the body en route to and from ABC, had thought of doing the same. Her experience was documented in the book *Journey of Heart*[1] in which she exposed the true violent nature of being killed in an avalanche.

In 2016 an equally large number of teams assembled to attempt the mountain but another avalanche at the dangerous Camp 3, which buried tents, stored equipment and oxygen, resulted in all summit bids being abandoned once again. The only positive side was that, unlike 2013, no one was at the camp at the time. This failure meant that, since the disaster of 2008, there had only been two successful years of summits of K2, in 2012 and 2014, from the main Pakistan side in the past eight years – a statistic re-enforcing the mountain's high risk and low reward status.

In 2017 conditions were once again extremely poor, with avalanches striking Camp 3 and even ABC, fortuitously also with no one present at the time. As a result nearly all expeditions on the mountain, fewer than previous years, once again concluded that K2 was too dangerous to climb. One team, however, mounted a risky

---

[1] Sequoia Schmidt, *Journey of Heart*, Di Angelo Publications (2015).

summit attempt in a narrow weather window, and seven Sherpas and five foreign climbers summited K2 on 28 July 2017. Those of us from 2013 couldn't help observing the same 'one team went up, everyone else came down' analogy. The 2017 contemporaries got away with it but, undoubtedly, the story could equally have had the same tragic ending as the Schmidts. The fine line between life and death once more displayed on the most extreme terrain on earth.

In 2018, buoyed by the first excellent weather and snow conditions since 2014, a record number of climbers (60 plus) summitted K2, pushing total numbers of summiteers to over 400. Those numbers were helped considerably by SST finally managing to replicate their Everest model – namely a high level of Sherpa support (2:1 to team climbers), subsequent high levels of supplementary oxygen, and fixing lines to the summit. The successes, marred by two further deaths, inevitably resulted in mixed responses from the climbing community, however. Those with negative views were reinforced by news that some climbers had undertaken the minimum of rotations up the mountain before their summit push – a circumstance only possible with overly generous levels of oxygen supplementation. Suspicion was further raised by a Pakistani Liaison Officer stumbling upon 90 vials of dexamethasone in a team's Base Camp. Given that Dexi is usually the drug of last resort in treating pulmonary or cerebral oedema, it would be usual to carry a few vials in a team for emergency use only. Without passing any judgement, dexamethasone is also a banned performance-enhancing drug…

With well-known Everest expedition organizer, Russell Brice, additionally planning a future K2 expedition at $300k per head for high net-worth individuals, there will be many who feel that mountaineering ethics have now been completely lost in the quest for a 'summit at all costs'. I would only add that this is merely a consequence of the main topic in chapter one of this book, namely the social media-fuelled drive for significance, which is distorting and affecting our lives in an unhealthy manner beyond comprehension.

On the positive side, the 2018 season witnessed the first ever ski descent of K2 by Polish climber Andrzej Bargiel – who had summitted via the Cesen route without supplementary oxygen.

His amazing feat was greatly assisted by a drone, flown by his brother at Base Camp, used for route finding on the descent. The drone was also used a few days earlier in a remarkable rescue attempt on Broad Peak to locate injured Scottish climber Rick Allen, who had been missing for three days after a fall.

For my 2014 team members, Luo Jing went on to scale a further six 8,000-metre peaks and only has one remaining (Shishapangma) to become one of the very few women in the world to summit all fourteen. Meanwhile, Chris Burke, Lakpa Sherpa and Al Hancock all attempted Annapurna, the dangerous tenth highest mountain in the world, in spring 2015. Yet again, Al defied death or injury when he was hit by an avalanche whilst in his tent at Camp 4 - requiring him to dig through a metre or more of snow to escape. The expedition was aborted after the Nepal earthquake of April 2015. The mountain had killed Finnish K2 2014 colleague Samuli Mansikka and a Sherpa a few weeks earlier.

Chris and Lakpa, along with Matt Du Puy from the American team of K2 2014, returned to Annapurna in 2016 and summited on 1 May 2016, bringing her and Lakpa's total to nine 8,000-metre summits. They, together with the three Sherpanis, Maya, Pasang and Dawa, then attempted Kanchenjunga, the third highest mountain in the world in 2017, but the expeditions were aborted due to a shortage of ropes. Chris and Lakpa successfully summited the mountain in 2018 in horrific and tortuous circumstances, with Lakpa once again showing his skills as one of the most accomplished climbers in Himalayan mountaineering.

My erstwhile teammate, Al Hancock, instead of joining the Kanchenjunga expeditions, decided on a last minute quest on Lhotse (the fourth highest mountain) in 2017 and, to my delight, managed to summit at the end of May 2017. He has now completed seven eight-thousanders and is well on his way to becoming the first Canadian to complete all fourteen, for which I wish him every success.

For my own expedition postscripts, I tried to form a team to attempt Kanchenjunga in April 2015, my rationale being that, having climbed the two highest mountains on earth, I may as well continue working down the list! As I experienced in the two previous years, I failed to get a team together so, instead, launched a double attempt on number five, Makalu, followed by number four, Lhotse. We only managed to reach Camp 1 on Makalu before the Nepal earthquake of 25 April struck. After all teams agreed to abandon their expeditions, I ventured on a six-week personal quest in the hills and mountains of the country, using my knowledge of Nepali, medical training and equipment, acclimatization and expedition supplies to the fullest effect. Mindful of what I have previously written about significance, I was (and am) hesitant to make a big thing of it, but felt the benefits of publicity outweighed my reticence. It is the project MIRA Himalaya (Medicine in Remote Areas, Himalaya) that it has created, however, through follow-up medical outreach missions and medical centres, that is the real benefit and the major 'expedition' work in my life now (see Annexure F).

A spate of injuries since 2015, together with, sadly resumed ongoing personal life challenges, prevented any further expeditions in 2016 and 2017.

On my accompanying personal journey, my son Nicklas was born in California in October 2014. Notwithstanding being many miles away, I love him to bits and see him regularly. And, lastly, the hardest challenge of my entire life – that of the five years of struggles to see my beloved children – was finally concluded in July 2017. Although never about custody, my daughter Charlotte now lives with me, is my complete and total priority and, as such, major expeditions have been put on hold for the time being. I still await my oldest son Alex to return, and I look forward to a day in the future when, like the ending to the film *Seven Years in Tibet*, I am belaying him up an Alpine peak, along with Charlotte and Nicklas.

One chapter, and a five-year monumental journey of parallel paths, has subsequently closed, but a whole new adventure has just begun.

APPENDICES A-F

A: THE WORLD'S 8,000-METRE MOUNTAINS

MOUNTAIN	HEIGHT (M)	COUNTRY	FIRST SUMMIT	FIRST SUMMITEERS
1 Everest	8,848	Nepal/China	29 May 1953	Edmund Hillary (New Zealand) Tenzing Norgay (Nepal)
2 K2	8,611	Pakistan/China	31 July 1954	Achille Compagnoni (Italy) Lino Lacedelli (Italy)
3 Kanchenjunga	8,586	Nepal/India		George Band (UK) Joe Brown (UK)
4 Lhotse	8,516	Nepal/China	18 May 1956	Fritz Luchslnger (Switzerland) Ernst Reiss (Switzerland)
5 Makalu	8,485	Nepal/China	15 May 1955	Jean Couzy (France) Lionel Terray (France)
6 Cho Oyu	8,201	Nepal/China	19 Oct 1954	Joseph Joechier (Austria) Pasang Dawa Lama (Nepal) Herbert Tichy (Austria)
7 Dhaulagiri 1	8,167	Nepal	13 May 1960	Kurt Diemberger (Austria) Peter Diener (Germany) Nawang Dorje (Nepal) Nima Dorje (Nepal) Ernst Forrer (Switzerland) Albin Schelbert (Austria)
8 Manaslu	8,163	Nepal	9 May 1956	Toshio Imanishi (Japan) Gyalzen Norbu (Nepal)
9 Nanga Parbat	8,126	Pakistan	3 July 1953	Hermann Buhl (Austria)

10 Annapurna I	8,091	Nepal	3 June 1950	Maurice Herzog (France) Louis Lachenai (France)
11 Gasherbrum I	8,080	Pakistan/ China	5 July 1958	Andrew Kauffman (USA) Pete Schoening (USA)
12 Broad Peak	8,051	Pakistan/ China	9 June 1957	Fritz Wintersteller (Austria) Marcus Schmuck (Austria) Kurt Diemberger (Austria) Hermann Buhl (Austria)
13 Gasherbrum II	8,035	Pakistan/ China	7 July 1956	Fritz Moravec (Austria) Josef Larch (Austria) Hans Willenpart (Austria)
14 Shlshapangma	8,027	China	2 May 1964	Hsu Ching (China) Chang Chun-yen (China) Wang Fuzhou (China) Chen San (China) Cheng Tien-liang (China) Wu Tsung-yue (China) Sodnam Doji (China) Migmar Trashi (China) Doji (China) Yonten (China)

B: K2 2013 TEAMS

JAPANESE (2 NON-CLIMBERS)

Kitamura Seiichi
Endo Hirotaka
Sasaki Rihito
Oyabe Akira
Katayangi Norio
Higashiyama Takashi
Otomo Teruko
Yoshida Michiko

BRITISH/CANADIAN

Adrian Hayes
Al Hancock
Lakpa Sherpa
Mingma Sherpa
Chheji Nurbu Sherpa
Nima Sherpa

SPANISH

Alex Txikon
Felix Criado
Benjamin Salazar (Mexico)
Mingma Gyabu Sherpa
Jangbu Sherpa

GREEK

Alexander Aravidis
Nikoiaos Mangitsis
Pasang Namgyai Sherpa

SWISS

Mike Horn
Koby Reichen
Fred Roux

NEW ZEALAND/AUSTRALIAN

Marty Schmidt
Denali Schmidt
Chris Warner

MACEDONIA

Zdravko Dejanovic

C: KARAKORAM 2013 SEASON FATALITIES

NANGA PARBAT (8,126 M)

Badav Kashayev (Ukraine)
Dmytro Koniayev (Ukraine)
Ihor Sverhun (Ukraine)
Anton Dobes (Slovakia)
Peter Sperka (Slovakia)
Chunfeng Yang (China)
Janfeng Rao (China)
Hongiu Chen (USA-China)
Ernestas Marksaitis (Lithuania)
Sona Shepa (Nepal)
Ali Hussain (Pakistan) (cook)
All killed on 22 June 2013 by Taliban terrorist attack at Base Camp

BROAD PEAK (8,051 M)

Heidi Dana (Germany), died 7 July 2013 failing into glacial river at
Base Camp
Pouya Keivan (Iran), summited 16 July 2013, went missing on descent
Mojtaba Jarrahi (Iran), summited 16 July 2013, went missing on descent
Aidin Bozorgi (Iran), summited 16 July 2013, went missing on descent, last
    call received on 20 July 2013

GASHERBRUM 1 (8,080 M)

Artur Hajzer (Poland), died 9 July 2013 due to a fatal fall
Xavi Comez (Spain), summited 21 July 2013, went missing on descent
Abel Alonso Gomez (Spain), summited 21 July 2013, went missing on descent
Alvaro Paredes (Spain), summited 21 July 2013, went missing on descent
Zdenek Hruby (Czech Republic), died 9 August 2013 in fail on descent after
    unsuccessful attempt on new SW Face route

K2 (8,611 M)

Marty Schmidt (New Zealand), died 27 July 2013 in avalanche at Camp 3
Denali Schmidt (New Zealand), died 27 July 2013 in avalanche at Camp 3

D: K2 2014 TEAMS

SST INTERNATIONAL TEAM

Al Hancock (Canada)
Adrian Hayes (UK)
Chris Jensen Burke (New Zeaiand/Australia) Lakpa Sherpa (Nepal)
Pasang Lhamu Sherpa (Nepal)
Dawa Yangzum Sherpa (Nepal)
Maya Sherpa (Nepal)
Luo Jing (China)
Plus Sherpa support

MADISON MOUNTAINEERING TEAM (CO-LOCATED)

Garrett Madison (USA)
Alan Arnette (USA)
Matthew Du Puy (USA)
Rick Sylvester (USA)
Plus Sherpa support

OTHER TEAMS

Czech Republic
Greece
Italy
Pakistan
Polish
Spain
International Team

E: THE DENALI FOUNDATION

The Denali Foundation's purpose is the preservation of the artwork of Denali Schmidt and the ongoing support for the expansion of the minds of young artists. Current programmes for the Denali Foundation include, but are not limited to, exhibitions of the artwork of Denali Schmidt and the artistic preservation of the name and lifestyle of freedom led by the young artist Denali Schmidt. Scholarship programmes have been set up in the name of Denali Schmidt so that young artists may experience life adventures and are encouraged to creatively express those adventures through their art.

The Foundation is currently involved in expanding artistic expression of Nepali children in the Khumbu Valley region. This is being accomplished through the development and construction of an artistic and educational facility in Nepal. Future plans will include sending out ambassadors to provide art supplies and instructional programmes related to artistic creation on a local and global level, and to hold fundraising events in order to provide supplies and assistance to those schools and communities unable to afford the funding for their young generation to express themselves through art, regardless of their race, ethnicity or religion.

F: MIRA HIMALAYA

Medicine in Remote Areas, Himalaya (MIRA Himalaya), is an ongoing project to provide medical outreach camps, along with health and hygiene education, in hill and mountain communities in Nepal.

While medical treatment appears to be well catered for at road head locations and major settlements in Nepal, there is an ongoing shortfall and requirement for treatment and general health and hygiene education in the more remote hill regions of the country. Due to this remoteness and terrain, neither government or aid agency medical staff are generally able, or willing, to cover all needs from main medical bases and, for minor ailments, many villagers are not inclined to walk for many hours to reach such bases for treatment.

The project – set up by Adrian Hayes in conjunction with the Kathmandu based NGO, Mission Himalaya – aims to set up a lightweight logistics medical camp every year in the remote regions of the country. Accompanied by a Nepalese doctor, the remit is to treat and help prevent the major ailments affecting villagers, namely throat and chest infections; skin ailments (eczema, lesions, infections); skin abrasions; gastric infections and conditions; and eye infections. More serious cases are referred to road head locations. At the same time, the parties visit each school en route to deliver a short presentation on hand sanitization, coughing practices and water sanitation – the main lapses of the hill-dwelling Nepalese that are responsible for spreading these conditions.

The project may be expanded to other Himalayan countries in due course.

ACKNOWLEDGEMENTS

I wish to sincerely thank the following people and organizations for their generous support, assistance, inspiration, involvement or financing in both the completion of this book and on K2 itself:

THE BOOK

Sir Ranulph Fiennes for writing the Foreword to the book; Sequoia Schmidt for initiating the project; Eberhard Jurgalski, Bob A. Schelfhout and Fabrice Imparato for K2 statistics and history; Tess Kazim for a 'second pair of eyes' on my work; Al Hancock for additional pictures and information; Chris Burke for additional information; and Tracey Katz for helping me put it all together.

THE K2 EXPEDITIONS

IN PAKISTAN: *the 2013 Team*: Al Hancock, Lakpa Sherpa, Mingma Sherpa, Chheji Nurbu Sherpa and Nima Sherpa; *the 2014 Team*: Al Hancock, plus the wider team of Chris Burke, Lakpa Sherpa, Luo Jing, Maya Sherpa, Pasang Sherpa and Dawa Sherpa; *Seven Summits Treks*: Dawa Sherpa, Tashi Sherpa plus our Sherpa support for 2014, in particular Lakpa Sherpa and Chheji Nurbu Sherpa; *Nazir Sabir Expeditions*: Nazir Sabir, Sultan Khan, Rehmat Ali and their teams; Manzoor Hussain; and Sher Ali .

IN UAE: *My hiking colleagues*: John and Barbara Young, Jon and Helen Rodd, Wolfgang and Sonja Aeugle, Darryl Chiles, Kevin West, Sean James, Cath Todd, Tanya Appleyard, Rachel Delaunay and Giles Richardson; *My rock climbing colleagues*: John Gregory, Dee McEnery, Aiden Laffey, Tim Richards, Philip Delaunay and Shahan Contractor.

ELSEWHERE: Fabrice Imparato; Henry Todd; Lisa Read; Bexta Tierney; and Frances Ber.

SUPPORT SPONSORS: JA Resorts and Hotels (David Thomson); Thuraya (Raouf Khalifa); Xtra-Link (Hans Kruijt); California Chiropractic and Sports Medicine Centre (Charles Jones); Ten Twenty (Patrick De Jong); ZSI Trading / Marmot (Dewald van der Wath); MEFITPRO (Greg Boucher); and Dubai Podiatry Centre (Michelle Champlin).

GLOSSARY

abseil – The process by which a climber can descend a fixed rope. Also known as rappel.

alpine climbing – Climbing with the primary aim to reach the summit of a mountain, by ascending high rock faces or pinnacles.

alpine style – Lightweight, fast climbing that emphasizes the role of speed in safety; to climb and return quickly during a window of good weather.

AMS (acute mountain sickness, hypoxemia, hypoxia) – Low blood oxygen due to high altitude, with symptoms of headache, loss of appetite, nausea, vomiting, malaise and disturbed sleep.

anchor – A point where the rope is secured to the snow, ice or rock to provide protection against a fall.

approach – The non-technical section of the climb that leads to the technical part of the climb.

arête – A small ridge-like feature or a sharp outward facing corner on a steep rock face, usually formed by glacial erosion.

ascend – To climb a rope using aid device. To move, climb or go upward.

ascender (jumar, clog) – A safety device used to clip into and ascend a fixed line.

avalanche – Movement down the mountain of previously stationary snow, rock or both.

belay – A safety technique where a stationary climber provides protection by means of ropes, anchors and braking devices or techniques, to an ascending or descending partner.

benightment – An unscheduled overnight bivouac.

bivouac – A temporary camp without tents or cover, used especially by soldiers or mountaineers.

bolt – A substantial metal pin drilled in the rock to provide permanent protection.

buttress – A prominent feature that juts out from a rock or mountain.

chimney – A fault line on a rock route large enough for the climber to fit inside and use the relative wealth of holds from both sides of the chimney.

clean – To remove protection (cams, pickets, etc.), usually the responsibility of the last climber in a rope team.

clipping in – Using a karabiner to connect to belays and anchors or to connect ropes to protection.

cornice – Wind-sculpted snow overhanging a ridge, a hazard avoided by not walking on the cornice or in the fall line below it.

couloir – A gully, sometimes a potential route. A chute or bowling alley is steep enough for rock or ice fall to be a concern.

crag – Any large expanse of rock.

crampons – Spiked metal devices that attach firmly to climbing boots to provide reliable footing on ice and firm snow slopes. An archaic term for grappling hook.

crevasse – A crack in a glacier surface. Crevasses vary in width and depth and are often concealed by surface snow that forms a snow bridge. Concealed crevasses are the main hazard on glaciers.

descender – A device for controlled descent on a rope. Also called a rappel device. Many belay devices may be used as descenders, including ATCs, figure eights, or even karabiners.

Diamox – A drug used to inhibit the onset of altitude sickness. Otherwise known as acetazolamide.

edging – A rock climbing technique where the edges of the climbing shoes are used to stand on small footholds. By contrast, smearing uses as much of the sole of the climbing shoe as possible to a rock slab to achieve maximum friction.

eight-thousander (or 8,000er) – One of the fourteen mountains in the world, all in the greater Himalayas, whose elevation exceeds 8,000 metres above sea level.

exposure – The distance from a climber to where he/she would likely stop in the event of an unprotected fall.

first ascent – The first successful completion of a route.

fixed rope or fixed line traverse – The practice of fixing in place bolted ropes to assist and protect climbers in exposed mountain locations, left in place for others who follow.

free climb – To climb using only one's hands and feet

without artificial aids. A belay rope may be employed.

HACE (high altitude cerebral oedema) – Swelling of the brain due to cell death and fluid increase, the most serious form of altitude sickness.

HAPE (high altitude pulmonary oedema) – Fluid build-up in the lungs. Can lead to HACE if descent is not immediate.

harness – A strong belt with leg loops made of nylon webbing used to secure the climber to the rope, often with loops to hold climbing hardware.

headwall – A precipice rising above the floor of a glacial cirque; a steep slope forming the head of a valley.

hypothermia – Low body temperature caused by cold ambient temperature, more likely when having become wet and when not carrying a heat source.

ice axe – A mountaineering tool for snow and ice climbing, pointed at the base of the shaft and with a head consisting of a pick and an axe.

ice screw – A threaded piton designed to bore into ice securely enough to serve as an anchor.

icefall – A steep part of a glacier like a frozen waterfall.

karabiner – Forged aluminium devices of various shapes (oval, D, etc.) with a spring-loaded gate through which a climbing rope can be threaded, used to connect to protection or to provide connections in an anchor.

moraine – A random accumulation of boulders, rocks, scree and sand carried down the mountain and deposited by a glacier.

overhang – A section of rock or ice that is angled beyond vertical.

phlebitis – Inflammation of the walls of a vein.

rappel – To descend a fixed rope, usually by means of a braking device.

saddle – The lowest point of elevation between two peaks. Saddles are common waypoints in routes to eliminate unnecessary elevation gain and loss.

scree – Small loose rocks. Difficult to ascend, like climbing a slope of loose sand, scree slopes are often used for descents.

self-arrest – A technique using an ice axe that works in some snow conditions on moderate slopes to bring a fall to a stop.

serac – A large ice tower.

Sherpa – A person of the ethnic group of the same name that is located in the Himalayan mountains. Also a generic term for mountaineering porters in Nepal (usually those working at or above base camp) regardless of their ethnic group.

sling – A length of nylon webbing or cord either sewn or tied into a loop used in conjunction with the rope and anchors to provide protection. A daisy chain is a sling sewn into loops so its length can be adjusted easily. A quickdraw is a sewn sling with a karabiner at each end.

spur – A rock or snow rib on a mountain, a lateral ridge.

summit – (noun) The high point of a mountain or peak. (verb) To reach such a high point.

traverse – Moving laterally across terrain instead of ascending or descending, usually using karabiners or, on steeper traverses, an ascender.

ABOUT THE AUTHOR

Adrian Hayes is a British, record-breaking adventurer, author, keynote speaker, business coach, documentary presenter and sustainability campaigner.

An Arabic- and Nepali-speaking former British Army Gurkha Officer and Special Forces reservist, he has conquered Everest, K2, the North and South Poles, the length of Greenland by kite-ski and the Arabian Desert by camel amidst a lifetime of adventure, setting two Guinness World Records, writing two books and featuring in three documentaries to date.

One of the few extreme adventurers in the world with a senior corporate background, including formerly an Airbus Middle East Sales Director, Adrian is an internationally acclaimed keynote and motivational speaker and professional leadership, team, and executive coach and consultant, delivering speeches, seminars, and programmes worldwide.

He is an ambassador on economic, social and environmental sustainability and a patron of several organizations and charities, speaking, writing and campaigning on related contemporary world issues. As a former paramedic, he is also involved in an ongoing project providing medical treatment and health and hygiene education in the remote areas of the Himalayas.

Adrian has featured in three documentaries: *The Greenland Quest* in 2011 for the National Geographic Channel, *Footsteps of Thesiger* in 2013 and *In Inner Mongolia* in 2017 for the Discovery Channel, and is now an established television and documentary presenter. His first book, *Footsteps of Thesiger*, was published in 2013, and details his forty-four-day journey across the Arabian Desert.

Outside of mountaineering and expeditions, his interests include all sports, particularly rugby union, athletics, cycling and triathlon, personal development, politics and international affairs, medicine, health and nutrition, astronomy, film and music, and he is still an occasional singer and guitarist in a rock band.

www.adrianhayes.com

f adrianmhayes

y adrianhayes

⊙ adrianmhayes

▶ adrianmhayes